Stephen Crane
and Literary Impressionism

The camera obscura is in Ocean Grove. It really has some
value as a scientific curiosity. People enter a small wooden
building and stand in a darkened room, gazing at the surface
of a small round table, on which appear reflections made
through a lens in the top of the tower of all that is happening in the vicinity at the time. One gets a miniature of everything that occurs in the streets, on the boardwalk or on the
hotel-porches. One can watch the bathers gambolling in the
surf or peer at the deck of a passing ship. A man stands with
his hand on a lever and changes the scene at will.

Stephen Crane, "Joys of Seaside Life"

The interior of the church was too cavelike in its gloom for
the eyes of the operating surgeons, so they had had the altar-
table carried to the doorway, where there was a bright light.
Framed then in the black archway was the altar-table with the
figure of a man upon it. He was naked save for the breech-
clout, and so close, so clear was the ecclesiastic suggestion,
that one's mind leaped to a fantasy that this thin pale figure
had just been torn down from a cross. The flash of the impression was like light, and for this instant it illumined all
the dark recesses of one's remotest idea of sacrilege, ghastly
and wanton. I bring this to you merely as an effect—an effect
of mental light and shade, if you like; something done in
thought similar to that which the French Impressionists do in
color; something meaningless and at the same time overwhelming, crushing, monstrous.

Stephen Crane, "War Memories"

A worshiper of everything beautiful in life, he [Stephen
Crane] could see rosy lights under the most sordid clouds and
had the moral courage to write his true impressions[. H]e
said: "The true artist is the man who leaves pictures of his
own time as they appear to him."

Cora Crane

Stephen Crane
and Literary Impressionism

James Nagel

The Pennsylvania State University Press

University Park and London

Library of Congress Cataloging in Publication Data

Nagel, James.
  Stephen Crane and literary impressionism.

  Includes index.
  1. Crane, Stephen, 1871–1900—Style.   2. Impressionism.   I. Title.
PS1449.C85Z75   813′.4   80-16051
ISBN 0-271-00266-0

Designed by Glenn Ruby

Printed in the United States of America

for Gwen

Contents

Preface

This book is the result of a decade of exploration of two concerns that became increasingly related as the study developed. The first was a general interest in Impressionism as a cultural movement, especially in America. I was astonished to discover that the *Literary History of the United States*, Fourth Edition, does not even mention the term, implying that despite the enormous impact of Impressionism on painting and music, the movement had no influence on American literature whatever. My feeling was that this view, all too common among literary scholars, was in need of dramatic modification. The second concern was to assess Stephen Crane's role in the development of the "modern" impulse in American literature, an involvement I found in need of more precise definition. I found that definition in Impressionism.

The search for an understanding of the role of Impressionism in the fiction of Stephen Crane was an invigorating and rewarding enquiry, one that brought me into contact with scores of colleagues, students, and friends who contributed in significant ways to this study. Although it is impossible to acknowledge everyone who assisted my labors, a few people deserve special expressions of gratitude. No one served as a more joyful source of encouragement and wise counsel than Roland Nadeau of Northeastern University, whose work on Impressionism in music helped to shape my own thinking. I am deeply indebted to Maria Kronegger of Michigan State University both for her excellent book *Literary Impressionism* and for her helpful comments in response to the manuscript and to a lecture I presented as part of an interdisciplinary colloquium in Boston. My oldest debt is to Clarence Glasrud of Moorhead State University, who first introduced me to Crane over twenty years ago, and whose life and sensitivity to literature have had a constant influence on me. Ellen Benoit, Alan Rooks, Laura Dunn, among other of my students, helped me in many ways over the years, and I am pleased to acknowledge their dedicated assistance. Catherine Ezell, my Editorial Assistant for *Studies in American Fiction*, has for several years played an important role in nearly every level of my work. Her patience and understanding have been remarkable, as has her keen insight into literature. Harrison T. Meserole (Pennsylvania State University), James J. Martine (St. Bonaventure University), and James B. Colvert (University of Georgia) all read the manuscript and offered valuable suggestions for improving it. John M. Pickering and Peter Ross Sieger of Pennsylvania State University Press have been continually gracious and professional in the production of this book.

My work was assisted by a grant from the Research and Development Fund of Northeastern University and by a Fulbright Lectureship at the University of Waikato in Hamilton, New Zealand, where my graduate seminar on Crane and Hemingway provided me with an opportunity to explore the thesis of this book. A lecture tour for the United States Information Service allowed me to present my ideas before learned audiences in New Zealand, India, and Germany and to benefit from their comments and suggestions.

I am grateful to the University Press of Virginia for permission to quote from *The Works of Stephen Crane*, now the standard text. Two portions of this book appeared previously in rather different form: "Stephen Crane and the Narrative Methods of Impressionism," *Studies in the Novel*, 10 (1978), 76–85, and "Impressionism in 'The Open Boat' and 'A Man and Some Others,'" *Research Studies*, 43 (1975), 27–37. I am grateful to these journals for permission to reprint sections of these articles. My one regret about this project is that after years of constant support, P. S. Nagel did not live to see the publication of this study. Finally, I express my most profound indebtedness to my wife, Gwen, whose insight and sensitivity made all the difference. My dedication says in two words what I could never fully acknowledge here.

Wellesley, Mass.   J.N.

I

Backgrounds and Definitions:
Conrad's "Complete Impressionist"

In early December of 1897, only two months after their first meeting, Joseph Conrad wrote a letter to Stephen Crane expressing his appreciation of "A Man and Some Others" and "The Open Boat," both of which had appeared earlier that year.[1] After voicing his enthusiasm for the two stories, Conrad went on to say that

> you are an everlasting surprise to one. You shock—and the next moment you give the perfect artistic satisfaction. Your method is fascinating. You are a complete impressionist. The illusions of life come out of your hand without a flaw. It is not life—which nobody wants—it is art—art for which everyone—the abject and the great—hanker—mostly without knowing it.[2]

Four days later, on December 5, 1897, Conrad wrote to Edward Garnett revealing similar sentiments:

> I had Crane here last Sunday. We talked and smoked half the night. He is strangely hopeless about himself. I like him. The two stories are excellent. Of course, "A Man and Some Others" is the best of the two but the boat thing interested me more. His eye is very individual and his expression satisfies me artistically. He certainly is *the* impressionist and his temperament is curiously unique. His thought is concise, connected, never very deep—yet often startling. He is *the only* impressionist and *only* an impressionist.[3]

Conrad was perhaps overly restrictive in suggesting that Crane was "only an impressionist" for, indeed, Crane wrote in a wide variety of styles. Nevertheless, Conrad's assessment apparently impressed Garnett a great deal for a year later, in "Mr. Stephen Crane: An Appreciation,"

1

perhaps the most important critical study of Crane's Impressionism published in his lifetime,[4] Garnett himself took the view that Crane "is the chief impressionist of our day."[5]

It is historically important that both Conrad and Garnett regarded Crane, without qualification, as an Impressionistic writer, especially in view of the stature of these two men in English letters of the late nineteenth century. But they were not the earliest of his readers to consider his work in those terms. As early as 1895 reviewers had noted, sometimes obliquely, Impressionistic ideas and techniques in his fiction. Nancy Huston Banks, for example, in reviewing *The Red Badge of Courage* in the *Bookman* in 1895, suggested that the novel "may perhaps be best described as a study in morbid emotions and distorted external impressions. . . . The few scattered bits of description are like stereopticon views, insecurely put on the canvas. And yet there is on the reader's part a distinct recognition of power—misspent perhaps—but still power of an unusual kind."[6] Banks' concern for "impressions" was developed a few months later by George Wyndham in the *New Review*. His essay clarifies the contemporary view of Crane's use of impressions and of their singularity in the fiction of the day:

> Mr. Crane, for his distinction, has hit on a new device, or at least on one which has never been used before with such consistency and effect. In order to show the features of modern war, he takes a subject—a youth with a peculiar temperament, capable of exaltation and yet morbidly sensitive. Then he traces the successive impressions made on such a temperament, from minute to minute, during two days of heavy fighting. He stages the drama of war, so to speak, within the mind of one man, and then admits you as to a theatre.[7]

Beyond psychological realism, Wyndham stressed Crane's use of sensory imagery to create an immediacy of scene:

> The sights flashed indelibly on the retina of the eye; the sounds that after long silences suddenly cypher; the stenches that sicken in after-life at any chance allusion to decay; or, stirred by these, the storms of passions that force yells of defiance out of inarticulate clowns; the winds of fear that sweep by night along prostrate ranks, with the acceleration of trains and the noise as of a whole town waking from nightmare with stertorous, indrawn gasps—these colossal facts of the senses and the soul are the only colours in which the very image of war can be painted. Mr. Crane has composed his palette with these colours, and has painted a picture that challenges comparison with the most vivid scenes of Tolstoi's *La Guerre et la Paix* or of Zola's *La Débâcle*.

Crane's imagistic density seems to have impressed Wyndham as being especially effective in creating a sense of "reality" in the novel, for he comments that the book is filled with "sensuous impressions that leap out from the picture" leaving "such indelible traces as are left by the actual experiences of war."[8] Perhaps it was this same sense of reality, born of sensory images, that led Sydney Brooks to conclude in his review that "certainly, if his [Crane's] book were altogether a work of imagination, unbased on personal experience, his realism would be nothing short of a miracle."[9]

The precise nature of Crane's literary "miracle" was difficult for some contemporary reviewers to define, and it eluded many. Rupert Hughes maintained that *The Red Badge* showed Crane to be a "slap-dash impressionist."[10] John Barrow Allen found it hard to come to grips with the novel and finally concluded that a "serio-comic effect seems to be intended throughout."[11] Jeannette L. Gilder, the sister of Richard Watson Gilder, the editor of *Century*, reviewed Crane's war novel for the New York *World* and offered the memorable comment that "at present Mr. Crane is living with a brother at a place called Hartwood, in Sullivan County in this State. He spends a great part of his time out of doors and writes just as little as he can. In this he shows good sense."[12] Perhaps it was thinking of this kind that Crane was responding to when he wrote to Nellie Crouse that "there is only one person in the world who knows less than the average reader. He is the average reviewer. I would already have been a literary corpse, had I ever paid the slightest attention to the reviewers."[13]

But most early reviews were favorable and many alluded to some aspect of Crane's Impressionism, frequently equating Crane's style with devices in painting and photography and even, in one instance, with the phonograph. Harold Frederic, soon to become a close friend of Stephen and Cora, commented in the New York *Times* on Crane's "battle painting" and concluded that "it is [the] effect of a photographic revelation which startles and fascinates one in *The Red Badge of Courage*."[14] Charles Dudley Warner maintained that Crane's attempt in the novel was to "make every page blaze with color, in order to affect the mind through the eye. It is all very interesting. Every page is painted, perhaps I should say saturated, with this intensity of color."[15] Other reviews described Crane's techniques in similar terms. A writer in *Godey's Magazine* described *The Third Violet* as an "impressionistic sketch in dabs of primary color"[16] and another, reviewing *Wounds in the Rain* in the New York *Times* in 1900, saw Crane as an Impressionist who "tries to record, as would a phonograph, not so much action, as the sounds of the small arms and the boom of the big guns."[17] And John D. Barry, commenting on *The Black Riders* in 1901, wrote that "perhaps an explanation may be suggested by the association of Mr. Crane at this period with a group of young American painters, who had brought from France the impressionistic influences, which with him took literary form."[18]

The most significant comments from this period on Crane's Impressionistic techniques appeared in two notable essays: Edward Garnett's "Mr. Stephen Crane: An Appreciation," which ran in the *Academy* in December of 1898, and H.G. Wells' "Stephen Crane: From An English Standpoint," which appeared in *The North American Review* in August of 1900, just two months after Stephen's death. Garnett argued that "the rare thing about Mr. Crane's art is that he keeps closer to the surface than any living writer, and, like the great portrait-painters, to a great extent makes the surface betray the depths." After enthusiastic praise of *George's Mother*, "The Bride Comes to Yellow Sky," and *The Red Badge of Courage*, he remarked:

> His art does not include the necessity for complex arrangements; his sure instinct tells him never to quit the passing moment of life, to hold fast by simple situations, to reproduce the episodic, fragmentary nature of life in such artistic sequence that it stands in place of the architectural masses and co-ordinated structures of the great artists. He is the chief impressionist of our day as Sterne was the great impressionist, in a different manner, of his day. If he fails in anything he undertakes, it will be through abandoning the style he has invented.

Garnett's perception that life is inherently "episodic" and "fragmentary," and that these qualities inform the structural principles of Impressionistic fiction, constitutes an important step in the critical description of the nature of Crane's art. Garnett clearly regarded the "invention" of Literary Impressionism by Crane to be a monumental achievement, for he concluded his essay with the comment that "of the young school of American artists Mr. Crane is the genius—the others have their talents."[19]

H. G. Wells echoed both Garnett's praise of Crane's work and his sense that Crane had "invented" a new form of fiction, calling *The Red Badge* "a new thing, in a new school." Wells was also sensitive to the influence of the Impressionistic painters on Crane's fiction:

> For the great influence of the studio on Crane cannot be ignored; in the persistent selection of the essential elements of an impression, in the ruthless exclusion of mere information, in the direct vigor with which the selected points are made, there is Whistler even more than there is Tolstoi in "The Red Badge of Courage."

Wells also praised Crane's use of imagery, especially color imagery, in such stories as "The Open Boat," a work Wells regarded as the "crown" of Crane's fiction. Again, however, Wells' emphasis was on artistic control: for him the story had "all the stark power of the earlier stories, with a new element of restraint; the color is as full and strong as ever, fuller and stronger, indeed; but those chromatic splashes that at times deafen and confuse in 'The Red Badge,' those images that astonish rather than enlighten, are disciplined and controlled." In all of this, he saw Crane's work as a radical departure from traditional fiction and as a precursor of a new direction in literature. Crane, Wells concluded, "is the first expression of the opening mind of a new period, or, at least, the early emphatic phase of a new initiative—beginning, as a growing mind must needs begin, with the record of impressions, a record of a vigor and intensity beyond all precedent."[20]

These early reviews and comments on Crane's art are useful in revealing the contemporary understanding of Crane's fiction as Impressionistic and for a sense, stressed especially by Wells and Garnett, that Crane had developed a vibrant new style. But any definition of Literary Impressionism based solely on these reviews would be fragmentary and suggestive at best. Nevertheless, a number of important points were established in these early comments: reality is perceived as fragmentary; fiction that portrays real life will therefore be episodic; artistic control rivaling that of painters is needed to render fiction in this style; controlled patterns of imagery, especially sensory imagery, are essential for recording the impressions of the characters; such methods produce a startling illusion of life, especially in visual terms; and these qualities in Crane's works, handled with artistic skill, point to a new direction in literature. In effect, what these writers saw in Crane's work was remarkably close to what Hamlin Garland predicted as the new wave of literature in his *Crumbling Idols*:

> [T]he novel of the future will be shorter and simpler and less
> obvious in its method. It will put its lessons into general effect
> rather than into epigrams. Discussion will be in the relations of
> its characters, not on quotable lines or paragraphs. Like impres-
> sionism in painting, it will subordinate parts to the whole. . . . It
> will teach . . . by effect; but it will not be by direct expression, but
> by placing before the reader the facts of life as they stand related
> to the artist. The relation will not be put into explanatory notes,
> but will address itself to the perception of the reader.[21]

What Garland in 1894 had predicted for the future, Stephen Crane was already employing in his fiction.

Despite the number of these early essays, and the insights that they provided, nearly a half-century passed before there was any important development in the critical interpretation of Crane's work as Impressionistic. Part of the reason for this delay may well have been the lack of rigor in the critical terminology of the time, in which distinctions among Realism, Naturalism, and Impressionism were not clearly defined. As a result, although there was general agreement about Crane's basic themes and techniques, scholars variously found his work to be representative of all three of these modes and of Symbolism as well. Another variable was the range and complexity of Crane's fiction. Certain critics, looking primarily at *Maggie, George's Mother,* and the *Bowery Tales,* concluded with some justification that they closely resembled works of Naturalism. Richard Chase, for example, argued as late as 1960 that "like the other significant new writers of his generation—Frank Norris, Jack London, and Theodore Dreiser—Crane is, generally speaking, of the 'naturalist' school."[22] This view, with some complications, has been widely held, even in recent scholarship.[23] Although Alfred Kazin has proclaimed rather categorically that Crane was a "naturalist by birth,"[24] most critics have sensed in Crane's work a number of elements not accounted for in traditional descriptions of either Realism or Naturalism. The result has been a confusion of terms, an uncertainty of critical assertions, and a simplification of the understanding of Crane's work. In *The Poetry of Stephen Crane,* Daniel Hoffman is led to assert that "in technique he [Crane] is comparably varied, essaying impressionism, naturalism, fantasy, realism, and symbolism. . . ."[25] Other equally acute Crane scholars have grappled with the dilemma of a descriptive term for Crane's art, often with less than conclusive results. Joseph Katz, for example, reflected that

> Crane is difficult to label. In his own time he was called either an impressionist or a decadent; but as later criticism sought a perspective on the literary nineties he was variously considered a realist, a naturalist, a symbolist, a parodist, and even a romantic.[26]

Thomas Gullason, in harmony with Katz, maintains that "though he is still called a realist, naturalist, symbolist, impressionist, and existentialist, Crane cannot truly be labelled."[27] What both Katz and Gullason are responding to is, perhaps, the confluence of the diversity of Crane's literary production and the historical application of inconsistent and incomplete definitions of critical terminology.

The record of the scholarship on Crane as an Impressionist provides ample testimony to this problem. Thomas Beer, for example, in his influential *Stephen Crane* (1923), stressed that Crane "was in full flight from the codes of naturalism" and made several references to Impressionistic tendencies in his work, but Beer offered neither a definition of his terms nor a development of his thinking.[28] In contrast, Harry Hartwick, writing in *The Foreground of American Fiction* in 1934, elaborated his views in what is still an important, if often overlooked, discussion of Crane and Impressionism.

Hartwick implies that literary Impressionism derives from painting, specifically from Monet's *Impression, Sunrise* (1872), which presented an image rather than a narrative. He sees the analogous literary manifestation of this mode in the verse of the French Symbolist Mallarmé and in the fiction of Joseph Conrad and Stephen Crane. This type of fiction, he explains, "is a sequence of pictures, visual, aural, olfactory, or tactile. . . ." He continues:

> Impressionism is a sensory kodaking, a confused mosaic of details, a rivulet of hyphenated photographs, which the reader himself must fuse into some eventual relationship. . . . Experience becomes a series of "intense moments"; plot loses in importance; and from an interest in the larger aspects of his product, the author turns to an interest in "the bright, particular world."[29]

The introduction of scientific objectivity and analysis, he suggests, has its humanistic expression in ethical relativity and the leveling of social rank: "Democracy, impressionism, and relativity in morals are all yoked together, and follow in the track of science." Impressionism violates tradition and suggests

> the collapse of consistency in thought and literature. . . . Experience, it insists, should be broken into fragments, each fragment to be respected for its own sake, each passing moment or passion to be welcomed individually and squeezed dry before it can escape us.[30]

Hartwick's discussion was the dominant statement on Crane and Impressionism for almost three decades, until Sergio Perosa's study in 1964. During the intervening years, however, occasional comments touched on the subject. For example, in his *Stephen Crane* for the American Men of Letters Series in 1950, John Berryman introduced the subject of Impressionism and quoted a statement Crane supposedly made to a "friend" in New York in 1893: "'Impressionism was his faith. Impressionism, he said, was Truth, and no man could be great who was not an impressionist, for greatness consisted in knowing truth. He said that he did not expect to be great himself, but he hoped to get near the truth.'"[31] Hailing Crane as one of the "few manifest geniuses the country has produced," he nevertheless concludes that Crane is a Naturalist whose work contains Realistic elements at the same time that he states that "Crane was an Impressionist."[32] In a more extended analysis, Charles C. Walcutt, in *American Literary Naturalism: A Divided Stream* (1956), solved the difficulty of clarifying distinctions among movements by simply making Impressionism one of the styles of Naturalism. As a result, he can see Crane's works as an "early and unique flowering of pure naturalism. It is naturalism in a restricted and special sense, and it contains many non-naturalistic elements, but it is nevertheless entirely consistent and coherent."[33] Walcutt's contradictory synthesis is representative of scholarship on this subject. And R. W. Stallman did not clarify matters in his *Stephen Crane: An Omnibus* when he introduced the term "prose pointillism," an interesting but nebulous phrase. Stallman argued that *"Crane's style is prose pointillism.* It is composed of disconnected images, which coalesce like blobs of color in French impressionistic paintings, every word-group having a cross-reference relationship, every seemingly disconnected detail having inter-relationship to the configurated whole."[34] This description has essentially metaphoric reference and does little to clarify the modality of Crane's work, especially since Stallman also contends that "Crane's *Maggie* is par excellence the exemplar of literary naturalism."[35]

But the major documents of the study of Crane's Impressionism to 1970 are four articles by Sergio Perosa, Orm Øverland, Stanley Wertheim, and Rodney O. Rogers which appeared between 1964 and 1969.[36] Perosa's "Stephen Crane fra naturalismo e impressionismo" explores the thesis that Crane's work presents a "symbiosis" of Naturalistic ideas and Impressionistic methods. He sees the origins of both movements in a common matrix: the development of artistic modes based on scientific principles. As a result, they retained a common bond discernible at the heart of Crane's fiction. Perosa maintains that the major influence on Crane was Hamlin Garland, especially his theory of "Veritism" and his discussion of Impressionistic painting in *Crumbling Idols* (1894). The painters were engaged in an "attempt to apply to traditional painting the new optic discoveries on the nature of colors and on the decomposition and recomposition of light on the retina to produce them." Naturalistic fiction, on the other hand, was concerned with the "principles of physiological heredity and social determinism, together with the concept of a scientific, photographic, and documentary reproduction of life, even at its lowest, to serve the purpose of social denunciation. . . ." Meanwhile, Literary Impressionism attempts to portray the

> apprehension of life through the play of perceptions, the significant montage of sense impressions, the reproduction of chromatic touches by colorful and precise notations, the reduction of elaborate syntax to the correlation of sentences, which leads to a sketchy, and at the same time evocative, kind of writing.

Having established this theoretical base, Perosa then discusses *Maggie* and the Bowery tales, *The Red Badge*, and, very briefly, a few of the best known stories.[37]

Orm Øverland supplied much of the detail of definition and analysis that Perosa's essay lacked with the publication of "The Impressionism of Stephen Crane: A Study in Style and Technique" in *Americana Norvegica* in 1966. Øverland apparently wrote without knowledge of or benefit from Perosa's earlier work, a persistent circumstance in essays on Crane's Impressionism. Apart from the concern of both scholars for perception in the technique and theme of Impressionistic fiction, Øverland's essay almost directly contradicts Perosa's contentions. Øverland stresses the distinction between Naturalism and Impressionism, especially in underlying philosophy. Naturalists, he contends,

> believed that reality *could* be seized upon, while the impressionists went one step further toward "realism" and "objectivity." . . . To the susceptible mind of the impressionist the surrounding world viewed at large is not simple and well ordered, but an indistinct and obscure picture made up of an irresistible flood of confused and ever changing sense impressions.[38]

Øverland's discussion, broader than Perosa's, ranges throughout the canon providing precise documentation of the elements of style, syntax, and structure that represent Impressionistic techniques. He is especially perceptive in demonstrating Crane's use of fragmented scenes to form episodes, the restriction of narrative comments to perceptions rather than logical conclusions, the use of substitutionary speech, and the unique quality of Crane's imagery.[39] In detailed analysis, Øverland documents examples of Impressionistic methods in Crane's works. However, his essay does not provide a close analysis of an entire work by Crane to demonstrate the full effect of his approach on an understanding of a story or novel.

Stanley Wertheim's "Crane and Garland: The Education of an Impressionist" covers familiar biographical matters with a new emphasis. In a few pages, this essay discusses Crane's association with artists, the influence of Hamlin Garland on his literary creed, and the role of Garland's Veritism in *The Red Badge of Courage*. Impressionism, Wertheim contends, has to do with the "subjective rendering of experience," the employment of an "episodic narrative structure," and an emphasis on images of color. Wertheim underscores the importance of Crane's exposure to Garland's lectures at Avon-by-the-Sea in 1891, which Crane covered for the New York *Tribune*. Wertheim maintains that these lectures were not only the source of Crane's Impressionism but also the "starting point of literary impressionism, which stresses the replacing of theoretical knowledge with visual experience as the goal of realistic writing."[40]

Rodney O. Rogers, in his "Stephen Crane and Impressionism," which appeared in *Nineteenth-Century Fiction* in 1969, argues cogently that the link between Impressionistic painting and fiction is not so much a matter of technique, as R. W. Stallman's "prose pointillism" thesis would imply, as a view of the nature of reality. Both painters and writers of the Impressionistic mode base their work on the premise that "Impressionism is a realistic style of description precisely because reality is ephemeral, evanescent, constantly shifting its meaning and hence continually defying precise definition." The effect of this conception on Crane's fiction, Rogers contends, is the creation of a narrative perspective that is distinct from and often even contradictory of the protagonist's sensibility. The modulation of this disharmony in point of view undercuts the stature of the protagonist, displaying his illusions, posings, and naiveté. Hence the manipulation of point of view not only links Crane ideologically to the French Impressionistic painters but also generates the central themes of his fiction.[41]

Taken as a body of work, these essays on Crane's Impressionism, for all their virtues, do not cohere into a unified definition of the mode. Rather, they indicate the need for a more substantial definition of Impressionism as a prelude to a consideration of his work in these terms.

The modern usage of the term "Impressionism" to describe an artistic tendency derives from an exhibition of the *Société anonyme des artistes, peintres, sculpteurs, et graveurs* in the Paris studio of the photographer Nader in 1874. The exhibit contained pieces by thirty artists (among them Cézanne, Degas, Monet, Pissarro, and Renoir), works previously rejected by the conservative selection judges at the Official Salon in Paris. Among the paintings shown was Claude Monet's *Impression, Sunrise*, painted in 1872, a work sometimes credited with giving the name to the movement. In addition, art critic Louis Leroy used the word "impressionist" in his review of the exhibition, and it was quickly adopted as a term of derision. The currency of "Impressionism" to describe this new mode was assured with the formation of an artistic journal entitled *The Impressionist* in 1877.[42]

A good deal of confusion surrounded Impressionism from the first. Emile Zola persisted in referring to these artists and works as Naturalistic, perhaps originating the linking of the two modes still perpetuated in modern scholarship. Renoir resisted the term "Impressionist" because it implied a "school" of painting, and Degas found it difficult to see how the term could be applied to his own work.[43] Conceived in disharmony, nurtured in derision and confusion, and applied without precision, it is understandable that "Impressionism" has had less than clear meaning over the past century. This early lack of clarity contributed to the dissatisfaction of the artists with the movement, and its first wave lasted only until the Eighth Exhibition of 1886, when the term was formally renounced by the artists of the original 1874 exhibit.

Although the terminology of the movement was controversial from the first, a spectrum of ideas and methods gave the group cohesion without the formalized rules of a "school" of art. Its fundamental concept was a rejection of preconceptions about the nature of reality and an attempt to paint what was actually seen, what sensory impressions were available to the individual painter at a given time and place. The concern for immediate impressions required an intense interest in the fluctuations of light and color, with the effect of a more accurate "realism" in the rendering of nature as it is perceived.[44] This position had its intellectual antecedents: Comte, the originator of Positivism, had also distrusted *a priori* assumptions and had stressed the importance of empirical data. A French chemist, Eugène Chevreul, had explored the scientific basis for the modifying influence of juxtaposed colors in *The Principles of Harmony and Contrast of Colors, and Their Application to the Arts* in 1839.[45] And there was a good deal of work in philosophy relevant to Impressionistic ideas, including that by David Hume and the British empirical philosophers on the theory of knowledge, perhaps best represented by Hume's *A Treatise on Human Nature* (1739–40).[46] Despite such influences, however, the Impressionistic movement was not essentially philosophical or scientific; it derived from the minds of artists whose principal concerns were for artistic effect rather than intellectual coherence.

Indeed, as Diego Martelli argued in *Gli Impressionisti*, a pamphlet published in Pisa only six years after the first Impressionist Exhibition,

> Impressionism is not only a revolution in the field of thought, but it is also a physiological revolution of the human eyes. It is a new theory that depends on a different way of perceiving the sensations of light and of expressing the impressions. Nor do the Impressionists fabricate their theories first and then adapt the paintings to them, but on the contrary, as always happens with discoveries, the pictures were born of the unconscious visual phenomenon of men of art who, having studied, afterward produced the reasoning of the philosophers.[47]

And four years before, in 1876, Edmond Duranty had defended the Impressionists in his *La Nouvelle Peinture: A propos du groupe d'artistes qui expose dans les Galeries Durand-Ruel* against the charges that their works were mere "sketches and abbreviated summaries." He countered, especially with regard to Degas' work, that by means of a back, we want a temperament, an age, a social condition to be revealed; through a pair of hands, we should be able to express a magistrate or a tradesman; by a gesture, a whole series of feelings. . . . *A man opens a door; he enters; that is enough: we see that he has lost his daughter.* Hands that are kept in pockets can be eloquent.[48]

Duranty's remarks are pertinent not only to the painters he was defending but also to the dramatic mode of the writers who were to follow, especially in the role of suggestion, the restriction of expository background information in a scene, and the use of synecdoche.

The variety of concerns represented by the concept "impressionism" is easily suggested by the works and comments of the French painters themselves. Cézanne indicated the "sensational" nature of Impressionism, as well as its distinction from Realism, when he declared, "'I have not tried to reproduce Nature: I have represented it. . . . Art should not imitate nature, but should express the sensations aroused by nature.'"[49] On another occasion he wrote to Emile Bernard, "we must render the image of what we see, forgetting everything that existed before us."[50] As Cézanne suggests, visual emphasis is the most striking feature of Impressionistic painting, from the dominant red sun, pasted in the sky like a wafer, shimmering across the bay in Monet's *Impression, Setting Sun*, to the more delicate pastels in his *Sailboats at Argenteuil.* Of particular interest is the obscuring of vision in Impressionistic painting, a systematic limitation of the sensory reception of the essentials of scene. Such obscuring is generally the result of natural phenomena (trees, fog, snow, darkness, distance) or, less often, problems arising from human civilization (smoke, flags, buildings, crowds). So Pissarro, a defender of Neo-Impressionism, will portray a river on a misty and fog-laden morning, as in *L'Ile Lacroix, Rouen.* Claude Monet shows not simply a train depot in *La Gare Saint-Lazare, Paris* but a depot seen through the heavy smoke pouring from the locomotives. In *Boulevard Montmartre, Night,* Pissarro renders the obscured effect of lights along a street in the evening. Distance reduces the background figures in Degas' *Carriage at the Races* to the same kind of "tiny riders on tiny horses" that Henry Fleming perceives across a battlefield in *The Red Badge of Courage.* The effect of distance on vision, especially when viewing human forms, is equally pronounced in Monet's *Vétheuil.*

Another striking dimension of Impressionistic painting that links it to literature of the same mode is the concern for the transience of reality, or, more correctly, the ineluctable flux in human perceptions of even the most stable of objects. Monet will present numerous paintings of haystacks from the same perspective at different times and under differing light conditions: the color, the emphasis, the essence of "reality" has changed. He presents the same phenomenon in *Rouen Cathedral in Full Sunlight* and *Rouen Cathedral in Sunlight*; only the light effects have altered, and yet the nature of the reality portrayed has changed dramatically. In these and other paintings the fundamental ideology is clear: reality is a matter of perception; it is unstable, ever-changing, elusive, inscrutable.

The implications of this new artistic mode in France were not lost on American intellectuals. As early as 1870, for example, the French opera singer Madame Ambre, in America for engagements with Colonel Mapelson's Italian Opera Company in New York and Boston, brought with her Edouard Manet's *Execution of the Emperor Maximilian*. Four years later the Foreign Exhibition in Boston displayed works by Monet, Manet, Pissarro, Renoir, and Sisley in the first important Impressionistic show in America, although their appearance came at a time when the American public was not quite prepared to receive them.[51] And in 1886 Durand-Ruel came to New York with a large collection of Impressionist paintings which were praised with enthusiasm.[52] In this year as well, James F. Sutton of the American Art Association arranged an exhibition in April in New York of over 300 paintings, most of them by Degas, Monet, Manet, Pissarro, and Renoir.

By the late 1880s, Impressionism in painting had been displayed to American society and had become an important topic of discussion and debate. Many Americans, having studied in France, had adopted the mode themselves and were active representatives of the movement. Among the first of these was Theodore Robinson, who returned to the United States in 1888 and displayed his work at the Society of American Artists; later, in 1895, his works were on exhibit at the Macbeth Gallery in New York. Similarly, James Whistler had studied in Paris during the rise of Impressionism and had brought these new ideas back to England and America, as did Mary Cassatt, who encouraged American collectors to buy and show Impressionistic works still scorned by Parisian conservatives. By 1895, in fact, there were enough American Impressionistic painters for John Twatchman and Childe Hassam to form an exhibition of American Impressionists, entitled "Ten American Painters," and to establish with other artists, among whom J. Alden Weir and Willard Metcalf are perhaps the most important, the Academy of American Impressionism.[53]

This activity in painting was familiar to American writers. In 1892, when Stephen Crane was living in the Art Students' League in New York, Cecelia Waern published a brief but important essay, "Some Notes on French Impressionism," in the *Atlantic Monthly*. The thrust

of her remarks makes it easy to understand why literary critics of the
time would show a certain flexibility in their use of the term "Impressionism" throughout the decade. Waern began with the assertion that

> Impressionism, like most new things, great or small, is at present
> more discussed than understood. The word itself is elastic, and
> covers a variety of significations; the teachings of the school, in
> themselves narrow and definite, are only vaguely known and ap-
> prehended even by many professional critics.

Attempting to narrow and clarify the term, she nonetheless concedes
that Impressionism sometimes refers to the conception of a work of art
and at other times to its technique. Painters, she says, also differ in the
degree of clarity they give to objects. But the one thing she sees in all
Impressionism is the "visual unity of their picture." Thus, she implies,
Impressionism is largely a technique based on optical effect; it is not a
school of philosophy. Still, she suggests, there is an underlying idea
behind Impressionist art: "The great secret of all impressionism lies in
aiming to reproduce, as nearly as possible, the same kind of physical
impression on the spectator's eye that was produced on the eye of the
artist by the object seen in nature. . . ."[54] Waern's aesthetic of Impressionism in painting embraced principles of form and unity, of the
relation of reality to aesthetic production, and of the "effect" of art on
the viewer. The literary equivalent of Waern's concept was just beginning to appear in American literature, and it was remarkably close to
her definition.

French Impressionist painting attracted the attention of a number of
writers who became intimates of the group and apologists for the
movement. Emile Zola, for example, had early joined the meetings at
the Café Guerbois, which included Monet, Renoir, Pissarro, and, especially important for Zola, Edouard Manet and Paul Cézanne.[55] Other
important French writers became involved with the lives and philosophies of these artists, among them the brothers Goncourt, Baudelaire,
who became a companion of both Monet and Courbet, Jules Laforgue,
who defended the painters in a series of articles, and Mallarmé, whose
works show influence from Impressionistic painting and music.[56] In
America the literary articulation of the movement in painting came
largely through the efforts of Hamlin Garland, who, basing much of
his thinking on the work of Eugène Véron, lectured on Impressionism
and wrote about it in his *Crumbling Idols: Twelve Essays on Art
Dealing Chiefly with Literature Painting and the Drama*. As is well
known, Garland was an acquaintance of Stephen Crane's as early as
1891, and his views indicate the exposure to Impressionistic ideas available to Crane in the formative years of his career.

Garland regarded the fundamental idea of Impressionism as a structural principle: "A picture should be a unified impression. . . . [It] should be the staged and reproduced effect of a single section of the world of color upon the eye." Garland's views are remarkably close to those of Cecelia Waern: that the sensory *effect* of reality, not reality itself, is the subject of such art; that the desire to portray the immediacy of experience excluded basically historical subjects; that the Impressionist aesthetic, although not a formal philosophy, "indicates a radical change in attitude toward the physical universe. It stands for an advance in the perceptive power of the human eye."[57] Garland's literary expression of these concepts he called "Veritism," and, although he was never to fully employ these concepts in his own fiction, his ideas were an important influence throughout the 1890s.

Precisely how much of the discussion of Impressionism in painting and literature Stephen Crane had read or heard is not known, but there is no doubt that he knew painters and painting in the 1890s and that he was particularly aware of Impressionism. From his early childhood, painting had surrounded him. His older sister, Mary Helen Crane, was an artist herself and taught art during the 1880s and 1890s in Asbury Park, New Jersey. As a freshman at Syracuse University Crane had several Impressionistic paintings by Phebe English on the walls of his room.[58] Many of Crane's closest friends and roommates during his early career were painters. Even Cora Taylor, who lived with Crane as his wife, had family ties with painting: "Her father, John Howarth, was a Boston artist, and her great-grandfather, George Howarth, had been an art dealer."[59] Other aspects of Crane's life indicate an almost continuous involvement with painting. In a particularly intriguing episode, R. W. Stallman has recorded that in 1897 Henry Sanford Bennet had brought his young French wife to visit Crane at Ravensbrook. She had known Seurat and spent the evening discussing his work with Crane and Ford Madox Ford. And after Stephen's death in 1900, one of Cora's problems was moving all the paintings they had acquired.[60]

The key period in Crane's life for his involvement in painting was his experience in 1892-1893 of living in the Art Students' League with a group of young painters. Here he came to know Frederick Gordon, R. G. Vosburgh, David Ericson, Nelson Greene, W. W. Carroll, Edward S. Hamilton, and Corwin Knapp Linson, who kept a journal of life in the League, and who was both a painter and an illustrator. Before long Crane had been introduced to Henry McBride and Gustave Verbeek as well. During this period, he not only lived and dined with these men but participated in their artistic discussions. As Melvin H. Schoberlin revealed in a letter in 1949, they frequently explored the topic of Impressionism.[61]

Corwin Knapp Linson's record of these years was finally published in 1958. Linson, born in Brooklyn in 1864, had studied in Paris at the Julian Académie and, more importantly, under Léon Gérôme, Lafebvre, and Laurent, at the École des Beaux-Arts, where one of his fellow students was Paul Gauguin.[62] By 1891, when he first met Stephen Crane, Linson was dividing his time between "pure" art and sketches for books and magazines, including *Harper's Weekly* and *Scribner's*, for which he sketched the Olympic Games in Athens. Looking back on this period, Linson acknowledged a uniquely "artistic" quality in Crane's fiction: "Had not Stephen Crane been an artist in words he must have used color with a brush." He was especially struck by Crane's use of color to create an "impression" of a scene, particularly in his Cuban sketches. Linson also commented that "Crane's was peculiarly the genius for distilling from a given situation its very essence, fixing it on the page in swift impressionistic sentences tingling at times with a perfect expression, always alive." Indeed, Linson saw the quality of painting in a great deal of Crane's work, even in his description of the Scranton coal region. In return, Crane paid indirect homage to Linson in *The Third Violet*: the painting described as "cows in a wintry barnyard around a central haybox" was by Linson and hung on the wall of his room where Crane used to see it.[63]

There is also evidence from other sources about Crane's awareness of painting and Impressionism. In 1896 Herbert P. Williams, a friend of Crane's and a reporter for the *Boston Herald*, recalled in an interview for the *Illustrated American* that Crane had several Impressionistic landscapes on the wall of his apartment in New York. He added that he believed that these "Impressionistic paintings had been with him since his college days."[64] More recently, Daniel Hoffman has reflected that when Crane was working on the poems for *The Black Riders*, his closest companions were the students of the Art Students' League:

> These young men were studying with the first generation of American art teachers to have brought home the doctrines of Monet, Cézanne, and Seurat. Crane often slept on cots in their studio, and in several stories he drew upon the discussions of artistic theory he overheard—and probably took part in—as well as the difficulties of his artist friends in earning their daily dinners.[65]

And R. W. Stallman recorded in his *Stephen Crane: An Omnibus* that

> Crane knew Albert Pinkham personally; he knew not only Ryder's paintings, but some of Monet's, Winslow Homer's, and Frederic Remington's drawings, and he had Brady's poignant photographs

to brood over, Coffin's illustrations to *Si Klegg*, and the appren-
ticeship paintings of Linson and of Crane's fellow lodgers at the
Art Students' League, where he lived during the period when he
was composing his own impressionistic paintings: *Maggie* and
The Red Badge.[66]

Another important study of Crane's relationships with painters during
this period is Joseph J. Kwiat's "Stephen Crane and Painting." Kwiat
explores the biographical record of Crane's acquaintance with painters
and his use of artists and their work in his fiction. He mentions not
only Mary Helen Crane but also Phebe English, an art student Stephen
became infatuated with at Claverack Academy between 1888 and 1890.
She gave him some of her paintings and the two remained friends until
at least 1892, when Crane became involved with art students in New
York.[67]

These studies provide a good deal of information about Crane's
involvement with painting, which seems circumambient in his life.
These experiences are reflected in his fiction as well. Beyond *The Third
Violet*, which has as its protagonist a young painter named Bill
Hawker, there are numerous references to painting in general and to
Impressionism in particular. Perhaps the most direct comment is in
"War Memories," Crane's journalistic recollections from Cuba of the
Spanish-American war:

> The interior of the church was too cavelike in its gloom for the
> eyes of the operating surgeons, so they had had the altar-table car-
> ried to the doorway, where there was a bright light. Framed then
> in the black archway was the altar-table with the figure of a man
> upon it. He was naked save for a breech-clout, and so close, so
> clear was the ecclesiastic suggestion, that one's mind leaped to a
> fantasy that this thin pale figure had just been torn down from a
> cross. The flash of this impression was like light, and for this
> instant it illumined all the dark recesses of one's remotest idea of
> sacrilege, ghastly and wanton. I bring this to you merely as an
> effect—an effect of mental light and shade, if you like; something
> done in thought similar to that which the French Impressionists
> do in color; something meaningless and at the same time over-
> whelming, crushing, monstrous.[68]

Other passages in Crane's works suggest his considerable awareness of
art and the artistic world. In "Avon's School by the Sea," for example,
he mentions Professor Conrad Diehl, who in 1865 had gone to "Paris
and entered Gérôme's atelier classes at the École des Beaux Arts" (VIII,
504). Indeed, these remarks about Diehl, as well as those about developments in music, reveal a great deal more cultural sophistication than
Crane has generally been thought to possess.[69] Other journalistic essays

on similar subjects, including two more articles on art at Avon-by-the-Sea,[70] further suggest his awareness of current controversies in art criticism.

In the first of his war dispatches from Greece, pertinently entitled "An Impression of the 'Concert,'" he reports that "Crete spread high and wide precisely like a painting from that absurd period when the painters each tried to reproduce the universe on one canvas. It merely lacked the boat with a triangular sail and a pie-faced crew occupying the attention in the foreground" (IX, 5). Again, in "Death and the Child," he portrays the reflections of Peza:

> Peza remembered his visit to a certain place of pictures, where he had found himself amid heavenly skies and diabolic midnights— the sunshine beating red upon the desert sands, nude bodies flung to the shore in the green moon-glow, ghastly and starving men clawing at a wall in darkness, a girl at her bath with screened rays falling upon her pearly shoulders, a dance, a funeral, a review, an execution, all the strength of argus-eyed art; and he had whirled and whirled amid this universe with cries of woe and joy, sin and beauty, piercing his ears until he had been obliged to simply come away (V, 129).

The paintings here described cannot be specifically identified from the brief descriptions given, but several by Degas would work for the dance and for the girl at bath, and Manet's *Execution of the Emperor Maximilian* (1867), which Emilie Ambre had brought on her concert tour of the United States in 1879, could provide a well-known reference for the execution.[71] In brief, references to painting abound in Crane's works, appearing in such unlikely pieces as *George's Mother* and "One Dash —Horses" as well as in the stories involving painters as characters, such as "Great Grief" and "The Silver Pageant."

Unfortunately, there is no statement by Crane to directly link his knowledge of painting with his fictional aesthetic, at least nothing so direct as Ernest Hemingway's comment that he "learned to write looking at paintings at the Luxembourg Museum in Paris."[72] What remarks exist are often reported second-hand and contain frequent contradictions. Some of the most pertinent are in Linson's recollections in his journal.

Linson reports that the first comment he ever heard Crane make about his literary creed was his rejection of sentimentality and his assertion that "a story should be logical in its action and faithful to character. Truth to life itself was the only test, the greatest artists were the simplest, and simple because they were true." This realistic code contained, as Linson remembers, two important qualifications: that the "truth" portrayed would not necessarily be a scientific analysis of reality but rather a "simple fidelity to a man's own vision"; that beyond realism there needed to be an aesthetic element: "His art—of course he must be an artist—could take care of the rest." The one other matter that Linson could recall was Crane's emphatic denunciation of didacticism in any form.[73]

These comments, which Linson recorded in 1892 and 1893, are basically consistent with what Crane said about literature throughout his lifetime. Beyond such brief statements, however, there is no evidence that Crane formulated a precise and coherent theory of his craft to guide him in his writing. As Joseph Conrad later recalled, "we were no critics, I mean temperamentally. Crane was even less of a critic than myself."[74] Nonetheless, the extant record of Crane's principles indicate a general "Realism" qualified by the variable of one's impressions. He could state, on one hand, that one should attempt to portray "life" and at the same time profess, as he did before the "Society of the Philistines" in 1895, that he was a writer "who was trying to do what he could 'since he had recovered from college' with the machinery which had come into his hands—doing it sincerely, if clumsily, and simply setting forth in his own way his own impressions."[75] Crane's indirect confirmation of the accuracy of this statement of his views comes in the fact that he clipped an account of them from a newspaper and sent it to Nellie Crouse.

What is unique about Crane's brand of Realism is his awareness that the apprehension of reality is limited to empirical data interpreted by a single human intelligence. As a result, he can echo William Dean Howells' views of Realism but stress that a novelist should be "true to himself and to things as he sees them."[76] How well he can see them, Crane writes in "The Mexican Lower Classes," is limited: "He can be sure of two things, form and color" (VIII, 436). Form and color are as much aesthetic as epistemological, however, and the fact that only they seem verifiable implies severe limitations on an artist's ability to portray life realistically. In Crane's "War Memories," a correspondent named Vernall complains that it is impossible to capture the reality of war in art, to get the "real thing." He explains that this is so "because war is neither magnificent nor squalid; it is simply life, and an expression of life can always evade us. We can never tell life, one to another, although sometimes we think we can" (VI, 222).

Crane's understanding of his art, these comments suggest, transcends the purely mimetic functions of slice-of-life Realism in favor of a representation of how things are "seen." But nowhere in Crane's comments are these matters fully developed or made consistent. At times he will assert an affinity with the principles of Howells and Garland, attributing to them an artistic mimesis. In 1895 he asserted: "I decided that the nearer a writer gets to life the greater he becomes as an artist, and most of my prose writings have been toward the goal partially described by that misunderstood and abused word, realism. Tolstoi is the writer I admire most of all." The word "partially" is significant here, especially when taken in the context of Crane's admiration for Ambrose Bierce's story "An Occurrence at Owl Creek Bridge," which is a decidedly Impressionistic story rendering sensory data and fantasy as one, dramatically restricting the sources of information, and stressing confusion over what is real. Crane said that "nothing better exists. . . . That story contains everything."[77] There is some reason for believing, therefore, that Crane's deviations from the norms of Realism were toward a still-developing theory of fiction closely associated with artistic Impressionism.

Thus James B. Colvert reasoned well in "The Origins of Stephen Crane's Literary Creed" in contending that Lars Åhnebrink was short-sighted in viewing Crane's work as simply an extension of French and Russian Naturalism.[78] Colvert, however, is too limiting in his attribution of Crane's theories of art to the aesthetic credo of Dick Heldar, the protagonist of Rudyard Kipling's *The Light That Failed*, which appeared in serial form in *Lippincott's Magazine* in 1891. Dick Heldar, like Crane's Will Hawker to follow, is an Impressionistic painter who experiments with color, especially with its potential for evoking mood. Despite this similarity to Crane's own work, there is no direct evidence that restricts influences on him to this source; it would be more reasonable to suggest that Kipling's novel was one element in a matrix of concepts that influenced Crane's thinking. Indeed, Kipling's ideas may have reinforced, rather than inspired, Crane's developing aesthetic.

But contrary to the historical assumption that Crane was a reluctant browser into literature, an "untutored genius" who sprang into life fully armed, as Howells would have it, Crane was in fact a serious reader.[79] He had an extensive library and was reasonably conversant in recent literary history. Despite his frequent disavowals of any knowledge of literature, there is evidence that he had read, for example, Anatole France, Henry James, George Moore, Mark Rutherford, Bierce, Hardy, Twain, and Kipling.[80] But his knowledge of literature was a good deal wider than this list and would certainly have included the works of his friends Joseph Conrad, Ford Madox Ford, and Harold Frederic. Of these, James, Moore, Bierce, Conrad, Ford, and Frederic play a role in the development of Literary Impressionism. Indeed, Ford said, some years after Crane's death, that "it was perhaps Crane of all that school or gang—and not excepting Maupassant—who most observed that canon of Impressionism: 'you must render: never report.'

You must never, that is to say, write: 'He saw a man aim a gat at him'; you must put it; 'He saw a steel ring directed at him.' "[81]

Ford's remarks imply a dramatic literature in which direct sensory experience is rendered without expository intrusion into the flow of sensation. No narrative intelligence asserts the existence of a gun in Ford's passage; the reader must interpret the sensory data himself. This method is at the heart of Impressionism in literature.

As Herbert Muller has observed, Impressionism requires the suppression of traditional concepts that have the effect of subordinating the sensory impulses of actual life in favor of a narrative generalization of that life, some abstraction of its "meaning." The purpose of Impressionistic writing is not polemical, often not even "thematic" in the sense of organizing the details of fiction to point toward a predetermined idea, but rather to render the sensory nature of life itself, especially to make the reader "see" the narrative described.[82] The effect, as Crane's comments often suggest, is to convey to the reader the basic impressions of life that a single human consciousness could receive in a given place during a restricted duration of time. The qualification on the "reality" of these impressions is that they necessarily filter through the intermediate minds of character and narrator and may be subject to distortions from either restricted data or faulty interpretation of it. In effect, the impressions may be rendered with meticulous fidelity; or they may not; the reader is forced to exercise a continuous skepticism about the reliability of narrative assertions of judgment and of fact.

Fiction thus presented implies a philosophic base, one well described by Paul Ilie:

> The assumption is . . . that the immediate is in an incessant state of rapid flux, with an infinite number of sensory phenomena occurring in as many moments in the time continuum. Ultimate reality, however, belongs to the realm of human consciousness, whose instruments for monitoring those phenomena are the sensory faculties, through the medium of sensation. Impressionism, consequently, is the technique by which one moment of reality is comprehended after the sensation has been modulated by consciousness and arrested in time.[83]

Given a slightly different formulation by Page Stegner, the philosophy of Impressionism

> establishes reality entirely in the stream of sensations. Fundamentally, impressionism is a statement of the subjectivity of reality and the variety of human responses to . . . experience. Memory, imagination, and emotion guide the mind in its ordering of indi-

vidual consciousness and become the basis for artistic representation of experience.[84]

Implicit in art based on the confluence of sensation with secondary interpretation is a necessary distinction between reality as perceived and reality itself. The two may be harmonious, an assumption central to Realism, but more often there is discord caused by factors within reality that distort its sensory signals (distance, fog, obscure sounds, darkness, obstructions) or within the receiving interpretive intelligence (fears, dreams, fantasy, preoccupations). The logic of Realism depends on a consistent reliability of both interpretation and perception; the logic of Impressionism suggests that this correspondence is never certain and that the inscrutability and flux of life *are* its fundamental reality. Impressionistic fiction involves the constant interplay between experience and comprehension, the "apprehension of life through the play of perception,"[85] qualified by the constant awareness that any description or presentation of reality is dependent upon the clarity with which it is perceived.[86]

Depending upon emphasis, an Impressionistic writer can modulate his fiction between the "objective" stance of presenting sensations at the instant of reception, and before cognitive processes have begun to interpret and formulate them into patterns of meaning, and the "subjective" stance of recording the internalization of sensory experience, what a given mind understands having received and analyzed the data. An extension of objective Impressionism would lead to a photographic Realism, one with a high order of fidelity to the external world. An extension of subjective Impressionism would lead to an emphasis on the internal world, to psychological Realism, and to stream-of-consciousness in narrative technique. In practice, Impressionistic fiction tends to blend these possibilities.

Fiction based upon these concepts necessarily creates difficulties in the generation of themes, for empirical sensation does not organize itself around consistent ideas and often stops short of thematic or teleological implications. However, in both its central premise and narrative modalities, Impressionism suggests that "reality is ephemeral, evanescent, constantly shifting its meaning and hence continually defying precise definition."[87] As a result, the characters in Impressionistic fiction are constantly in a state of having to interpret the world around them and to distinguish the "real" from their own views of it.[88]

The truth-illusion theme in Impressionism has been perceptively defined by H. Peter Stowell in his discussion of Chekhov as an Impressionist who presents characters who "perceive only the limited, ambiguous, and ultimately unknowable surfaces of a reality of the senses."[89]

The thematic center of such fiction concerns itself with a character's ability to understand reality, most often presented in terms of the metaphor of vision: a character's ability to "see" becomes synonymous with his ability to interpret experience correctly. Comprehension is presented in narrative terms as apprehension.[90] A character might persist throughout a work in being unable to perceive reality accurately, thus living in a world of illusions and blindness. He might receive restricted, disordered, or ambiguous signals from the external world and be limited to perpetually tentative judgments. He may also reason quite logically from unreliable and incomplete data and arrive at an inaccurate formulation. At best, he might accumulate bits of data that ultimately coalesce into a unified generalization consistent with the sensations he has received, at which point he experiences a sudden moment of insight in a Joycean "epiphany."

Beyond the central truth-illusion theme, a number of important subordinate themes appear in Impressionistic fiction. One of these is the isolation that results from the individualistic nature of empirical limitations. Basically, in Impressionism, each character lives alone, alienated from other characters, uncertain of reality. If a character is forced to an ethical choice, his awareness of the limitations of his knowledge forces him to a point of crisis and despair. As Marston LaFrance explains the concept,

> morality must be the creation of man's weak mental machinery alone; but even the best of men, the most personally honest, is prone to error and thus liable to bring misery upon himself and others because the mental machinery often distorts that reality which he must perceive correctly if his personal honesty is to result in morally significant commitment.[91]

To state it briefly, Impressionism is focused on the central truth-illusion theme, modulated by differences in individual abilities to perceive reality and to interpret it.

A fictive mode that presents such themes must render its reality in an aesthetically compatible form, in a manner which itself suggests a restriction of knowledge and shifting, uncertain views of the world. Impressionistic writers have experimented with nearly every dimension of standard fiction, creating dramatic and ironic modes of narration, plots that violated chronology, and narrative lines that are associative, retrospective, or discontinuous. Life, as Joseph Conrad and Ford Madox Ford stressed on several occasions, presents a series of disjointed sensory experiences. Fiction that shows life must be evocative and dramatic, limiting exposition and authorial intrusion, and presenting the sensory life of a character. The narrator evokes these sensations in a highly controlled style which seeks *le mot juste* and *l'épithète rare*, presenting a scene in the fewest possible words: "Lightning is a match struck against the sky and the sun is a red wafer."[92] The focus is on episodes of isolated activity rather than lengthy patterns of coordinated events; characters are developed dramatically rather than through expository description; the emphasis is on the minds and actions of the characters rather than on the interpretive analysis of the narrator.[93]

The crux of these devices is the method of narration, the central concern of Impressionistic literature. The basic concept was aptly stated by Ford: "[W]e saw that life did not narrate, but made impressions on our brains. We in turn, if we wished to produce on you an effect of life, must not narrate but render. . . ."[94] The point of rendering life rather than narrating it, of showing rather than telling, relates to the realization that "to hear an event is more immediate than is hearing about an event."[95] It is a sense of immediacy, the process of perception, which gives Impressionism its unique quality and which leads to its coordinate devices. Sensory perception necessarily implies a receiving intelligence; the identity of that intelligence can vary according to a variety of patterns within the Impressionistic mode. One stratagem that is inconsistent with the idea and themes of Impressionism, however, is the presence of the author in fiction. The perceiving intellect must seem to be that of the character, a fictive personality serving as narrator, or a number of characters who see reality in different terms.

In general, Impressionistic fiction is not often written in traditional first person because the standard first-person narrator does not describe the immediacy of experience; he is recapitulating rather than experiencing, using memory rather than sensation.[96] First-person narratives enjoy spatial immediacy but temporal dislocation. There is customarily a double time: the time of the action presented from the time of the telling. This distance creates a sense of remoteness from the experience itself, one difficult to render Impressionistically. First person is, however, reconcilable with Impressionistic ideas in a number of ways: the dichotomous times of telling and action can be presented as a dramatic "present" time. This device demands a suspension of disbelief in that the reader must be convinced that the sensations described are being recorded the instant they occur by a person who is acting and not writing. Another alternative is the juxtaposition of two or more narrators describing the same pattern of events so that the concern is on the way in which their minds differ in perceiving reality. But both of these are relatively sophisticated devices that were not common in Impressionism until the twentieth century.[97] A third narrative mode of Impressionistic first person is the complex device of uncertain or unreliable narration, in which the narrator searches for the truth of his own experience, for the meaning of what has happened, for implications unrealized at the time of action. These variations, however, do not play an important role in the fiction of Stephen Crane.

A similar problem exists with the use of an omniscient narrator, for the basic implications of omniscience are irreconcilable with the notion of a limited view of reality and of the relativity of empirical data. As a result, omniscience is not common in Impressionism, although it can play a role if its function is not to state the truth, not to intrude with evaluation or comment, not to provide background information for its own sake, but rather to qualify the consciousness with which the dominant narrative mind is identified or to provide a context for its activity. To be consistent with Impressionism, such comments could describe the conditions that cause the other narrators or characters to perceive experience in a certain way or provide a point of contrast, a superior perspective from which the characters' thoughts become ironic. Omniscience used in this way implies not so much comprehensive knowledge as the diminished reliability of an alternative narrative consciousness.

The norm in Impressionistic narrative devices, however, is the creation of a narrative intelligence that is as restricted in interpretive power as any of the characters. As a result, narrative assertions beyond scenic description are limited to sensational experience, reflective moments, and musings that carry no guarantee of authenticity beyond their occurrence as thought. The constant unreliability of this mode lends itself to two basic modulations: the possible inaccuracy of narrative assertions, whether sensory or interpretive, can be explicitly acknowledged in statements of uncertainty, qualifications that the data "seems" to suggest a given conclusion or that an event "must have" taken place. This device is generally reserved for occasions in which the character has difficulty perceiving an event, is not present, or in some other way is denied access to primary impressions. The other tendency, to report data as though there were no qualifications on its reliability, creates a subtle irony when the reader recognizes that the assertions are not necessarily true, especially when they involve some degree of evaluative judgment.[98]

This device generally takes the form of the identification of the narrative intelligence with the mind of the protagonist, rendering his sense impressions, judgments, memories as though all were fact. The character becomes the center of intelligence, replacing author and narrator, and as the narrator-character distinction diminishes so does the distinction between illusion and reality.[99] As a result, the reader has no access to data outside of the sensory awareness of the protagonist, no reliable information against which to measure the judgment of the narrator other than the narrator's revelations themselves. The reader is forced to the uncomfortable realization that

> the impression of the perceiving mind is quite distinct from the phenomenon stimulating the impression, and although impressions may be the only source of human knowledge, the perceiving intelligence in recognizing the stimulus apprehends it in terms formulated by the mind itself.[100]

The result is a persistent unreliability of narrative stance similar to what Robert Browning presented in the form of the dramatic monologue. The reader cannot supersede the epistemological level of the center of intelligence and thus receives fragmented and potentially unreliable information which is often distorted and ambiguous.

Even within this realization a distinction may be drawn between the objective and subjective modes. In the objective method, the fictive data derives from the primary level of sensory reception, before cognitive processes have analyzed and organized it into comprehensible patterns. There is a high degree of reliability that the data received reflects the world the character experiences. Such narrators function as "receptors" of life, presenting experience with little reflection or comment. The narrator's role is objective in all but one sense: impressions are rendered in terms of language. Verbal evocation implies some degree of understanding, memory, and conceptualization on the basis of existing categories of knowledge. Even the simplest sensory experience undergoes some evaluation and reconstruction to be formulated in words.[101] This process represents the irreducible medium of expression, one which has its corollary in all forms of art. To represent life in art, some conceptual activity, whether associative or discriminatory, is inescapable. With this qualification in mind, the mode of rendering primary perception can be regarded as the "objective" pole on a continuum of narrative methods.

The "subjective" pole presents impressions after the data has been received and filtered through the narrator's mind. In the process, the reliability of the data diminishes in that the additional level of mental activity adds a "subjective valuation superimposed upon sensory objectivization." As Paul Ilie has indicated, in this method "concomitant feelings [are] evoked at the same time that the sensorial impressions are being registered, or else they are sentiments that arise in response to the stimulation of those sensations."[102] The subjective valuation represents the judgment of the narrator and possesses only a tentative validity; it does, however, reveal important information about the character who forms the center of intelligence, revealing his emotions, sapience, illusions, sensitivity, prejudices. This is especially true when the subjective judgment is at odds with the objective impressions. In these cases the first can be measured against the second to provide a qualitative expression of a character's comprehension of the world.[103]

Another variation of Impressionistic narration is the device of "parallax," the method of presenting a scene as perceived by multiple narrators.[104] There are many possibilities for the identity of the two or more narrators: an unidentified narrator may be contrasted to a character acting as a center of intelligence, or characters may be contrasted to each other, both resulting in a narrative irony that juxtaposes views. A work rendered through parallax develops a conflict in the mere statement of what is real, making it an expression of the very concept of Impressionistic thought. In all forms, however, Impressionistic narrative methods are related to the conception of life as apprehensible only through empirical data; any narrative judgments are necessarily restricted and potentially unreliable. Whether the method of presentation is objective or subjective, whether it presents parallax or stream of consciousness, the central concern implied by the method itself is epistemological and relates the methodology of the fiction to its thematic content.

The central theme and basic narrative methods of Impressionism also have some influence on the types of characters portrayed and on the way they are presented. For example, since the protagonists often serve as centers of intelligence, as the receptors of sensory experience, they must be mobile and percipient to provide a wide range of sensory awareness. If they are treated ironically, as blind to experience, incapable of new realizations, they have an antipathetic relationship to the more sensitive reader. But most often, Impressionistic characters are organic, ceaselessly in the process of becoming themselves, as Maria Kronegger states it. Characters who are in the process of forming their understanding of reality are capable of experiencing an epiphany, the central plot development for most Impressionistic fiction.

Impressionistic characters are presented dramatically. Since, with the exception of centers of intelligence, there is no narrative capacity to enter their minds or to explore their backgrounds, what is known about them must emerge from what they do, from what they say, and from what other characters say about them. If the narrative voice is identified with the mind of the protagonist, as is often the case, there is access to one fictive mind and the capacity for direct psychological depth in one character. Since this is a severe limitation in comparison to various omniscient modes, Impressionistic fiction has a tendency to seem shallow, to present the surface of character and action without the depth of narrative analysis.

This sense of shallowness takes several forms. For one thing, the names of characters have no means of introduction until they are mentioned in the dialogue or until the narrator has some reason to think of them in terms of names. As a result, characters are often known by descriptive epithets developed from their most observable characteristics. A character will be labeled the "cowboy" if he is the only such in a group, or the lieutenant if his rank distinguishes him among soldiers, or the "little man" if he is smaller than his compatriots, or the "oiler" if his occupation is his primary distinction. Under some conditions, at night or in a fog, characters may be referred to simply as "figures" or "forms," since sensory data provides no means of determining that they are human beings.[105] Once a character is identified, however, once he is seen clearly or his name is spoken, his name and specific identification become part of the knowledge of the narrator and serve from that point onward as the reference to the character.

The narrative methods of Impressionism also have an impact on the employment of figurative devices. Since the source of data is restricted to the interaction of a limited intelligence with the phenomenological world, the empirical nature of that experience is rendered in images. Indeed, since reality is largely sensory, the images that formulate sensation are the basic unit of narration. Human experience is not projected as an organized continuum of thought and action but rather as a series of images in sequence which may or may not suggest a coherent whole. As Orm Øverland has postulated:

> Seeking an expression for an ever changing and transitory appearance the impressionist's images naturally tend to be particular and personal rather than general and universal. They do not profess to reveal about the objects or situations described any deep and hidden truth which will be valid for all time. The aim is merely to convey the immediate impression evoked by a certain set of circumstances, the interplay of which would most probably occur only on that one and unique occasion.[106]

This reasoning further implies that an Impressionistic writer would tend not to use symbols in fiction, for symbolism requires an abstract and consistent frame of reference that provides extensional meaning for the literal vehicle. The use of a dominant symbol, as is common in Naturalism, implies a more reliable and organized view of reality than would be consistent with the philosophy of Impressionism. Such referential associations as suggest themselves from context might accrue to an image; organic metaphor is possible; but symbolization, by virtue of its referential method, is rare and potentially inconsistent with the assumptions of Impressionism.

The imagery used in Impressionism is related to its source in the narrative consciousness. If the narrative method is objective, limited to sensory evocations of scene and action, the images tend to be descriptive, verbal equivalents of experience. Although all of the senses may be involved, the dominant sensory images are visual and involve various modifications of sight: light, shadow, color, form, depth.[107] The imagery is suggestive rather than definitive, recording brief sensations without organization and interpretation (the glint of the sun on a rifle, for example), sometimes without indications of understanding. It is this mode of imagistic evocation that most clearly resembles the effects of Impressionistic painting, and it may have been this effect that R. W. Stallman had in mind in using the phrase "prose pointillism."

The subjective tendency of narrative method, in which narrative data derive from the mind of the narrator after interpretation has begun, allows for greater variation in the nature of imagistic expressions. The imagery suggests not only sensory experience but how it is perceived and understood. The objective description of war would present images of the sights and sounds and smells of the scene; the subjective image of war might translate the enemy soldiers into monsters if the protagonist's mind perceives them as such. In the subjective mode, the images derive their significance not from their description of the external world but from what they suggest about the mind of the character. The subjective imagery of Impressionism tends toward Expressionism; the more general handling of figurative devices in Impressionism resembles Imagism and recalls T. E. Hulme's contention that images were the "real substance of experience" and Ezra Pound's idea that an image is a device "which presents an intellectual and emotional complex in an instant of time."[108] But basically, Impressionistic imagery presents the verbal equivalents of sensory experience and the subjective values of that experience as formulated by the mind of the protagonist.

The employment of plot and structure in Impressionism also derives from the implications of the narrative method. The writer is faced from the beginning with the problem of creating a coherent work of art based on the fragmentary episodes the protagonist experiences. Since human life is composed of the "movement of discontinuous momentary fragments,"[109] fiction that attempts to reproduce life must render it in terms of brief episodes, abbreviated narrative units that cover a single experience in the center of intelligence. If the narrative method is largely objective, the episodic units are likely to be discrete and related to one another only by the continuity of scene and character. Sometimes, however, the episodes lead to a cumulative significance which the character experiences as epiphany.

Episodic structure also lends itself to narrative parallax and the juxtaposition of scenes from various points of view. A related device is time shift; since episodes do not imply a continuum of activity, they may be presented in virtually any order, even in violation of chronology. Each episode is basically a time shift unexplained by expository comment and determinable largely through internal data, the movement of the sun, people, or other events that require time to occur. In the subjective mode of narration, however, there is room for the associative arrangement of episodes as the interplay between experience and memory relates scenes to one another. The principle of organization by psychological time, by thematic association which selects the episodes to be presented and gives them a developmental order, creates the potential for a structural unity in Impressionism despite its focus on isolated impressions. As Hamlin Garland suggested about painting, even isolated episodes may be arranged to give the whole of a work a satisfying artistic order, a sense of design that transcends the limitations of episodic structure.

As a total aesthetic, the themes and techniques of Impressionistic fiction derive their coherence from the assumption that human life consists of the interaction of an individual intelligence with a world apprehensible only in terms of sensory experience. The narrative methods may present the objective experience of the reception of sensation, or the subjective interpretation of sensation, or two or more modes in narrative counterpoint. The characters, especially protagonists, are in a continuous state of flux, never fully comprehending themselves or the world around them, never able to grasp a generalization that explains life to them. They are subject to uncertainty and delusion, to diminution of stature, to ironic and satiric treatment, but they are also capable of percipient states in which they realize something new about their lives. The figurative devices tend to be sensory images that serve as the correlatives of empirical data and derive their meaning from context; since there is no stable referential schema, there are few symbols. The narration proceeds by means of fragmentary episodes of discontinuous awareness which achieve unity through continuity of scene or character, juxtaposition, association, or theme. The result in a total work is a fiction that resembles the sensory nature of human experience, no more necessarily teleological than life itself, and no less dramatic and meaningful.

This brief postulation of the aesthetic of Literary Impressionism is theoretical, and no single work is consistent with this model in all respects. Nevertheless, even a tentative description of a literary mode is helpful in distinguishing among tendencies within a work and for making discriminations among modes within an historical period. Realism, Naturalism, and Impressionism, being nearly concurrent historically, share many characteristics: natural settings, an anti-

Romanticism that eschews mystification, and concern for the hard life of common Americans. But there are also distinctions among them, differences obscured by a general confusion in terms. Lars Åhnebrink's comment in *The Beginnings of Naturalism in American Fiction* indicates the depth of the problem:

> During the nineties and even after, the discussion of literary theories was confusing because of the looseness of terms used. In general, in the eighties and nineties the movement usually called naturalism went under the name of realism. . . .[110]

Åhnebrink's sense that the terms of the period lacked rigor is unassailable, but perhaps some disorder is inevitable when a disparate group of scholars employ ill-defined verbal indicators to a diverse body of work. Another problem is that critics rarely discuss the same aspects of art when they speak of a movement. Some regard a movement as basically historical, others as the expression of philosophical principles, still others as artistic categories, and some as sociological developments. In addition, many authors, Stephen Crane among them, experimented with several modes and rarely wrote anything with complete fidelity to one school. Nevertheless, recognizing that a definition of a literary mode describes tendencies rather than absolutes, it is essential to provide some indicators for distinguishing Impressionism from Realism and Naturalism.

Many aspects of Naturalism are distinct from those of Impressionism, especially in narrative method, imagery, and theme. If Impressionism derives its themes and techniques from the premise that reality is apprehensible only through empirical experience, Naturalism develops from the concept of determinism. The specific deterministic agent in Naturalism varies from genetic to environmental, but in either form it is usually pessimistic.[111] Heredity functions not only to instill personality traits in the characters but also to link them atavistically to the primitive, animalistic origins of human life, to a time when irrational feelings dominated cognitive abilities. The environmental forces in Naturalism are generally socioeconomic, resulting in a tendency to depict lower-class characters struggling for survival in an alien and often hostile society. As Åhnebrink summarizes these ideas,

> *Naturalism* . . . is a manner and method of composition by which the author portrays *life as it is in accordance with the philosophic theory of determinism* (exemplified in Zola's *L'Assommoir*). In contrast to a realist, a naturalist believes that man is fundamentally an animal without free will. To a naturalist man can be explained in terms of the forces, usually heredity and environment, which operate upon him.[112]

The artistic techniques of Naturalism derive from these ideas. The portrayal of forces beyond the control and comprehension of individual characters cannot easily be rendered in terms of the activity of their minds. As a result, the tendency in Naturalism is for an omniscient narrative consciousness which tells rather than shows its story and which provides voluminous expository data about the characters and events. Naturalistic fiction is often "accumulative and ponderous," scientifically analyzing the forces that drive the characters toward their destinies.[113] Since determinism precludes individual choice, the ethical behavior of the characters is not a prime concern, nor is their individualism, for they function largely as representatives of social and economic groups. All of this is in direct contrast to Impressionism, in which reality is established through an individual's view of it and which restricts narrative data to the mind of a character. Naturalism also allows for greater implementation of characters who remain static for the entire work. Indeed, since they are frequently victims of external forces, they are often grotesques, or derelicts from the lower class, or compulsive monomaniacs.[114]

Since the philosophy of Naturalism implies a stable conception of reality in which influences can be analyzed and documented, it is possible to use this frame of reference as a basis for symbolization. Symbolism depends upon stable abstractions for its extensional meaning; in Naturalism those abstractions are suggested through symbols of animalism, depravity, lust, or greed, when the referent is a genetic force, or the jungle, or machinery, or primitive humanity when describing the environment. Often the imagery of Naturalism, rather than its themes, reveals its Darwinian influences. Plot development in Naturalism tends to portray a history of causality for human tragedy; the figurative devices suggest the specific agents that impel the plot.

Although all of these characteristics are rarely found in precisely this form in any single work of fiction, a story such as Frank Norris' "A Deal in Wheat" can serve as an example of the mode. The protagonist is a simple, well-intentioned farmer who struggles hopelessly against economic forces beyond his control. The omniscient point of view is essential for revealing the economic system that ruins him; his particular case is emblematic of the ills of unchecked capitalistic power; the plot contrasts his hopeless plight against the barons of industry and reveals the inevitable human tragedy that results from their competition; and the tone of pessimism underscores the deterministic themes.

If the relationship between Naturalism and Impressionism is one of ideological and artistic antithesis, the distinctions between Impressionism and Realism are much more subtle. W. W. Sichel, writing in the *Quarterly Review* in 1897, maintained that "what is vulgarly known as

'Realism' has indeed nothing necessarily in common with impressionism at all."[115] Unfortunately, Sichel's concept of Impressionism was
based on the artist's need to "recall an emotion," an indicator so nonrestrictive that he could discuss Donne, Sterne, and Keats as Impressionists. More recently, Jacob Kolb has discussed the difficulties of
using "Realism" with precision:

> The term "realism" has had a remarkable vogue, although its
> popularity seems to be inversely proportional to the precision with
> which it has been used. It is a term which is in great need of
> clear definition, not only because of its constant general and crit-
> ical use, but also because of the importance to literary study of the
> concepts which the term implies.[116]

The sorts of nonrestrictive indicators that Kolb complains about are
present in Åhnebrink's definition: *"Realism* is a manner and method
of composition by which the author describes *normal, average life* in
an accurate and truthful way (exemplified in Howells' *The Rise of
Silas Lapham*)."[117] Although Howells' novel may well be a model of
Realism, the more general attribution of mimesis to Realism ignores
the fact that Realism, Impressionism, and Naturalism are all essentially mimetic, although they may differ in their assumptions about
reality. And of course this definition indicates nothing of the fictional
methods employed to present a mimetic portrait.

In basic philosophy, Realism seems to differ from Impressionism in
holding three coordinate postulations:

1) that there is a real world (independent of man's knowledge)
2) that it is possible to know this world, and
3) that it is possible to write about it accurately in fiction.[118]

The difficulty of determining what the "real world" consists of is
solved in principle by invoking what Edwin Cady calls the "theory of
common vision" and by attempts to "approximate the norm of experience." As a result, Realism embraces an essentially "Benthamite doctrine that the most real is that which is experienced by the greatest
number."[119] At a meeting of the Modern Language Association in 1967,
six essential characteristics of Realism were isolated: "fidelity to actuality, objectivity (or neutrality—the absence of authorial judgment),
democratic focus (particularized ordinary characters), social awareness
(and critical appraisal), reportorial detail, and colloquial expression."[120] If the "fidelity to actuality" premise creates certain
philosophical difficulties, it is nevertheless useful in reaffirming that
Realism presumes to describe reality and that, unlike Impressionism,
determining what is real is not a central issue.[121]

As the central idea at the heart of Naturalism is Determinism, and the underlying issue of Impressionism is epistemology, so the dominant themes of Realism, beyond mimetic concerns, involve ethical crises. Moral choices are excluded from Naturalism by its deterministic emphasis, and to some extent from Impressionism by its problems in assessing what is real. Realism, on the other hand, assumes that a character knows what is real and that he is free to choose among alternatives presented to him, thus assuming full moral responsibility for his actions. As Åhnebrink suggests, the central decision made by Silas Lapham is representative of this theme, as are the decisions made by Marcia Gaylord in *A Modern Instance* and by Huck Finn in Twain's novel.

In Realism, the conflicts are often those moral and social dilemmas which grow out of bourgeois life and manners. As Jacob Kolb suggests, the ethics of *Huck Finn* are based upon the "confrontation of human beings in a humanely created social environment." As Realism subscribes to a normative common vision, it follows that the characters portrayed will also closely approximate the norm. As Kolb says,

> the realists write about the common, the average, the unextreme, the representative, the probable. They concern themselves with ordinary human lives seen in the context of normal social relationships. They concentrate on what people are rather than what they ought to be, on men rather than Man.[122]

One qualification that might be placed upon Kolb's description is that although Realistic characters are representative, they are also individualized, facing unique crises of intense moment drawn from within the range of probable human experience. They act as individuals, not as representatives or specimens. In this, characterization in Realism is not dramatically distinct from Impressionism, which emphasizes somewhat more the development of personality and ideas rather than their expression in moral judgment.

In narrative methodology, Realism demonstrates a great deal of variation. If nearly all Naturalism employs an omniscient narrator, and nearly all Impressionism some form of restrictive central intelligence, Realism tends toward Impressionism in its objectivity, eschewing omniscience and narrative intrusions. However, the effect of Realism is not generally to emphasize the limited knowledge of a character but to define his personality. First or third person limited, both usually identified with the mind of the protagonist, are the normative forms. This methodology allows for a natural definition of personality and for the documenting of the conflicts that give rise to the themes of Realism.

The structure of realistic fiction moves forward from character definition to ethical conflict, with the character's decision providing the climax and resolution of plot. Requiring neither the episodic units of Impressionism, nor the loose and baggy ramblings of Naturalism, Realism can employ a great deal of structural variation. There is similar flexibility in the handling of figurative devices. Realism focuses on character and conflict; its frame of reference is personal rather than mythic and abstract. Realistic referential devices, therefore, grow out of context, and these are usually images and organic metaphors rather than symbols.[123] For example, the houses in *The Rise of Silas Lapham* have a significance beyond themselves but one unique to Silas and his life, his social aspirations, his limitations. The same houses in other novels would have rather different values when related to characters of varying backgrounds. In short, the mimetic devices and themes of Realism relate to the basic concept of an ordinary character placed in a situation of ethical conflict. The fictional techniques, narrative methods, plot, and structural devices all derive from this underlying idea.

If these theoretical models of Realism, Naturalism, and Impressionism are artificial in their purity and imperfect as descriptions of individual works, they nevertheless postulate distinctions among the modes in theme and methodology. These lines of discrimination are crucial for an assessment of the works of Stephen Crane, who has been described variously as an innovative Impressionist, as the first American Naturalist, and as a central figure in the growth of Realism. Crane's work is sufficiently broad and varied so as to invite a variety of responses, but this variety deepens rather than vitiates the need to give his work a close reading in terms of discrete categories of literary modality. This is especially true for Impressionism, which has never received a full discussion in terms of Crane's work. His stories and novels need to be examined to determine which of them are essentially Impressionistic and what implications Impressionistic tendencies have for understanding the body of Crane's literary production. Crane, whom R. W. Stallman said "perfected more works than either Poe or Twain,"[124] played a key role in the development of American fiction, especially in its transition from traditional thought and methods to what is now regarded as Modernism. A detailed examination of his fiction should help to define precisely what that role was and how it has influenced modern literature.

II

Narrative Methods:
"The eyes of the world"

When *The Red Badge of Courage* appeared in 1895, some of the British reviewers, assuming that they were reading a Realistic novel, announced that Stephen Crane was a veteran of the American Civil War and that only a person who had actually experienced these events could possibly have presented them so vividly.[1] But Crane had not been to the war, and in an important sense he was not a Realist. With the exception of a few of the Bowery tales, he did not write what he had seen, with fidelity to actuality, in the way he had seen it. Indeed, in terms of sharpness of detail, his stories of war written after he had observed battle are inferior to those which were purely imaginative. Crane's gifts were not simply the photographic skills of journalism but the qualities of imagination of a creative fictionist. His English reviewers had been misled by his Impressionism, his ability to approximate immediate sensory experience and a believable psychological flow. Crane's war novel had applied Impressionistic ideas to fiction with a precision never before seen in American literature.[2]

If the central proposition of Impressionism is the fictional rendering of sensory experience, the qualifying variable is the mind that perceives the sensations. This problem did not affect Impressionistic painting because there was no presumed creation of human consciousness, only of the scene being perceived: the assumption is that what is depicted is rendered as the *painter* saw it, in *plein air*, in a *vistazo*. Similarly, in music, especially that of Claude Debussy and Maurice Ravel, the general assumption is that the impressions evoked through tones are those of the composer. But this assumption is not present in fiction because of the interjection of an intermediary center of intelligence which functions as narrator and which often records not what it sees but what is perceived by one of the characters. The effect is a distancing, an objectivity, which makes more difficult the illusion of sensory activity. The limitation of narrative data to the narrator's projection of the mind of a

character is essential to the concept of Impressionism since it ultimately reveals that reality is not fully comprehended by a single human
mentality. It implies that views of reality are dependent upon the perceiving mind; the accuracy of the portrayal relies upon the quality of
the observer and the limitations his immediate position may place
upon him. Although Stephen Crane wrote no essays on the theory of
literature, he did occasionally comment indirectly about various technical matters in fiction. For example, in *Active Service* the narrator
reflects, somewhat gratuitously,

> the war-correspondent arises, then, to become a sort of cheap tele-
> scope for the people at home; further still, there have been fights
> where the eyes of a solitary man were the eyes of the world; one
> spectator whose business it was to transfer, according to his abil-
> ity, his visual impressions to other minds (III, 172).

The awareness that what the viewer transmits is his visual impressions
of the scene is a central proposition in Impressionistic aesthetics, one
easily extended from a war correspondent to the narrator of fiction.

Although Crane's works exhibit a general commitment to this
method of narration, he was capable of experimenting with a variety of
forms. Indeed at the time of his death he was at work on a long first-
person novel, *The O'Ruddy*, written somewhat in imitation of the
eighteenth-century British picaresque. On the other hand, given the
quantity of fiction he wrote in his brief career, there is remarkably little
deviation from basic Impressionistic narrative stances. Beyond *The
O'Ruddy*, for example, only a few works are written in first person, and
many of those manipulate access to fictive data in an Impressionistic
way. One of the most fascinating of these works is a story entitled "A
Tale of Mere Chance," a piece related to the dramatic monologue in its
ironic revelations of personality. This brief story is told by a murderer
after his capture and imprisonment. The narration concentrates not so
much on the action of the killing and capture as on the unconscious
revelation of the mind of the murderer, whose opinions of himself are
inconsistent with the events he relates. The opening lines establish the
tone of the narrative:

> Yes, my friend, I killed the man, but I would not have been de-
> tected in it were it not for some very extraordinary circumstances.
> I had long considered this deed, but I am a delicate and sensitive
> person, you understand . . . (VIII, 100).

As these lines indicate, the heart of the story is in the persistent dis-
closure of the arrogance and self-deceit of the narrator. When people
pass him, he contemplates "their stupidity with a sense of satisfac-

tion." He demonstrates not his "delicacy" but the aberration of his mind.

One expression of his derangement is his surrealistic personification of inanimate objects. After the murder, according to his account, the chair moves to block the door; the clock speaks to betray his alibi; his bloodstained coat clings to him, revealing incriminating evidence; the tiles, on which the victim's blood flowed, pursue him relentlessly, shrieking his guilt. All of these events are related as facts by the narrator; there are no comments of compensatory interpretation. To evade the pursuing tiles, he invents various schemes: "I am an ingenious person, and I used every trick that a desperately fertile man can invent" (VIII, 101). He recalls these events, but he does not know fully what to make of them: "Who can be sure of the meaning of clamoring tiles?" But it is clear at the end that driven by guilt, insane to the point of hearing the voices of the tiles continuously, he is captured and imprisoned. The story is in first person but in a variety of that device closely related to the unconscious revelations of the dramatic monologue technique, stream of consciousness, and the psychological values of Impressionism. Beyond its affinities to the stories of ratiocination by Edgar Allan Poe, "A Tale of Mere Chance" is an alarmingly effective story that demonstrates one of the ways Crane could adapt first person to the needs of uncertainty and relativity.

Most of Crane's other first-person works are more typical of the traditional uses of the technique. Solomon Bennet narrates three of the *Tales of the Wyoming Valley*, "The Battle of Forty Fort," "The Surrender of Forty Fort," and "'Ol' Bennet' and the Indians," stories without artistic distinction but with continuously ironic comments by the narrator:

> If people had thoroughly known my father, he would have had no enemies. He was the best of men. He had a code of behaviour for himself and for the whole world as well. If people wished his good opinion they only had to do exactly as he did and to have his views (VIII, 148).

Several of the *Whilomville Tales*, such as "The Angel-Child," employ a first-person narrator identified only as the "unfortunate writer,"[3] but little is made of his identity. Slightly more is done with the Major in "A Freight Car Incident" who tells about his encounter with a character named Luke Burnham, who is later killed in a saloon (VIII, 105–09). "The Camel" is told by a youthful narrator who repeats the antecedent first-person tale told by Uncle Clarence, but again there is little development of the implications of having the story filtered through two levels of consciousness.

Beyond these stories there is one uniquely Impressionistic story, "An Illusion in Red and White," and occasional first-person intrusions into essentially third-person narratives. Such intrusions are generally casual, carrying no thematic implications beyond ironic comment on the action. This is the case in "The Clan of No-Name" and "One Dash—Horses," in which the narrator interjects, "My friend, take my advice and never be executed by a hangman who doesn't talk the English language" (V, 15). *The O'Ruddy* is more intriguing in narrative terms because of the persistency of self-conscious statements by the narrator[4] and for the indications of the restrictions of data. The narrator, a somewhat older O'Ruddy than the one involved in the action, is aware of the limitations of his experiences and of the significance of these restraints, a matter of no little import in assessing Crane's consciousness of these matters in the last year of his life.

In telling about a scene in the Red Slipper, the narrator concludes, "at least this is the way matters appeared to my stupefied sense" (IV, 130). The restriction of his access to information always modifies what is told about a scene:

> A little later, a great shindy broke out in the darkness and I heard voices calling loudly for a rally in the name of some guild or society. I moved closer but I could make out little save that it was a very pretty fight in which a company of good citizens were trying to put to flight a band of roughs and law-breakers. There was a merry rattling of sticks. Soon enough, answering shouts could be heard from some of the houses and with a great slamming of doors, men rushed out to do battle for the peace of the great city. Meanwhile all the high windows had been filled with night-capped heads and some of these people even went so far as to pour water upon the combatants. They also sent down cat-calls and phrases of witty advice. The sticks clattered together furiously; once, a man with a bloody face staggered past us; he seemed to have been whacked directly on the ear by some uneducated person; it was as fine a shindy as one could hope to witness and I was deeply interested (IV, 129).

Despite assertions of his interest, the narrator is limited to reported sounds and events without precise definition. Often his vision is restricted by objects and distance, and he must speculate about what he sees:

> I paced the lawn for a time, and then took seat in the summer-house. I had been there but a moment when I perceived Lady Mary and the Countess come into the garden. Through the leafy walls of the summer-house, I watched them as they walked slowly to and fro on the grass. The mother had evidently a great deal to

> say to the daughter. She waved her arms and spoke with a keen
> excitement.
>   But did I over-hear anything? I over-heard nothing. From what
> I knew of the proper conduct of the really thrilling episodes of
> life, I judged that I should have been able to over-hear almost
> every word of this conversation. Instead, I could only see the
> Countess making irritated speech to Lady Mary (IV, 59).

The O'Ruddy's problem of knowing, of having to speculate and sur-
mise in terms of uncertainty, is typical of the emphasis Crane developed in his first-person narratives.

But the problem of interpreting reality is given its most complex
development in first-person in "An Illusion in Red and White." The
story is Impressionistic in two dimensions: the narrator is uncertain
about the events and speculates about what "must" have occurred; the
characters, although present at the precipitating event, come to believe
an account of it which they have been told and which becomes fixed in
their imaginations. The narrator, a correspondent reporting on the
Cuban blockade, recalls the tale with some question of its authenticity:
"'Now this is how I imagine it happened. I don't say it happened this
way, but this is how I imagine it happened. And it always struck me as
being a very interesting story'" (VIII, 154).

The initial incident is that Farmer Jones murders his wife with an
axe one morning in the kitchen in full view of his four children. Then
he orders them to bed, buries his wife, and begins a series of suggestions
to the children that what they had seen was a man with red hair and
white hands, with large white teeth, take an axe to their mother. Soon
they believe it wholeheartedly, and the people in the area come to
believe it too. The narrator, however, does not, and he speculates about
how the children had become deluded. When Jones had denied to them
that he had been present,

> the children did not know how to reply. Their meagre little senses
> informed them that their father had been the man with the axe,
> but he denied it, and to their minds everything was a mere great
> puzzle with no meaning whatever, save that it was mysteriously
> sad and made them cry (VIII, 157).

The concern here for the "meagre little senses" of the children evi-
dences an explicit awareness by the correspondent of the inadequacy
and unreliability of the empirical data the children reject. That sensory
experience has "no meaning whatever" is an extension of the tenet of
Impressionism that experience is not necessarily teleological. In short,
the passage is a statement of basic Impressionistic ideas. The relativism
of perspective is made clear by the attitude of the infant Henry, who is

obsessed with his own needs. Despite the eventual conviction of the father and his subsequent confession, the eldest child, Freddy, never believes in the validity of the confession and lives with the hope that he will some day "meet the man with the red hair, big white teeth and white hands, whose image still remains so distinct in his memory that he could pick him out in a crowd of ten thousand" (VIII, 159). Imaginative data has replaced sensory data with a clarity that makes Freddy certain of its authenticity. Reality is a function of interpretation within the mind, and analyzed perception is subject to the distortions of memory and fantasy. Here, as elsewhere in Crane's works, the reliability of human comprehension is subject to error and distortion. In this story, as in "A Tale of Mere Chance" and *The O'Ruddy*, Crane was able to develop Impressionistic themes within a first-person narrative stance.

The technical antithesis of first-person narration, with its inherent limitations, is omniscience. Although much of Crane's work appears to employ an omniscient narrator, with access to all information, free of temporal and spatial restrictions, only a few of his narratives actually conform to this classification. *The Third Violet* and *Active Service*, two of what Lillian Gilkes called Crane's "potboiler" novels, are basically omniscient in method. In *Active Service*, for example, although the narrator is largely concerned with the actions and thoughts of the protagonist, Rufus Coleman, he is able to leave Coleman and roam freely among the other characters, occasionally entering their minds. The narrator, as narrator, is very much present:

> It may be curious to note here that all of Peter Tounley's impassioned communication with the inn-keeper had been devoted to an endeavor to learn what in the devil was the matter with these people . . . (III, 264).

Later, in a scene in which Coleman is absent, the narrator provides this information:

> Nora was silent for a time, while a gloom upon her face deepened. It had struck her that the theories for which she protested so energetically might be not of such value (III, 282).

In these and other instances it is clear that the narrator has access to the thoughts of several characters and can present even mental data with assurance.

The Third Violet is a more controlled novel, with greater limitation on the narrator's range. The information is restricted to the mind of Will Hawker and what can be observed about other characters. The stance implies a psychological restriction coupled with spatial freedom. Hawker is not present at the Inn, for example, when the women gossip about him and his family, so the narrator reports the surface only, relating dialogue and action but not thought (II, 37–39). The same device is used in other scenes not involving Hawker, as in Chapter 16 when Hollanden and Fanhall discuss Hawker. But beyond these two novels there is little of traditional omniscient narration in Crane's work except in such short pieces as "Henry M. Stanley," which is notable for being one of the few Crane works free of irony. In short, omniscience is inhospitable to Impressionistic ideas, and Crane wrote only a few omniscient works and these are among his least successful.

Another technique inimical to Impressionistic ideas is narrative intrusion, a device often used to provide background, to point to themes, or to provide information beyond the knowledge of the characters. Ford Madox Ford, in advocating Impressionistic fiction, warned against using a narrative presence that breaks the illusion of the dramatic presentation of life: "In vain does the fowler set his net in the sight of the bird."[5] Despite such cautions, and contrary to Joseph X. Brennan's assertion that Crane's intrusions occur "only in those works in which Crane chose to reveal the mental operations of his creations,"[6] Crane's fiction is less than perfectly controlled, and a good number of works contain narrative intrusions. For example, in "The Black Dog," in the midst of otherwise dramatic action, the narrator reflects that "in the final struggle, terror will fight the inevitable [death]" (VIII, 246). There are also gratuitous judgments in many other stories. In "A Man and Some Others," the narrator, after recalling Bill's history, offers his estimate that "by this time all that remained of his former splendor was his pride, or his vanity, which was one thing which need not have remained" (V, 55). Even in "The Blue Hotel," one of Crane's finest stories, there are intrusive expository comments at various points, one of them being the "space-lost bulb" observation. A more subtle intrusion occurs when Scully is showing the Swede the living quarters in the hotel. Scully is displaying some familial artifacts when the narrator comments that "there was revealed a ridiculous photograph of a little girl" (V, 150). There are no indications that the narrator is projecting a judgment drawn from any mind other than his own.

Other intrusions occur in *George's Mother* (I, 135, 142) and in "God Rest Ye Merry Gentlemen," in which the narrator tells the future beyond the conclusion of the action (VI, 148). In "The Angel-Child" expository digressions fill in the background of the barber, and in "The Price of the Harness" the narrator interrupts the action to reflect on duty, the pride of an officer, and the suffering of horses in battle, ideas already developed dramatically. In this story, the narrator generates the central metaphor for war out of his own mind: "It reminds one always of a loom, a great grand steel loom, clinking, clanking, plunk-

ing, plinking, to weave a woof of thin red threads, the cloth of death"
(VI, 109). Crane's most explicit employment of narrative intrusion
comes in the didactic conclusion of "Diamonds and Diamonds":

> If you are a politician and you allow a man to substitute a ring
> of paste and gold-plate for a two-hundred-dollar diamond ring and
> sell it to you for a hundred dollars merely because you have had a
> jeweler appraise the real diamond—if you are this kind of an ass
> and dwell in a live ward, let your idiocy be known. It will make
> you friends. People will laugh and vote for you out of a sense of
> humor. If you don't believe it, look at the returns and see who
> was elected last year to the board of aldermen from the 204th ward
> of the city of Boston (VIII, 118).

All these intrusions interrupt the dramatic flow of action and expound
on concerns already clear in the story itself. They indicate not so much
Crane's sense of the theory of fiction as the fact that he worked at times
with less than perfect control of his craft, with less than a firm grasp on
his own pronouncements about writing.

The narrative mode that Crane most often employed is third-person
limited, the natural expression of Literary Impressionism. As the most
objective and empirically controlled of the narrative devices he used, it
is also the one most consistent with what is known of his own articulation of his artistic goals. As Crane once said in a letter to John
Northern Hilliard,

> I have been very careful not to let any theories or pet ideas of my
> own creep into my work. Preaching is fatal to art in literature. I
> try to give to readers a slice out of life; and if there is any moral
> or lesson in it, I do not try to point it out. I let the reader find it
> for himself. The result is more satisfactory to both the reader and
> myself. As Emerson said, "There should be a long logic beneath
> the story, but it should be kept carefully out of sight."[7]

In general, Crane's dislike of didacticism and authorial presence in
fiction is remarkably close to Flaubert's dictum, one often applied to
the inception of Impressionism in French painting and literature, that
"the artist should no more appear in his picture than God does in
nature."[8] Crane's comment implies that fictive data should be rendered
as originating from within the fiction itself and as having been perceived by the narrator or one or more of the characters. The author
records what the center of intelligence experiences and thinks and
nothing else. Crane's description of the inside of the church in "War
Memories" (VI, 254), with its overt expression of affinities to Impressionistic painting, is a good example of how an established center of
intelligence can relate not only sensory data but cognitive and associ-

ative mental activity as well. Here, too, is a clear statement that Crane understood Impressionism to involve the presentation of the "effect of mental light and shade."

The projection of mental states, the rendering of apprehensions, makes special demands upon a writer. As Orm Øverland has pointed out, "one consequence of this technique with regards to Crane's style is the predominance of verbs of perception. Things are constantly 'seen,' 'heard,' and 'felt': they become real through the act of perception."[9] Sergio Perosa has explored these stylistic matters in depth in *The Red Badge of Courage*, a novel he describes as a "triumph of impression- istic vision and impressionistic technique." Perosa counts, in this brief novel, 350 verbs directly indicating visual sensations, another 200, such as "appear," suggesting visual phenomena, and numerous auditory and sensual verbs. His point is that the novel is rendered as sensory data at the moment of apprehension: "The total picture is the sum of the infinite touches and sense impressions, and must be focused anew at each step or turn of the process: it is the characteristic manner of impressionistic rendering."[10]

Crane's fiction is nearly always written in accord with Impression- istic strategies. The basic restriction of data for an individual character, and hence for the fiction itself, is well defined by a passage in "London Impressions":

> [E]ach man sat in his own little cylinder of vision, so to speak. It was not so small as a sentry-box nor so large as a circus-tent, but the walls were opaque, and what was passing beyond the dimen- sions of his cylinder no man knew (VIII, 683).

Although Crane is describing merely the experience of riding through London in a carriage, the limitation of sensory information, the restric- tion of point of view, provides a useful metaphor for the implicit epistemological condition in nearly all of his work. Regardless of intel- ligence or other factors, each character is limited to his own "cylinder of vision" and must base all of his conclusions and actions upon the limited information available.[11] What is lost in Crane's fiction by such narrative restriction is compensated for by intensity; as Seymour L. Weingart has commented, "the more limited the point of view, the more intense is the recapitulation of stimuli, wherein lies the strategy of the Impressionist."[12] Crane's fiction is replete with examples of restricted and yet intense narrative perspectives.

Perhaps the most dramatic representation of this method is "Three Miraculous Soldiers," in which the point of view is largely identified with the mind of the female protagonist, Mary Hinckson, who gains much of her information by peering through a knothole into a barn.

The opening of the story reveals Crane's typical method of progressive intensification: the first paragraph describes Mary and the room she is in from the viewpoint of the third-person narrator. "The girl was in the front room on the second floor, peering through the blinds" (VI, 22). The narrator is not omniscient: he speculates that two clay figures on the mantel are "probably" a shepherd and a shepherdess. Beyond introducing this element of uncertainty, the opening paragraph also defines Mary's initial angle of vision, which then controls the second paragraph:

> From between the slats of the blinds she had a view of the road as it wended across the meadow to the woods and again where it reappeared crossing the hill, a half mile away (VI, 22).

There are no comments beyond her knowledge; by implication, she is deeply concerned with activity on the road, of which she can see only part. By the third paragraph the narrative perspective is explicitly limited to Mary's mind, although formulated by the narrator, who retains a descriptive function:

> Mary's eyes were fastened upon the little streak of road that appeared on the distant hill. Her face was flushed with excitement and the hand which stretched in a strained pose on the sill trembled because of the nervous shaking of the wrist. The pines whisked their green needles with a soft hissing sound against the house (VI, 22).

The reader is presented with almost poetic sensory data in the view of the road, the feeling of the trembling hand, the sound of the pines in the wind.

The story progresses on these terms. When Mary speaks to someone downstairs, "a voice" answers. Only the dialogue reveals that the speaker is Mary's mother, after which the narrator provides this identification in subsequent references. When the soldiers first appear on the road, they do so at a distance, a fact rendered impressionistically: "Upon the yellow streak of road that lay across the hillside there now was a handful of black dots—horsemen" (VI, 23). It is characteristic of his method of presenting apprehension before cognition that Crane does not say that "soldiers" appeared in the distance. Mary's eyes perceive dots, which are then interpreted as horsemen, the next level of analysis, and finally as soldiers, distinguishing among other categories of horsemen.

To Mary's point of view is added another, one equally limited: "Rushing to the window, the mother scanned for an instant the road on the hill." The mother responds with fright, apparently from dread of the enemy, but it is evident that the soldiers are at some distance, for a moment later "the black dots vanished into the wood." Soon the girl can hear the "quick, dull trample of horses." When the soldiers appear, the forest suddenly "disclosing" men in blue uniforms, the situation is further clarified: Mary and her family are loyal Confederates living in the South; the Union army is advancing. The perspective briefly shifts to that of the officer in charge of the group, and the fear of the women is dramatically revealed to be groundless: the Union officer has no interest in the women. His insouciance is contrasted to the fear of the women, which distorts their view of the situation. When they hear the crackling of the fire in the kitchen, they are certain it is the soldiers, and they know that "these sounds [are] sinister." Apprehensive data is now mingled with interpretive distortions. The first section of the story ends when Mary goes to the barn to relieve her fear that her horse has been stolen and discovers three Confederate soldiers who have sought refuge from the Union advance. Again the narrative emphasis is on restriction: at first "the girl could not see into the barn because of the heavy shadows." In a moment, when her eyes adjust to the light, her perception is of "three men in grey" sitting on the floor. That the men are Confederate soldiers in hiding is left to the reader to induce from the description.

The next section of the story retains its restriction on the point of view to Mary's mind and what she is able to observe. As she speaks to the soldiers, seeking information about her father, and as a large group of Union cavalry ride into the yard, the emphasis is on how little Mary can perceive of the action. The trees and a henhouse obscure her view of the arriving troops; she has to leave the barn to get a better look at them; once in the house, she moves about from window to window, each revealing only a partial view of the scene. No clarifying information is introduced from any source other than Mary's mind. By the end of the section, she has hidden the three men in the feed box and the Union soldiers have decided to imprison another captured soldier in the barn.

At this point the story becomes increasingly vivid in its projection of sensory details as the scene becomes obscure and limited. As it begins to grow dark, Mary, now back in the house peering out the window, perceives the muted colors before her: "Tones of grey came upon the fields and the shadows were of lead" (VI, 34). The fires in the encampment shine more brilliantly, "becoming spots of crimson color in the dark grove." As the light fades even further, visual data become more indistinct: trees appear as black "streaks of ink"; groups of soldiers are "blue clouds" about the fire. A lantern hung in the barn distorts the view: "Its rays made the form of the sentry seem gigantic" (VI, 35).

Auditory sensation, of course, is not affected: the whinny of the horses, the hum of distant conversation, the calls of the sentries are all heard clearly. Mary's assessment of the scene in the orchard, with campfires glowing in the darkness, is that it is "like a great painting, all in reds upon a black cloth" (VI, 36). Finally, in the ultimate restriction of narrative data, Mary, stealing to the rear of the barn to determine the safety of her compatriots in the feed box, puts her eye to a knothole. Much of the rest of the story is rendered from this source of information.

There is a tense scene when a Union officer opens the feed box and finds nothing but grain. Mary, understandably, is startled. Incapable of accounting for the disappearance of the three men, she perceives the feed box as a mysterious object "like some dark magician's trap" (VI, 38). Through the knothole, the Union soldiers cast "monstrous wavering shadows" in the lantern light; the roof of the barn becomes an "inscrutable blackness." Mary's belief in sensory data is shattered: hearing sounds at her feet, she first "imagines" that she sees human hands protruding from under the barn and then she realizes that a man is, in fact, crawling out. Despite the dramatic plot, this scene emphasizes problems of perception and interpretation rather than action. The three Confederate soldiers escape only to learn that their Captain is being held within. They decide to rescue him.

As the soldiers return to the barn, Mary returns to her knothole. As she surveys the scene within, she searches "with her eyes, trying to detect some moving thing, but she could see nothing" (VI, 42). She thinks she can see a figure in the darkness, but she is not sure:

> At one time she saw it plainly and at other times it vanished,
> because her fixture of gaze caused her occasionally to greatly
> tangle and blur those peculiar shadows and faint lights. As last,
> however, she perceived a human head (VI, 43).

Her other sensations are equally uncertain. The sounds are incomprehensible: she can interpret them only in general terms as a "tumult," as the "scramble and scamper of feet," as voices yelling "incoherent" words. As the Union sentry moves into her vision, however, and as her sense of his danger from the creeping men within the barn grows, she focuses sharply on his "brown hair," "clear eyes," and the wedding ring on his finger. When the men finally leap upon the sentry, Mary's passive reception of details ends and she screams, inadvertently creating a diversion that allows the four Confederates to escape. The story concludes with the Union lieutenant reflecting on Mary's concern for the sentry, an indication that despite war some elements of compassion survive.

"Three Miraculous Soldiers" is no more an historical record of war than is *The Red Badge*. The story reveals Crane's best use of suspense in the narrative line, but even the suspense is a product of narrative method. Told from another point of view, there could have been little suspenseful interest. The story is artistically and ideologically a study in the limitation of sensory data, rendered, with some contrasts from other viewpoints, from the mind of a woman under conditions of extraordinary restriction. Although there are other elements of interest (the depiction of war from the point of view of a Southern woman, melodramatic plot development, and a concern for the father off at war), the fundamental themes and methods of this study are Impressionistic. Indeed the lengthy scenes based on what Mary can perceive through the knothole constitute one of the most remarkably limited narrative perspectives in American literature.

There are many other examples in Crane's fiction of sharply restrictive narrative perspectives in an Impressionistic mode. If Mary Hinckson's view through a knothole, under difficult light conditions, represents a physical constriction of vision, the conditions of sight in such works as *Maggie* demonstrate more complex problems with the reception and interpretation of sensory data.

In Chapter 10 of *Maggie,* in which Jimmie and his mother are so obsessed with self-righteousness that they fail to perceive any familial obligation to Maggie after her seduction, the point of view is largely identified with Jimmie. His moral blindness is metaphorically suggested in terms of literal problems of vision:

> Jimmie walked to the window and began to look through the blurred glass. It occurred to him to vaguely wonder, for an instant, if some of the women of his acquaintance had brothers (I, 43).

The blurred glass suggests his incapacity to see the situation clearly, especially since he has himself seduced at least two young girls. That he ponders this matter, albeit "vaguely," suggests a potential moral growth that is never realized, although he continues to "stare out the window for some time." This simple scene underscores the central, unifying theme of the novel: perceptual and moral blindness.[13]

Problems of vision, in both literal and metaphoric terms, are at the center of "The Little Regiment," in which the focus is on Billie Dempster's understanding of himself and his brother. The theme of limited knowledge is made explicit when Billie is stunned from a wound:

> Finally he looked around him at the corpses dimly to be seen. No change flashed into his face upon viewing these men. They

seemed to suggest merely that his information concerning himself was not too complete (VI, 20).

In "A Christmas Dinner Won in Battle" the point of view is identified with Tom's mind as he, in his ardent pursuit of Mildred, heir to her father's fortune, becomes embroiled in a railway strike. As Tom attempts to defend Mildred from the rioting strikers attempting to break down her door, he is stunned by a blow and knocked to the floor:

> Directly indeed they [the doors] crashed down and he felt the crowd sweep past him and into the house. He clung to a railing; he had no more sense of balance than a feather. A blow in the head had made him feel that the ground swirled and heaved around him (VIII, 86).

The story then proceeds on the basis of what Tom can perceive through his "half-closed" eyes. When he finally recovers and drives off the crowd long enough for the police to arrive, he is again struck: "He saw a stretch of blood-red sky flame under his lids and then sank to the floor, blind, deaf, and nerveless" (VIII, 87). Since Tom is unconscious, and his mind no longer receives external data, the perspective temporarily switches to the mind of the father until Tom awakens and is informed that he may now marry Mildred. The restriction of point of view to the visual sensations of a person who is knocked unconscious is a remarkable limitation, especially when the narrator includes the visual phenomena Tom's mind receives when his eyes are closed. This is precisely what William Faulkner does in the first section of *The Sound and the Fury* when the narrative perspective, restricted to the sensory data of Benjy's mind, renders the "bright, whirling shapes" as Benjy is struck on the head and the "smooth, bright shapes" his mind retains even after he closes his eyes.[14]

There is much of this method in Crane's fiction. In *George's Mother* the narrative data derives from George Kelcey's mind even as he enters into a drunken stupor. The quality of his sensory reception progressively deteriorates. As he falls, "blinding lights flashed before his vision." After another drink,

> he felt the room sway. His blurred sight could only distinguish a tumbled mass of shadow through which the beams from the light ran like swords of flame. The sound of the many voices was to him like the roar of a distant river (I, 147).

The formulation that "he felt the room sway" reveals that the narrator expresses George's interpretation without correction or compensation. A more important distortion of reality comes in George's assessment of events after he has been ejected from the gathering: "He, the brilliant, the good, the sympathetic had been thrust fiendishly from the party" (I, 149). The obvious implication of the narrative projection of data from the mind of a character, without compensatory comment by the narrator, is the potential for unreliable assertions. This is, in fact, the standard fictional situation in Crane's works.

Other examples of this method occur throughout Crane's fiction, as three instances will illustrate. In *The Red Badge*, Henry's visual experiences are recorded without correction for distance: "Once he saw a tiny battery go dashing along the line of the horizon. The tiny riders were beating the tiny horses" (II, 38). The narrator does not intrude to explain that these are normal beings perceived at a distance.[15] Nor does the narrator compensate for the visual illusion at the beginning of "The Bride Comes to Yellow Sky," other than to use the qualifier "seemed":

> The great Pullman was whirling onward with such dignity of motion that a glance from the window seemed simply to prove that the plains of Texas were pouring eastward. Vast flats of green grass, dull-hued spaces of mesquite and cactus, little groups of frame houses, woods of light and tender trees, all were sweeping into the east, sweeping over the horizon, a precipice (V, 109).

If the first sentence of this passage suggests a narrative qualification of its accuracy, the second presents the illusion as fact. Nor is there any compensation for distance in "Stephen Crane in Mexico (I)," in which the phenomenon is stated in terms of size, as it was in *The Red Badge:*

> The burden and its carriers grew smaller and smaller. The two Americans went out to the curb and remained intent spectators until the six men and the piano were expressed by a faint blur (VIII, 439).

One means of Crane's handling of narration is thus the objective presentation of the sensory and interpretive experiences of a character at the primary level without compensatory correction by the narrator. The effect is one of psychological immediacy, of sharp sensory detail uncluttered by expository intrusions, but one inherently delimited and unreliable.

Another variation of this method is the objective presentation of sensory data as it is received, in cinematic terms, by a "camera eye," as in the fight scene in "The Blue Hotel":

> During this pause, the Easterner's mind, like a film, took lasting impressions of three men—the iron-nerved master of the ceremony; the Swede, pale, motionless, terrible; and Johnnie, serene yet ferocious, brutish yet heroic (V, 159).

Limited to the vision of the Easterner, a small man fraught with guilt and anxiety, looking into a snowstorm, the narrator can present only fragmentary glimpses:

> For a time the encounter in the darkness was such a perplexity of flying arms that it presented no more detail than would a swiftly-revolving wheel. Occasionally a face, as if illumined by a flash of light, would shine out, ghastly and marked with pink spots (V, 160).

The logic of portraying this scene from the perspective of the Easterner seems to be twofold: as a sensory recorder, his view of the action is limited and provides the realistic intensity of observing a fight; as a participant in the preceding action, he has failed to acknowledge that he too saw Johnnie cheat, and the Easterner is ridden with guilt for permitting a fight that he could have prevented:

> To the Easterner there was a monotony of unchangeable fighting that was an abomination. This confused mingling was eternal to his sense, which was concentrated in a longing for the end, the priceless end (V, 160).

That the events constitute a "confused mingling" is a product of his viewpoint; that the end of the fight would be "priceless" represents a subjective projection of the Easterner onto the activity before him.

There is a similar device in "A Man and Some Others," in which another Easterner observes a fight to the death between a cowboy named Bill and a group of Mexicans who try to run him off the range. Again the narrative perspective is that of an observer rather than a participant in the action. The point of view constricts to record the confused and fragmentary view of the stranger:

> The lightning action of the next few moments was of the fabric of dreams to the stranger. . . . And so the fight, and his part in it, had to the stranger only the quality of a picture half drawn (V, 66).

The method of recording the action of the fight is again a restriction of sensory data to a center of intelligence within the story, a method that achieves the dramatic intensity of a person actually on the scene. Crane's fiction, as this passage implies, often has the quality of a picture half drawn.

In *Active Service*, Crane's longest but least successful novel of war, the narrator reflects that

> perhaps one of the first effects of war upon the mind is a new recognition and fear of the circumscribed ability of the eye, making all landscape seem inscrutable (III, 173).

This comment is intriguing because it suggests that one of the central concerns of war and, presumably, of fiction about war, is the problem of perception. In a heightened emotional ambience in which accurate interpretation of the environment can determine life or death, there is understandable emphasis on the "circumscribed ability of the eye" and upon any matter that appears "inscrutable." Indeed this rather innocuous remark from *Active Service* suggests a concern for the central narrative method of Crane's finest work, *The Red Badge of Courage*.

The point of view Crane employed in *The Red Badge* is basically that of a limited third-person narrator whose access to data is restricted to the mind of the protagonist, Henry Fleming, to his sensory apprehensions and associated thoughts and feelings. In typical Impressionistic manner, Henry's experiences are discontinuous and fragmented and result in a novel composed of brief units. These scenes do not always relate directly to juxtaposed episodes, nor do they always develop the same themes. Furthermore, Henry's view of the battle is severely limited. He knows nothing of the strategy of the battle; he frequently cannot interpret the events around him because his information is obscured by darkness, smoke, or the noise of cannons; rumors spread quickly throughout his regiment, heightening the fear and anxiety of the men. Often, preoccupied by introspection, Henry's mind distorts the data it receives, transforming men into monsters and artillery shells into shrieking demons that leer at him. In short, Henry's view of things is limited, unreliable, and distorted, and yet a projection of the working of his mind becomes a dramatically realistic depiction of how war might appear to an ordinary private engaged in a battle in the American Civil War.

In an important sense, narrative method is the genius of *The Red Badge*. Of their own, the central events of the novel are commonplace. What gives the novel its unique quality is the method of its telling, its restriction of information. As Orm Øverland has pointed out,

> throughout *The Red Badge* (except in the first paragraph where, as it were, the "camera eye" settles down on the camp and the youth, and the concluding one where it again recedes) we in our imagined roles as spectators never have a larger view of the field than has the main character.[16]

Many other Crane scholars have commented on this technique, and most of them invoke a visual metaphor, such as the "camera eye," to describe the method. Carl Van Doren, for example, wrote in the *American Mercury* in 1924 that Henry Fleming "is a lens through which a whole battle may be seen, a sensorium upon which all its details may be registered."[17] Although Van Doren is overgenerous in his analysis of how much of the battle Henry actually sees, he is essentially correct in classifying the methodology of its rendition. Indeed, even thirty years after its initial publication, *The Red Badge* must have seemed most remarkable, for no third-person novel in American literature previously published had so severely limited its point of view. That such restriction is Impressionistic has been well established by Sergio Perosa:

> *The Red Badge of Courage* is indeed a triumph of impressionistic vision and impressionistic technique. Only a few episodes are described from the outside; Fleming's mind is seldom analyzed in an objective, omniscient way; very few incidents are extensively *told*. Practically every scene is filtered through Fleming's point of view and seen through his eyes. Everything is related to his *vision*, to his *sense*-perception of incidents and details, to his *sense*-reactions rather than to his psychological impulses, to his confused sensations and individual impressions.[18]

There is somewhat more "telling" by the narrator than Perosa's comment suggests, and perhaps more interplay from Henry's "psychological impulses," but this formulation of the narrative method of the novel is essentially accurate. Although there are a few passages with an intrusive narrative presence, and a few other complicating devices involving temporal dislocations, the central device of the novel is the rendering of action and thought as they occur in Henry's mind, revealing not the whole of the battle, nor even the broad significance of it, but rather the meaning of this experience to him. The immediacy of the dramatic action is a product of the rendering of the sensory data of Henry's mind; the psychological penetration results from the mingling of experience with association, distortion, fantasy, and memory.[19] A further implication of this method, one that is unsettling but realistic, is that the world presented to Henry is beyond his control, beyond even his comprehension. His primary relation to it is not so much a matter of his deeds as of his organization of sensation into language and pattern.

No reading of *The Red Badge of Courage* can be complete, therefore, which does not deal with the significance of perception in the novel as both a methodological and thematic component. In this sense, the method of the novel is a rendering of Fleming's apprehension and his thoughts: its unifying and informing theme is the development of his capacity to *see* himself, in the context of war, more clearly. Henry's initiation into a nominal maturity becomes a function of his perception of life, death, and his own consuming, nearly incapacitating, fear.[20] After the opening of the novel, the concentration is on Henry's

mind. In the first paragraph, however, before Henry has been introduced, an abstract, third-person narrator presents an establishing
scene:

> The cold passed reluctantly from the earth and the retiring fogs
> revealed an army stretched out on the hills, resting. As the land-
> scape changed from brown to green the army awakened and began
> to tremble with eagerness at the noise of rumors. It cast its eyes
> upon the roads which were growing from long troughs of liquid
> mud to proper thoroughfares. A river, amber-tinted in the shadow
> of its banks, purled at the army's feet and at night when the
> stream had become of a sorrowful blackness one could see, across,
> the red eye-like gleam of hostile camp-fires set in the low brows of
> distant hills (II, 3).

This paragraph contains not only objective descriptive details but a
subjective and animating quality as well. The cold retreats "reluc-
tantly," suggesting a desire to remain, to the discomfort of the soldiers;
the fog, which has obscured the scene, now "reveals" the Union army
in the hills; the army, personified into a composite and singular entity,
"trembles" in response to rumors and casts its "eyes" across the scene.
It is an opening filled with tension and ominous suggestion. As J. C.
Levenson has pointed out, "the reader enters an animistic scene in
which red eyes gleam beneath the low brows of hills and the whole
world of consciousness is alive and active and menacing."[21] The characters, introduced in terms of their sensory indicators (the tall soldier,
the loud soldier, the youth) to a narrative mind free of prior knowledge,
behave nervously. Thus the opening ambience establishes the tone as
well as the topography of the novel.

As soon as Henry Fleming is introduced, the center of intelligence
becomes his: "There was a youthful private who listened with eager
ears to the words of the tall soldier and to the varied comments of his
comrades" (II, 4). From this point on, the central concern of the novel
is the literal and figurative dimensions of his perception. The most
obvious examples of this mode are narrative assertions about Henry's
eyes and what he can see. The thrust of the novel is on Henry's mind
rather than on the battle itself, and these comments are essentially
revelations of character. For example, several passages reveal his ego-
tistic conception of his superior vision, as when he concludes that
"there was but one pair of eyes in the corps" (II, 25), or when, after his
desertion, he feels that the limitations of his comrades "would not
enable them to understand his sharper point of view" (II, 46). Of
greater thematic significance are those passages which relate knowledge in terms of vision, as when Henry realizes that Wilson has
changed from a "loud young soldier" to one of quiet confidence:

> The youth wondered where had been born these new eyes; when
> his comrade had made the great discovery that there were many
> men who would refuse to be subjected by him. Apparently, the
> other had now climbed a peak of wisdom from which he could
> perceive himself as a very wee thing (II, 82).

Significantly, Wilson's development of insight, of true self-knowledge,
precedes Henry's. Wilson, who functions in some ways as Henry's
alter-ego in the second half of the novel, has experienced his perceptual
initiation by Chapter 14; Henry's does not come until Chapter 18, at
which point it is formulated in terms of a similar visual metaphor:

> These happenings had occupied an incredibly short time yet the
> youth felt that in them he had been made aged. New eyes were
> given to him. And the most startling thing was to learn suddenly
> that he was very insignificant (II, 101).

For Henry, this passage has a function beyond its metaphoric value.
For the first time he is able to see clearly:

> It seemed to the youth that he saw everything. Each blade of the
> green grass was bold and clear. He thought that he was aware of
> every change in the thin, transparent vapor that floated idly in
> sheets (II, 105).

The psychological implication of Henry's transformation is that his
preoccupation with fear, and his projection of heroic stature for his
brave deeds, had obscured reality and prevented him from seeing himself in context. Now that he sees himself as one with his fellows, as an
individual no more significant than any other, within the impersonal
machinations of war, he develops the capacity to comprehend his
environment: "His mind took mechanical but firm impressions, so
that, afterward, everything was pictured and explained to him, save
why he himself was there" (II, 105). The conclusion of the novel, which
marks a juncture not in the battle but in Henry's development, continues the concentration on vision. In the final scene, Henry's "eyes
seemed to open to some new ways. He found that he could look back
upon the brass and bombast of his earlier gospels and see them truly"
(II, 135). In visual terms, there is no doubt that Henry has undergone
significant development: he has relinquished his dreams of "Greek-like
struggles" as well as his fear, which had become "the red sickness of
battle," in favor of a more mature and balanced picture of himself as
part of humanity.

As might be expected from the narrative stance of the novel, there is a
stress on sensory faculties. The reader, like the viewer of an Impressionistic painting, is presented with an array of sensational details

from a scene: the colors, sounds, feelings of a given experience.[22] In Chapter 3, for example, after a visual passage in which Henry keeps "his eyes watchfully upon the darkness" (II, 21), other senses come into play: the smell of the pines is pervasive; the sounds of insects and axes echo through the forest; and Henry's sensations of touch become acute:

> His canteen banged rhythmically upon his thigh and his haversack bobbed softly. His musket bounced a trifle from his shoulder at each stride and made his cap feel uncertain upon his head (II, 22).

But the predominant sensory emphasis is on vision, so much so that Harold Frederic, himself a skilled novelist, called *The Red Badge* a "battle painting" in his review in the New York *Times* in 1896.[23] Sensitive to Crane's narrative method, Frederic remarked that as readers "we see with his [Henry's] eyes, think with his mind, quail or thrill with his nerves.", Frederic concluded that this method of "photographic revelation" accounts for the fascination of the novel. Frederic's comments have more than figurative significance, for there is a good deal of narrative "picturing." One expression of this device is subjective, generated within Henry's mind, as in the opening chapter: "His busy mind had drawn for him large pictures, extravagant in color, lurid with breathless deeds" (II, 5). The method is essentially expository, evoking no coordinate image but rather a generic sense of the workings of Henry's mind.[24] Paradoxically, most of the passages labeled pictures by the narrator constitute internal rather than external renderings. In general, when Henry is confused and under stress, his mind seeks resolution through imaginative portraits. One such instance occurs in Chapter 11, in which Henry, filled with guilt for his desertion and remorse for the death of Jim Conklin, sees "swift pictures of himself, apart, yet in himself . . ." (II, 64). The first image he conjures is of himself in a heroic moment of death, standing bravely, "getting calmly killed on a high place before the eyes of all." He imagines as well the "magnificent pathos of his dead body." This image temporarily expiates his sense of shame and for a few moments "he was sublime." He constructs a more sustaining image of himself at the front of battle, then loses confidence in his capacity for heroic action (II, 65). Thus one function of narrative picturing is the projection of Henry's internal fantasy, creating visual correlatives for his heroic striving and compensatory fears of cowardice and death. So it is with Henry's "visions" and "pictures" in the opening chapter and his "dreams" throughout the novel.

To some extent, Henry is forced to imaginative picturing to find coherence and unity in his experience, for his sensory data is confused and incomplete. During the battle in which he deserts, smoke blankets the battlefield, as it does often, and allows him only "changing views" of the action (II, 41). One of his central problems throughout the novel is that he cannot perceive enough to construct a reliable interpretation of his situation: his comrades appear to him as "dark waves" and the enemy as "grey shadows" in the woods (II, 69). A "clouded haze" obscures almost every important scene. In the absence of congruent information about the events, Henry's mind interprets the limited data in terms of his fear. He never has access to all he would like to see:

> The youth leaned his breast against the brown dirt and peered over at the woods and up and down the line. Curtains of trees interfered with his ways of vision. He could see the low line of trenches but for a short distance (II, 89).

In another scene, in which Henry is so close to the rebel troops that he can momentarily distinguish the features of individual men, his view is changed before he can act:

> Almost instantly, they [the Southern troops] were shut utterly from the youth's sight by the smoke from the energetic rifles of his companions. He strained his vision to learn the accomplishment of the volley but the smoke hung before him (II, 114).

It is clear throughout the novel that given limited information, Henry must struggle to understand his circumstances. After one battle, in which it seemed to him that he had covered a great deal of ground, he has an opportunity to survey what has actually happened: "He discovered that the distances, as compared with the brilliant measurings of his mind, were trivial and ridiculous" (II, 117).

In most cases, however, Henry is not allowed to reflect upon the accuracy of his interpretations, and his fears and visions distort the data he receives. The most dramatic of these instances come during battle, and most of them involve Henry's perception of battle objects as dragons and monsters of various kinds. The first such image exemplifies his distortions: "From off in the darkness, came the trampling of feet. The youth could occasionally see dark shadows that moved like monsters" (II, 15). When he next peers across the river at the enemy camp fires, he sees them as "growing larger, as the orbs of a row of dragons, advancing." Even when his own regiment moves through the darkness the men appear to be "monsters" which strike Henry as "huge crawling reptiles." As a result, the early part of the novel is filled with "serpents," "monsters," "battle-phantoms," "dragons," and other fantastic manifestations of "war, the red animal, war, the blood-swollen god."[25] Significantly, Henry's distortions are consistent until Chapter 18, when he experiences a dramatic epiphany and "new eyes were given to him." Previously he had been capable of almost surrealistic projections, as when he imagines that the artillery shells arching over him have "rows of cruel teeth that grinned at him" (II, 42), or later, when coming upon some of his comrades in the forest,

> his disordered mind interpreted the hall of the forest as a charnel place. He believed for an instant that he was in the house of the dead and he did not dare to move lest these corpses start up, squalling and squawking (II, 80).

After his moment of recognition, in which he perceives his insignificance and loses much of his fear, there are no such distortions. It is then that he can see his earlier errors of interpretation: "Elfin thoughts must have exaggerated and enlarged everything, he said" (II, 117). He is still subject to sensory restriction and obscuring, as when a scene becomes a "wild blur" as he dashes across a field (II, 108), but he no longer creates monsters out of shadows.

Indeed much of the narrative emphasis is on his improved capacity to perceive:

> His vision being unmolested by smoke from the rifles of his companions, he had opportunities to see parts of the hard fight. It was a relief to perceive at last from whence came some of these noises which had been roared into his ears (II, 122).

As the narrator makes explicit, Henry's new sight is more than a literal clarity of apprehension; it involves cognitive factors as well. In the final chapter,

> gradually his brain emerged from the clogged clouds and at last he was enabled to more closely comprehend himself and circumstance. . . . He understood then that the existence of shot and counter-shot was in the past. . . . Later, he began to study his deeds—his failures and his achievements. . . . At last, they marched before him clearly. From this present view-point, he was enabled to look upon them in spectator fashion and to criticise them with some correctness . . . (II, 133).

The novel concludes with a visual emphasis. As Henry's "eyes seemed to open to some new ways," he is able to reflect on his earlier ideas and "see them truly" (II, 135).

In an important sense, *The Red Badge* is a novel of the growth of Henry's visual capacities. The narrative method, alternating from objective apprehensions presented in the manner of a motion picture camera[26] to the subjective rendering of his distortions, emotions, fantasies, and memories, is the single most innovative device in the novel. As J. C. Levenson has commented, Crane's

radical breakthrough came from his premise that mental life primarily consists in witnessing the vivid immediate presences within
one's own mind, that is, in the flux of consciousness. So far as
consciousness is concerned, self-projected images have equal status
with sense data.[27]

For Henry Fleming these "self-projected images" consist of both evocations generated out of internal need and interpretative distortions of
genuine sensory data, and he is largely unable to distinguish between
them.

Beyond these narrative methodologies, which dominate the novel,
there are several other strategies that play a role in individual scenes. If
the flashback technique can be theoretically reconciled with Impressionism in fiction as a narrative projection of thought, it is more difficult to establish congruence with Impressionism of moments that
jump forward, even if they present a future, retrospective time: "When
he thought of it later, he conceived the impression that it is better to
view the appalling than to be merely within hearing" (II, 42). It is even
more difficult to understand intrusive passages as part of an Impressionistic novel, and there are a few of them in *The Red Badge*. One
such passage occurs in Chapter 3: "But the regiment was not yet
veteran-like in appearance. Veteran regiments in this army were likely
to be very small aggregations of men" (II, 22). It seems unlikely that
this comment can be read as the narrator's statement of Henry's
thoughts since he is a raw recruit who has yet to see his first battle and
knows little of the size of battle-torn regiments. The later image of
"guns squatted in a row like savage chiefs" (II, 38) again seems to
derive from beyond Henry's frame of reference. But such passages are
rare and do not substantially qualify the Impressionistic method that
dominates the novel. It should be noted, however, that there is more
variation of narrative logic than has generally been acknowledged.
There is even one passage of direct thought as in stream of consciousness: "The youth pitied them [a group of artillery gunners] as he ran.
Methodical idiots! Machine-like fools!" (II, 43). Here, in an intensely
emotional moment, the intervening narrative consciousness disappears
to render Henry's thoughts precisely as they occur.

Despite these variations, the basic method of the "showing" of *The
Red Badge of Courage* is Impressionistic and consists of the sensations
and thoughts of a private engaged in a battle he does not comprehend
and cannot even clearly see. The drama of the novel is epistemological,
a matter of perception, distortion, and realization which finally culminates in Chapter 18 with Henry's epiphany. The genius of the novel
is its use of a narrative method that underscores the perceptual themes,
that forces the reader to participate in the empirical limitations of the

central character, and that creates a psychological reality on a level never before achieved in the American novel.

In general, there is a good deal of subtlety in Crane's handling of the narrator as an intermediary consciousness between character and reader. The obvious function of the narrator is to describe the scene; another more intricate role is to formulate and present the mental activity of the protagonist. The narrator presents thought without alteration, without comment, without verification that the thought has external validity; the presumption is that narrative assertions articulate the thoughts of the character. This methodology stresses the limitation of sensory perceptions and the reduced reliability of interpretations of experience. The meaning of data is often as much a product of interpretation as it is of physical reality. As Peter Sloat Hoff described Impressionistic narration,

> the reader is placed at the same epistemological level as the confused characters who serve as centers of consciousness. The reader becomes to some degree a receiver of temporally fragmented sense impressions rather than organized narration. The information which reaches the reader of an Impressionistic novel is potentially incorrect, for it often comes through an observer who may be mistaken, and it is information often broken and distorted.[28]

The mode of unreliable narration describes almost exactly Crane's means of presenting Henry Fleming's heroic view of himself, the plains rushing eastward in "The Bride Comes to Yellow Sky," and Maggie's view of Pete as a knight.

The close identification of the narrator's mind with a character has many unreliable manifestations in *The Red Badge*. One of those already noted is the narrator's insistence in rendering sensory impressions without correction, even in the case of distance, hence the formulation that "once he [Henry] saw a tiny battery go dashing along the line of the horizon. The tiny riders were beating the tiny horses" (II, 38). This scene represents the simplest form of unreliability in Impressionism in that it is the projection of raw, apprehensive data from the mind of a character. But it is also possible for the narrator to render subjective, judgmental thought as well, as is the case in *The Red Badge* when the lieutenant urges Henry to keep up with the ranks: "He [Henry] mended his pace with suitable haste. And he hated the lieutenant, who had no appreciation of fine minds. He was a mere brute" (II, 25). The irony of this passage results from the reader's sense of Henry's self-revelation, that the human weakness is not so much the lieutenant's brutishness as Henry's grandiose view of his own "fine mind."

The result of this mode in *The Red Badge* is a continuous pattern of distorted judgments by Henry projected faithfully by the narrator. In general, these statements reveal the extent to which Henry's mind, driven by doubt and shame, reconstructs the data of reality to create a context in which his actions can be seen in their most positive light. After Henry deserts, he begins to reflect that "his actions had been sagacious things. They had been full of strategy. They were the work of a master's legs" (II, 45). The narrator does not suggest the bias of Henry's view; the reader, seeing Henry's interpretation in context, must supply the countering qualification of Henry's delusions. The novel is replete with ironic assertions that point to Henry's immaturity, innocence, and distorted self-view.[29] Indeed, they build throughout the novel to a moment just before Henry's epiphany in Chapter 18, at which point they reach their most profound delusion: "He had been a tremendous figure, no doubt. . . . He had slept and, awakening, found himself a knight" (II, 97). After his epiphany, the narrative irony ceases. What the handling of this device suggests for Impressionism is that irony is a function of distance, of knowledge, of point of view; given the same data that Henry himself receives, the reader's interpretation is impossible to reconcile with Henry's. The resulting tension, born of interpretive distance, becomes one of the dominating factors in the novel.

Narrative irony is present in Crane's fiction from the very first. In the Sullivan County tales and even earlier, in "Uncle Jake and Bell-Handle," a story Crane composed when he was only fourteen, the most remarkable literary quality is the ironic perspective. In "Uncle Jake," for example, thematic and artistic concerns center on the contrast between the innocent yet self-aggrandizing perspective of Uncle Jake and that of the world-wise city folk who mock and condescend to him. The narrator plays on the conflict between angles of vision. From Jake's point of view, he is going to the city not only to sell his turnips but also to squire his niece about town as a cosmopolitan gentleman; he imagines himself doing so in a "lordly" way, giving her the benefit of his "experienced eye" (VIII, 3–7). The niece, Miss Sarah Bottomley Perkins, a delicate creature of "only twenty-eight years," shares Jake's naiveté, and together they are no match for the city and its mechanical marvels. But the humor of the story derives not so much from its titular incident (Jake pulls a bell-handle and mistakenly believes he has called out the fire department) as from its contrasting perspectives.

This contrast is marked from the beginning, when Jake, noticing the men peering out of saloons at him, believes that they "had heard he was coming to town and had 'knocked off' work to see him go past." Meanwhile, the perspectives of the men indicate that they are amazed at the rustic before them. Jake confronts them with his talk of crops and his wife's "plumbago"; they cheat him in the price for his turnips. Jake is clearly the butt of the joke, but the urban clerks also are treated ironically:

> Some of the clerks, understanding the old man and being gentle-
> men, listened politely and deferentially to his ramblings, while
> others who were not troubled that way, snickered behind his back
> at the other clerks, and pointed their fingers at him, while the old
> man beamed a world of peace and good will toward all men from
> the glasses of his spectacles (VIII, 5).

The narrative judgment here is not subtle: if Jake is a rustic, he is nevertheless basically kind and generous; the cynical clerks, not "troubled" by being gentlemen, are allowed their superior view and derision. The irony cuts both ways: Jake and the clerks hold views of themselves that exclude their most obvious flaws. For all its simplicity and indications of juvenilia, this story is remarkable for its irony and its interplay of multiple perspectives of reality, especially considering the age of its author.

Naive points of view have a propensity for error. This matter, so obvious in a story such as "An Illusion in Red and White," in which characters believe things counter to their direct experience, is present throughout Crane's works in a variety of ways. One method involves narrative qualification, in which a scene is described as it "seems" to the characters. For example, in "A Tent in Agony," in which a bear entangled inside a tent rolls down a hill, the event is perceived by three men who have no idea of what is taking place. The narrator projects their thoughts: "It seemed to them like a white-robed phantom pursued by hornets. Its moans riffled the hemlock twigs" (VIII, 254). On other occasions the narrator will present erroneous interpretations. After the fire in *The Monster*, for example, a team of physicians examine Dr. Trescott, Jimmie, and Henry:

> Almost at once they were able to know that Trescott's burns were
> not vitally important. The child would possibly be scarred badly,
> but his life was undoubtedly safe. As for the negro Henry
> Johnson, he could not live (VII, 29).

They are wrong, of course: not only is Jimmie not badly scarred but Henry lives, horribly disfigured, and his welfare becomes the central moral issue of the story.

This is essentially the method of the ironic passages in *The Red Badge*, *George's Mother*, and *Maggie: A Girl of the Streets*, perhaps Crane's most important ironic work. *Maggie*, Crane's first significant piece of fiction, is the most sardonic novel in American literature. Its irony is not so much the product of events, which vary from the grotesque to the comic, as of the way in which these events are viewed by the characters. The narrator projects the judgments of the characters without qualification; the irony generates from the reader's progressively sharp awareness that these judgments are irreconcilable with reality.

On the simplest level, the narrative method of *Maggie* is an Impressionistic series of brief but sensorially vivid episodes, often discontinuous, which represent something of the life of the Johnson family over a period of years.[30] The physical environment is rendered, in some detail, in terms of the sensory impressions it evokes: the first paragraph of the second chapter, which describes the tenement building, is a typical example. The sensory imagery evokes sight (the darkness, the dust swirling in the wind, the infants, the disheveled women and "withered persons"), sound (the gossiping of the women, the screams of their quarrels, the creak of the building), smell (the odors of food), and feeling (the building quivers). The image of the garments that "fluttered" from the fire-escape is, of course, synaesthetic, suggesting both auditory and visual evocations (I, 11).

Another brilliantly Impressionistic paragraph, one typical of Crane's introductions of important scenes, begins Chapter 7. Here the yellow of the "silk woman," the green of the hall, the kinaesthetic images of the waiters."sliding" through the crowd carrying trays, the "rumble of conversation" and the "clinking of glasses," and the synaesthetic image of tobacco smoke, both seen and smelled, create a vivid description of scene. These sensorial details draw the reader into a social ambience in which the value judgments of the characters can be accepted as congruent.

If the objective presentation of sensory details is a simple method, the underlying irony involving the values ascribed to the characters is more complex. In the opening scene the judgment that Jimmie, standing on a "heap of gravel" and "throwing stones at howling urchins" is fighting for the "honor of Rum Alley" must be read as the narrator's ironic statement of Jimmie's self-serving assessment. Indeed, all the sensory indicators suggest sordid activity incommensurate with concepts of honor. The first paragraph of the novel suggests the narrative method throughout, the almost continual ironic disparity between what is empirically recorded as fact and what the characters comprehend as being real. As J. C. Levenson has commented, even in his first novel Crane was writing as much of internal visions of life as of the physical realities of the world: "He had become a psychological novelist committed to dealing with the knower as well as the known."[31]

As Bergon suggests, *Maggie* is a psychological work that reveals the quality of mental activity not through narrative assertions of thought but through a projection in third person of what the mind perceives as the nature of reality.[32] Jimmie is described as the "champion of Rum Alley" because he sees himself as such. As does Henry Fleming in the first half of *The Red Badge*, Jimmie continually distorts reality to conceive of himself in heroic terms; he drives the horses of his wagon with "majestic contempt" for street cars, denouncing pedestrians from his "throne" (I, 22). Even the elements of his courtship are rendered ironically, and he is blind to his moral responsibilities to two different women who wail at him "about marriage and support and infants" (I, 23). In a brilliantly ironic line, Jimmie is reported to have once said "wonderingly and quite reverently: 'D' moon looks like hell, don't it?' " (I, 23). Jimmie's blindness to his own culpability in the seduction and pregnancy of the two women is but one facet of his limited realizations; another is his ready adherence to a simplistic moral code that brings him to reject Maggie and yet play the righteous role of her avenger as he seeks a vindictive fight with Pete. Through it all, Jimmie retains the conviction that his own behavior is beyond question and that he is a good fellow of the highest order.

The main thrust of the epistemological reduction of narrative consciousness comes in the scenes involving Maggie herself. The early chapters of the novel document the formative influences on Maggie's perspective; the second unit of action, Chapters 5–9, displays the final simplicity and innocence of her view of life. If it is true, as the narrator states, that Maggie "blossomed in a mud puddle," then that fact has at least two important implications: that she is a physically beautiful girl in a sordid environment; that she is somehow *in* but not *of* her world and is not able to benefit from its worldly lessons. Maggie's vulnerability is the result of her innocence and the moral blindness of Pete, Jimmie, and her mother. Her naiveté and fear, both evident in the early childhood scenes, cause her to admire Pete's assertiveness and arrogance. The narrator indicates that "Maggie observed Pete" and then presents her view of him as someone who "had a correct sense of his personal superiority" (I, 25). The narrative formulation implies no complicity in the judgment; "Maggie perceived that here was the ideal man" (I, 26). She not only sees him as a "cultured gentleman" but she interprets the romantic melodramas they attend as possessing "transcendental realism." Such passages serve to define her character psychologically and intellectually through indirection.

The same device is used for Jimmie and for Mrs. Johnson, revealing their impoverished estimates of the people and situations around them.

The ironic tone of the end of the novel is a fitting conclusion to the perpetual duplicity of narrative assertions. At the end Mrs. Johnson is blind to her role in the events leading to Maggie's suicide, and she clings to the religious bromides that bolster her sense of social respectability. These lead to her magnanimous gesture of the conclusion: " 'Oh, yes, I'll fergive her! I'll fergive her!' " (I, 77). With typical Impressionistic restriction, no narrative judgment points to the mother's self-righteous stance. The reader, from an involvement in the epistemological process the novel presents, must construct a countering interpretation of culpability.

The narrative irony is somewhat less pervasive in *George's Mother*, a novel Crane began early in 1893, just after the initial publication of *Maggie*.[33] As a companion piece to the earlier novel (it takes place in the same tenement as *Maggie;* Maggie Johnson appears in it) it has diminished thematic sophistication, its characterizations are not as well integrated, and its focus on the demon rum is something from the era of the temperance tract. However, in narrative terms it contains some of the most fascinating passages in the Crane canon. Despite the critical tendency to read the novel as a work of Naturalism, the emphasis is not on deterministic causes but on the theme of self-delusion. Further, its method of narration is patently Impressionistic.

The narrative stance is that of a third-person limited narrator whose mind is identified with George and his mother. The result is the revelation of the restricted, distorted, and self-serving perspectives of these characters and the limitation of their literal perceptions. For example, during Bleecker's party George becomes intoxicated, and during a "furious" attempt to waltz with Jones they fall and "blinding lights flashed before his vision." After another drink, his powers of perception become even further restricted, and his apprehensive faculties function with dimmed acuity: "At last he perceived a shadow, a form, which he knew to be Jones." Nearly stupefied with drink, he resents the efforts of the others to care for him: "He had never seen anything so vastly stupid as their idea of his state. He resolved to prove to them that they were dealing with one whose mind was very clear" (I, 148).

The capacity of his mind to perceive is extremely restricted, and the narrative intelligence, identified with it, becomes unreliable. As George struggles to his feet, he falls over a table and chairs to the floor. The narrator presents George's interpretation of these events: "He felt them hurl him to a corner of the room and pile chairs and tables upon him until he was buried beneath a stupendous mountain" (I, 149). The party scene is representative of the ironic method of the novel as a whole, indicating the continuous projection of George's impressions and judgments as fact. Only the first paragraph of the first chapter, which occurs before George is introduced, can be read as an objective presentation:

> In the swirling rain that came at dusk the broad avenue glistened with that deep bluish tint which is so widely condemned when it is put into pictures. There were long rows of shops, whose fronts shone with full, golden light. Here and there, from druggists' windows, or from the red street-lamps that indicated the positions of fire-alarm boxes, a flare of uncertain, wavering crimson was thrown upon the wet pavements (I, 115).

There is a self-conscious Impressionistic quality to the passage in its numerous color images (blue, gold, red) and visual effects ("swirling" rain, diminishing light at dusk, the "wavering" crimson on the pavement from the fire in the lamp) and in its reference to what is condemned in "pictures." The second paragraph differs somewhat in that it projects the elevated interpretation inhabitants of the city have of their environment, seeing its sordid qualities in heroic, medieval terms: the buildings, now in shadows (time has passed since the first paragraph), resemble "castles and fortresses"; the umbrellas wave "bannerlike"; men, aimlessly watching the passing life, resemble those who in an earlier age "used to prostrate . . . before pageantry." As is typical of Crane's openings, and similar to the initial passages of *The Red Badge*, the narrative method of the first chapter is one of progressive limitation: the scene is viewed from an objective distance, then from the perspective from which the group sees it, then from the vantage point of the protagonist.

The passages rendered from George's perspective uniformly reveal his pathetically restricted assessment of himself and those around him. His view of Charley Jones offers the first revelation of this pattern: George, who is not allowed to drink or associate with the local "jays," sees Jones as a pinnacle of worldly wisdom who understands the "complications" of life, who possesses a "vast knowledge," and whose association with bartenders has equipped him with an "habitual expression of wisdom" (I, 116). George's grand estimate of Jones is only the first instance in a pattern of interpretive causality that leads to his mother's death.

Another even more serious misinterpretation is George's view of himself, especially after he becomes a regular at the saloon and begins to enjoy the fellowship of the jovial group, which in some measure substitutes for the family he had known before his father and four brothers died. George's response to the gathering is characteristically self-congratulatory: "Presently he began to believe that he was a most remarkably fine fellow, who had at last found his place in a crowd of most remarkably fine fellows" (I, 127). Such thinking provides an analogue of Henry Fleming's view of himself in the early sections of *The Red Badge*, and it also suggests how misconceptions ultimately exact a price in confrontations with reality. As does Henry, George misreads himself and the others around him. He comes to see the saloon gang as possessing superior knowledge, as being universally respected, and he mentally faults his mother for not comprehending the "advanced things in life" (I, 163–65). It is this vision of things which leads George to embrace the gang, to lose his job, and to develop a nearly total insensitivity to the emotional needs of his mother, to whom he represents "family," the center of life.

Another strain of perceptive causality derives from Mrs. Kelcey herself. Her adherence to a bourgeois Protestant ethic and her emotional necessity to reconstruct reality to cast George as a sterling example of manhood, whose moral stature compensates for her lost family, distort her conceptions of the truth. Furthermore, as she elevates George, her own stature rises commensurately: "She became convinced that she was a perfect mother, rearing a perfect son" (I, 133). In contrast to George, however, the mother's illusions are less self-aggrandizing than compensatory, a wish that George will "become a white and looming king among men," one who will replace all she has lost. But the narrator, in one of the few judgmentally intrusive passages in the novel, makes explicit the context that impels this view: "Upon the dead altars of her life she had built the little fires of hope for another" (I, 135). Since all of her sense of value rests upon George, when he loses his job, takes to drink, and lies to her, her dreams are shattered. The narrator projects the substance of her disillusionment in primitive terms: "It was as if she had survived a massacre in which all that she loved had been torn from her by the brutality of savages" (I, 167).

As in Chapter 17 of *Maggie*, the narrative handling of the final scene in *George's Mother* is the most intriguing in the novel. It begins with the narrator identifying George's apartment as a "chamber of death," thus relieving the conclusion of suspense. It is clear that Mrs. Kelcey will die; what matters is the quality of mental activity in mother and son during her final moments. Throughout, the narrator refers to the boy as "Kelcey" rather than "George," underscoring his identification with his family, the loss of which has driven his mother to a despairing death. She has suffered brain damage, which affects her movement and speech, and she is lost within a dream that has a young George as its main concern:

> She was at a kitchen-door with a dish-cloth in her hand. Within

there had just been a clatter of crockery. Down through the trees
of the orchard she could see a man in a field ploughing. "Bill—o-
o-oh, Bill—have yeh seen Georgie? Is he out there with you?
Georgie! Georgie! Come right here this minnet! Right—this—
minnet!" (I, 177).

In counterpoint to his mother's fulfilling dream, George is beset with
guilt. When his mother screamed, "he saw crimson curtains moving
before his eyes." He concentrates on the sound of the clock, pounding
out the last moments of his mother's life. Significantly, the clock is no
longer described as "swaggering," as it had been earlier, a fact that
indicates, through imagistic dislocation, an alteration in George rather
than in the clock.[34] Indeed, the narrator's imagery in describing
George's thoughts is revealing: "Kelcey began to stare at the wall-
paper. The pattern was clusters of brown roses. He felt them like
hideous crabs crawling upon his brain" (I, 178). The faded color of the
roses reveals again the economic level the family has fallen to, and the
surrealistic crabs become a metaphor for his guilt and despair. Then,
placing this event in social context, the narrator records George's view
of the surrounding city and the sounds of a mother and son quarreling
down the hall. These two matters, juxtaposed to the final line, "the
little old woman was dead," comment on the social significance of
individual death and the continuing pattern of familial strife.

These subjective narrative renderings are unusual in Crane's fiction
and show a flexibility in his handling of point of view that he developed in other works, especially in *The Red Badge* and *The Third
Violet*. But Crane's basic method of narrative identification with the
limited and often erroneous perspectives of the characters is at the heart
of his ironic method.

Another of Crane's basic narrative methods, although not so ubiquitous as narrative irony, is the device of narrational "parallax," of
rendering a work of fiction from more than one point of view.[35] The
possibilities for variations of parallactic method are numerous but
center on two basic patterns: the juxtaposition of two or more limited
third-person perspectives; the contrasting of limited points of view
with that of a superior narrator. Other variations could include
numerous first-person perspectives, or combinations of points of view,
including stream of consciousness, to form the fundamental contrasts
of parallax, but the underlying point is the implicit relativistic philosophy that reality is a function of perspective. How a given situation is
perceived is qualified by the intelligence, mood, and angle of vision of
the viewer; hence, a scene narrated from contrasting points of view will
reveal not only a greater complexity than any one perceiver sees but the
values and mental life of the viewers as well. Ernest Hemingway's

"The Short Happy Life of Francis Macomber" and William Faulkner's
As I Lay Dying and *The Sound and the Fury*, to mention only three
examples, all employ variations of this method with artistic success.[36]

That Crane uses multiple points of view in many of his works has
not been an obscure point in American scholarship, although the implications of that device have never been fully explored. Crane made
the method explicit in his war dispatch "Crane at Velestino" by
writing that the sound of rifles firing

> was a beautiful sound—beautiful as I had never dreamed. It was
> more impressive than the roar of Niagara and finer than thunder
> or avalanche—because it had the wonder of human tragedy in it.
> It was the most beautiful sound of my experience, barring no
> symphony. The crash of it was ideal.
>
> This is one point of view. Another might be taken from the
> men who died there (IX, 20).

Here the disparity is obvious between the abstract philosophizing of
the first-person narrator and his awareness of the point of view of those
directly involved in the fighting, to whom the sound of gunfire would
have immediate and less hopeful import. Crane does not dramatize the
contrasting points of view in this passage, but he did so throughout his
career from such early efforts as "Uncle Jake and the Bell-Handle" to
some of his most substantial fiction, including "The Open Boat,"
"The Bride Comes to Yellow Sky," and "Death and the Child."

Scholars have long regarded Crane's juxtaposition of points of view
to be central to his art. Joseph X. Brennan, in his important essay
"Stephen Crane and the Limits of Irony," sees it as the source of much
of Crane's irony. Thomas A. Gullason has explored this matter in
Crane's journalism, as has Rodney O. Rogers in *The Red Badge of
Courage* in one of the most significant essays on the subject.[37] Rogers'
study proceeds from the contention that what links Crane to the French
Impressionistic painters is a view of reality as "ephemeral, evanescent,
constantly shifting its meaning and hence continually defying precise
definition." He establishes a congruence between the ontological assumptions beneath Crane's fiction and his device of narrating from
more than one point of view. Indeed, he asserts that "Crane's typical
story presses for its effect through his narrator's ironic modulations
between two or more contradictory points of view."[38]

Rogers illustrates one implementation of this method in "Flanagan
and His Short Filibustering Adventure," in which most of the story is
narrated from a consciousness identified with the shipwrecked
mariners but shifts at the conclusion to the perspective of a group of
people attending a "charming dance" at the Imperial Inn. Their point

of view is detached: they view the news of the shipwreck as an interruption of their festivities, unable to believe that genuine tragedy could occur while they were enjoying themselves. The narrator suggests the confluence of tragedy and flippant confidence in the concluding paragraph:

> Save for the white glare of the breakers, the sea was a great wind-crossed void. From the throng of charming women floated the perfume of many flowers. Later there floated to them a body with a calm face of an Irish type. The expedition of the *Foundling* will never be historic (V, 108).

Rogers' central point here is that "Crane's ironic use of the juxtaposition to suggest that man's experience of the world is multifaceted, marks this particular modulation as impressionist in concept."[39] The near zeugma of the verb "floated" creates yet another level of irony between the disparate concerns of the two groups.

As Rogers suggests, narrative modulation is central to one pattern of Crane's methods. The contrasting points of view are often roughly similar in their degree of limitation and reliability. Jimmie and Mrs. Johnson, for example, are no less deluded in their simplicity than is Maggie herself, although they regard their perspectives as invested with superior wisdom, virtue, and social respectability. The modulations between George and his mother suggest a similar mutual delusion, as does the shifting of perspectives from Jack Potter to the porters on the train, from the correspondent to the other men in the boat, from Rufus Coleman to the other characters in *Active Service*.

Another variation is the shift from the restricted perspective of a character to that of an omniscient narrator who is not only emotionally detached from the scene but capable of perceiving it from a great distance. An illustration of this method comes from the journalistic "Crane at Velestino" in which, at the conclusion of an especially bloody battle, the narrator reflects: "Scattered fragments slid slowly back, leaving the plain black with wounded and dead men and horses. From a distance it was like a game. There was no blood, no expression, no horror to be seen" (IX, 20). The imposition of narrative distance on a scene of intense emotional concern on the part of the participants creates an irony of perspective which suggests the isolation of individual human beings, their inconsequence in the universal flux of life, their diminution from a superior vantage point, and their countering inflation of the significance of their own lives and the events that surround them.

Two of the most famous of these passages occur in "The Blue Hotel" and "The Open Boat." The first of these is narrated essentially from a third-person limited point of view which is sometimes, as in the fight scene, identified with the mind of the Easterner. Following the dramatic and intense fight, and as the Swede leaves the hotel on his way to his death in the saloon, the narrative stance recedes to a removed perspective from which

> it was hard to imagine a peopled earth. One viewed the existence of man then as a marvel, and conceded a glamour of wonder to these lice which were caused to cling to a whirling, fire-smote, ice-locked, disease-stricken, space-lost bulb. The conceit of man was explained by this storm to be the very engine of life (V, 165).

This extraordinary passage suggests both a cosmic and a local application: that people in general delude themselves by seeing their lives and activities as important in a scope far beyond their true status; that the significance of the fight over the card game is in fact a petty squabble of little consequence beyond the "conceit" of those involved. The last line of this passage goes further to suggest that delusions of significance enable human beings to survive by providing a motivation for impassioned activity; had the characters a more objective sense of their true position in the cosmos, they might well be immobilized by a sense of nihilism. The structural position of the passage also suggests that the events to follow in the saloon derive from the Swede's intensification of such conceit: the refusal of the gambler to drink with him is too small an insult to precipitate physical conflict when viewed with balance and detachment. The intrusion of a comment from an extraordinary perspective forces the thematic concerns of the story into a focus informed by antithetical views of the action and based on vastly differing assumptions. This antithesis generates the most remarkable levels of irony in the story.

"The Open Boat" also employs ironic narrative juxtaposition, contrasting the preoccupations of the four men in the boat against a detached perspective. As the opening line of the story ("None of them knew the color of the sky") suggests, the men have a severely restricted view limited almost entirely to the waves that "menace" them.[40] In contrast, the omniscient narrator views the scene objectively and comments, somewhat abstractly and without utility, that "many a man ought to have a bath-tub larger than the boat which here rode upon the sea" (V, 68). A few paragraphs later in the story the limitations of the men become even more acute: "As each slaty wall of water approached, it shut all else from the view of the men in the boat . . ." (V, 69). Juxtaposed to their restricted view is a detached oservation by the narrator: "Viewed from a balcony, the whole thing would doubtlessly have been weirdly picturesque." The effect of the passage is not to stress the "picturesqueness" of the scene but to suggest that moments of great intensity vary in their significance according to the perspective from which they are seen. The reader is led to consider the plight of the men from both an abstract view and one closely identified with the situation in the boat. This is one of the ways that Crane was able to reconcile intrusive passages of omniscient comment with the restrictive assumptions of Impressionism. In fact, Kenneth E. Bidle sees this story as the epitome of aesthetic Impressionism in Crane's work:

> Perhaps nowhere else in Crane is impressionistic technique and credo as well illustrated as in "The Open Boat." Here we have a stringent control of point of view; use of unusual metaphors to convey the incredibility of man's plight in an indifferent universe; a swift juxtaposition of scenes; several settings described so that scenes resembling impressionistically rendered paintings are evoked; a frequent use of terse dialogue; and an almost total adherence to technical distance in presentation resulting in an objective detachment on the part of the author.[41]

One necessary qualification of Bidle's formulation is to attribute the detachment to the narrator rather than to Crane himself. As author, and especially as a man who had experienced similar events himself, Crane may well have had personal feelings and ideas beyond those expressed by the narrator and the characters.

One other story, "Death and the Child," deserves special comment for its emphatic modulations of point of view in Impressionistic parallax. The most obvious contrast in perspective in this story is between two characters who stand as observers amid a scene of battle in the Greco-Turkish war of 1897: Peza, a correspondent who becomes increasingly involved in the battle, and an abandoned child who continues to play his games oblivious to the maiming and destruction around him. But these are not the only perspectives, as a close look at the story will reveal.

The story opens with the perspective of a detached, third-person narrator describing the hasty flight of peasants from a battlefield. The implementation of terms of uncertainty (that the peasants "evidently" had forgotten how to count; that fewer bundles "seemed" to suffice for them) precludes omniscience as does the "constant babble of tongues," which are indecipherable. But the opening paragraph is a visual portrait that establishes a scene and suggests the motivating energy, fear, behind the frenzied activity.[42] The second paragraph withdraws to an even greater distance, that of a bird flying high above and observing the battlefield. The first sentence presents a visual panorama: "The blue bay with its pointed ships, and the white town lay below them, distant,

flat, serene" (V, 121). The next sentence describes a bird soaring above
the scene, and the third assumes the perspective of the bird and describes the scene again:

> Here on the height one felt the existence of the universe scornfully
> defining the pain in ten thousand minds. The sky was an arch of
> stolid sapphire. Even to the mountains raising their mighty shapes
> from the valley, this headlong rush of the fugitives was too
> minute. The sea, the sky, and the hills combined in their grandeur
> to term this misery inconsequent (V, 121).

As in "The Open Boat" and "The Blue Hotel," the imposition of an
objective, distant perspective serves to diminish the intensity of activity
as perceived by those more directly involved.

The third paragraph functions similarly with the introduction of
Peza, who is described from a distance and whose mind quickly becomes the center of intelligence. At this point he has some of the
objectivity of the bird: the peasants "seemed to him to wear merely the
expressions of so many boulders rolling down the hill" (V, 122). Peza's
father was Greek, he states in conversation, and he now wishes to
become involved in the fighting. The narrative reveals Peza's sensations and thoughts. Standing on a hill with a lieutenant, his eyes
perceive

> a green plain as level as an inland sea. It swept northward, and
> merged finally into a length of silvery mist. Upon the near part of
> this plain, and upon two grey treeless mountains at the sides of it,
> were little black lines from which floated slanting sheets of smoke
> (V, 124).

The description provides color and visual depth; it offers the first
glimpse of the armies in combat, the batteries firing across the plain.
Peza's associations vary from the "dreams of his childhood" about war
to his empathetic identification with the soldiers: "He felt here the
vibration from the hearts of forty thousand men" (V, 125). Peza, "alive
with despair for these men," loses his detachment and becomes emotionally involved. His empathy frees him from isolation, and he contemplates himself in the context of the vast destruction before him:

> In the moment some portion of egotism left him, and he modestly
> wondered if the universe took cognizance of him to an important
> degree. This theatre for slaughter, built by the inscrutable needs of
> the earth, was an enormous affair, and he reflected that the acci-
> dental destruction of an individual, Peza by name, would perhaps
> be nothing at all (V, 126).

In this passage, Peza experiences an epiphany closely related to that experienced by Henry Fleming in *The Red Badge* and the correspondent in "The Open Boat." Peza sheds his solipsism, his childhood glorification of war, and gains a realistic sense of his position in the universe: "He thought that if he was killed there at that time it would be as romantic, to the old standards, as death by a bit of falling iron in a factory" (V, 127).

All of this is in the first section of the story. It has presented a distant perspective of the scene, rendered Peza's exposure to the battle, and revealed something of his cognitive and emotional response. The second section, reminiscent of Ambrose Bierce's "Chicamauga," follows the same pattern of external description and subsequent narrative identification with a character, in this case a child. Interestingly, this child's point of view shows his capacity for imaginative distortion of sensory details into new patterns of meaning commensurate with the demands of his play. In this fashion the child, abandoned by his parents, is playing at shepherding with an aggregate of sticks and stones: "By a striking exercise of artistic license the sticks were ponies, cows, and dogs, and the pebbles were sheep" (V, 127). In his fantasy the child is detached from the battle below, and he interprets it from the perspective of his own knowledge and concern. He sees the movements of the men as strategies in herding; he hears the artillery bombardment as thunder; he is absorbed in the immediacy of his own world: "The stick in his hand was much larger to him than was an army corps of the distance" (V, 128). The child's perspective of the same scene that Peza had observed, and at roughly the same time, is a narrative counterpoint: Peza moves from detachment to involvement and abstraction; the child perceives no significance in the action beyond his own fantasy.

Section three returns to Peza's perspective and to a series of unusual narrative effects. The first is the narrator's projection of Peza's sense of estrangement from the immediate scene: "It was as if Peza was a corpse walking on the bottom of the sea . . . " (V, 129). The second is a description of what he would have known "if he had been devoting the full lens of his mind" to the scene, which reveals a peaceful nature indifferent to the battle. The use of the term "lens" to indicate the visual receptivity of Peza's mind is operative in the second paragraph in his remembrance of a "place of pictures" that presented him with similar visual intensity. Among the pictures described are several suggestive of Impressionistic paintings, especially "a girl at her bath with screened rays falling upon her pearly shoulders," which recalls several by Degas, and "an execution," which is insufficiently detailed to indicate a specific work but which might relate to one of the most dramatic

paintings of the age, Manet's *Execution of the Emperor Maximilian.*
In any event, Peza's memory creates a distance between the present and
the past, and he is able to see himself leaving the "place of pictures,"
lighting a cigarette, and walking toward a café. His temporal distance
from the scene of memory instills in him a sense of emotional distance
from the lives of the wounded men in the present: "Peza no longer was
torn with sorrow at the sight of wounded men" (V, 130). After the
lieutenant, who had been serving as a guide, leaves him, Peza realizes
the limitations of his own knowledge, as revealed by a sense of his
point of view as a man "groping in a cellar." He cannot perceive
enough of the battle to understand it: "The trees hid all movements of
troops from him. . . . " The point of view is restricted to Peza's mind,
and he is viewing the battle from a distance. After he encounters a
soldier whose jaw has been "half shot away," recalling a similar figure
in Bierce's "Chickamauga," he moves to a hill from which to see "this
great canvas, this tremendous picture" (V, 136). The scene is still visual
for him, still associated with the paintings at which he had marveled.
The narrator presents the action at Peza's level of apprehension: "From
the black lines had come forth an inky mass, which was shaped much
like a human tongue" (V, 137). What Peza comes to understand of this
action is that the Turkish infantry is steadily advancing, threatening to
overtake the Greek position.

As the story moves into section six, the last associated almost entirely
with Peza, the narrative identification with his mind alters somewhat,
becoming progressively internalized to the point of stream of consciousness. When Peza strips a bandoleer from a corpse and puts it on,
he feels the odd sensation "that the dead man had flung his two arms
around him" (V, 138). The emphasis is on Peza's lingering sensation of
the dead man's grasp, joined by the presence of the man who had
owned the rifle he now carries:

> He heard at his ear something that was in effect like the voices of
> those two dead men, their low voices speaking to him of bloody
> death, mutilation. The bandoleer gripped him tighter; he wished
> to raise his hands to his throat like a man who is choking. The
> rifle was clammy; upon his palms he felt the movements of the
> sluggish currents of a serpent's life; it was crawling and frightful
> (V, 139).

The reliability of what Peza's mind takes to be sensory experience is
now subject to question in that it no longer discriminates fantasy from
actuality and misinterprets sensory data, transforming the weight of
the bandoleer into an anthropomorphic "gripping." Esophageal constriction and perspiring palms indicate his fear, as does the imagistic

projection of a sinister serpent. When he spies another dead face, his sense of the immediacy of death becomes overwhelming:

> Peza could feel himself blanch; he was being drawn and drawn by these dead men slowly, firmly down as to some mystic chamber under the earth where they could walk, dreadful figures, swollen and blood-marked. He was bidden; they had commanded him; he was going, going, going (V, 139).

At this point the proximity between the narrator's formulation of thought and Peza's thought itself results in a stream-of-consciousness effect. Driven by his fantasy of the dead men, Peza deserts, as had Henry Fleming, to escape the unconquerable foe within his own mind. Similar to Henry's sense of surrealistic artillery shells leering at him, Peza's imagination dominates the scene and explains his motivation. As he runs some men see him bolting for the rear "tearing madly at the bandoleer," and the narrator adds the interpretation, "the dead man's arms."

If the narrative sections identified with Peza's mind work progressively toward internalization and subjectivization, those using the child's mind as a center of intelligence remain objective. Indeed, the final section of the story continues the child's view of the battle as "fantastic smoky shapes" that have no meaning for him. Finally, he is frightened by the sounds and sights before him, by the mystery of the unfamiliar, and he begins to weep. The narrator intrudes with a reflection at this point, saying that if the soldiers had greater vision they would have regarded the child as a "powerful symbol." The child then sees Peza climbing the hill and asks him, "are you a man?" Peza, stunned by this pointed question, gasps in the manner of a fish. The story ends with the narrator's revelation of Peza's thoughts at this dramatic juncture:

> Palsied, windless, and abject, he confronted the primitive courage, the sovereign child, the brother of the mountains, the sky and the sea, and he knew that the definition of his misery could be written on a wee grass-blade (V, 141).

Peza comes to the same realization of insignificance as Henry Fleming and the correspondent. The narrative method of the story, with its modifications of perspective, not only traces the progression of Peza's conceptual development but contrasts it with superior views (the bird and the objective narrator) and an inferior one (the child). The final impact of this powerful story is the product of a dramatic plot, the theme of insignificance, and especially the intensity of the contrasts of perspectives in its narrative counterpoint.

Crane's use of narrative parallax as one Impressionistic method re-

veals his experimentation with points of view and his stress on the
relativity of perspective. Beyond his concern for urban problems, his
vaguely existential themes, and his portrayal of the philosophical
diminution of human life, it is his narrative techniques that give his
works their distincly "modern" quality. This is especially true of those
passages which resemble stream of consciousness. As the passage regarding Peza's thoughts during his contemplation of the dead man
("he was going, going, going") suggests, there is a point on the continuum of Impressionistic narrative modulation at which the narrative
consciousness becomes so closely identified with the mind of a character as to begin recording the flow of thought without reformulation
by the narrator.

If the "objective" pole of Impressionistic narration is the rendering
of pure sensation, the "subjective" extreme is the revelation of mental
activity derived from the associations of sensory data, a method close to
stream of consciousness but short of Expressionistic modes in which
the mind radically distorts external reality, renders surrealistic images
without external impulse, and violates both spatial and temporal sequence in its representation of subjective states. Written prior to the
formal introduction of stream of consciousness and the development of
Expressionism, Crane's work in the 1890s exemplifies the intermediary
tendency to allow occasional subjective distortion of empirical data
rather than the full Expressionistic attempt at the objectification of
internal experiences. Although the "red sun pasted like a wafer" that
Henry sees in *The Red Badge* and the "hideous crabs" crawling on
Kelcey's brain in *George's Mother* might be seen as Expressionistic
images, most of Crane's fiction is controlled short of pure subjective
projection and within the parameters of Literary Impressionism.

As Leon Edel, among others, has suggested, stream of consciousness
is the logical extension of Impressionistic modes of narration.[43] As the
process of recording sensational responses gives way to rendering
mental activity, the fictional presentation of passages of thought seems
the next likely step. Although Crane's experimentation with this device
is not extensive, and is restricted to brief passages in works largely
rendered from more traditional perspectives, several scholars have commented on his use of this method. Gordon O. Taylor, for example,
devotes a chapter to Crane in his *The Passages of Thought*.[44] Daniel G.
Hoffman acknowledges Crane as a "pioneer" in the use of stream of
consciousness.[45] Benjamin D. Giorgio, writing in his dissertation,
"Stephen Crane: American Impressionist," comments more extensively:

> Although Crane's greatest achievements are in those means by
> which he rendered the "spectacle of the affair"—striking use of
> color, flashing imagery, cinema-like shifting of the points of per-

ception, phrases of synesthetic appeal, dialogue, cadenced sentences—he also took significant steps toward internal impressionism. Crane not only effectively conveys his characters' thoughts and feeling through narrative means and impressionist techniques, but he also displays an acute knowledge of the process of mental flow.[46]

It is not difficult to provide examples from Crane's work of the kind of internal Impressionism Giorgio describes. For example, one instance occurs in *The Red Badge* when Henry is struck on the head. The narrator states as fact the sensations Henry thinks he is experiencing; in actuality Henry receives a blow, which his mind formulates into external sensory data: "He saw the flaming wings of lightning flash before his vision. There was a deafening rumble of thunder within his head" (II, 70). The narrative identification with Henry's mind is so close that there is no suggestion of interpretive distortion. Other more simple presentations of mental flow occur in the flashback of the first chapter and in Henry's wishful regression to the quietudes of his boyhood home following his wound:

> He saw his clothes in disorderly array upon the grass of the bank.
> He felt the swash of the fragrant water upon his body. The leaves
> of the over-hanging maple rustled with melody in the wind of
> youthful summer (II, 72).

This passage of memory is projected in terms of sensory immediacy in the picture of the clothes, the feel and smell of the water, and the synaesthesia of the leaves that "rustle" on the maple.

Other passages in Crane's work go somewhat further in projecting thought. In "God Rest Ye, Merry Gentlemen," for example, one of the accounts of Little Nell and the correspondents covering the Spanish-American War, there are two sections of interest. The first deals with Little Nell's assumption of what the other correspondents are thinking:

> How curious that Tailor should be almost the first [wounded];
> how *very* curious; yes. But so far as arousing them to any
> enthusiasm of active pity, it seemed impossible. He was lying up
> there in the grass, was he? Too bad, too bad, too bad! (VI, 153).

There is a certain awkwardness in this representation of Nell's speculative rendition of what the individuals in the group of correspondents might be thinking, but inasmuch as it represents actual thought for Nell, the narrator renders it as such: mental activity transcribed directly. A less complicated instance follows closely in the narrator's representation of Nell's thoughts about his wounded colleague: "Never mind. Nothing was to be done. The whole situation was too colossal" (VI, 154). Here the narrator appears to be rendering the thought directly, without indication of additional formulation.

A more self-conscious representation of thought, and one of the most remarkable passages in Crane's work, is in "A Man by the Name of Mud," in which The Kid reflects on a series of actions that might have led his friend, also called Kid, into his present circumstance with a girl. The narrator introduces the passage by saying "perhaps it [The Kid's reflection] could be indicated in this fashion" (VIII, 122). What follows is an account of The Kid's musings in telegraphic prose: " 'Went to Comique, I suppose. Saw girl. Secondary part, probably. Thought her rather natural. Went to Comique again. Went again. . . .' " What is suggested here is The Kid's rapid survey of half-formed ideas imagining a sequence of action. Since The Kid is a correspondent, fluent in cablese, his mind can be assumed to work habitually in the mode of his professional correspondence. Thus the rapid workings of his mind are given their appropriate expression. In a related passage in "The Five White Mice," the narrator comments more explicitly on what is being represented. When the New York Kid and his friends confront a group of Mexicans in what threatens to be a gunfight, the narrator represents the mental flow of the protagonist: "His mind leaped forward and studied the aftermath" of his own death:

> The story would be a marvel of brevity when first it reached the far New York home, written in a careful hand on a bit of cheap paper topped and footed and backed by the printed fortifications of the cable company. But they are often as stones flung into mirrors, these bits of paper upon which are laconically written all the most terrible chronicles of the times. He witnessed the uprising of his mother and sister and the invincible calm of his hard-mouthed old father who would probably shut himself in his library and smoke alone (V, 48).

After more of this projected scene, the narrator intrudes to comment on the nature of these thoughts: "These views were perfectly stereopticon, flashing in and away from his thought with an inconceivable rapidity until after all they were simply one quick dismal impression" (V, 49). The narrator presents, in extended form, what is presumably an instantaneous flash of scene in the mind of the New York Kid. Such passages in this story led Giorgio to comment that "although little known, it is probably the finest example of Crane's success with internal impressionism and it also demonstrates Crane's understanding of the mental flow as delineated by William James."[47]

In depicting mental flow, Crane uses an even more startling

narrative device, the implementation of a narrative chorus. The standard modalities of fiction, especially Impressionistic fiction, seem irreconcilable with the implications of a chorus, a repeated refrain, a device more suited to verse or drama. However, Stephen Crane used a chorus in several instances in his fiction and in a number of different ways. In "The Pace of Youth," for example, there is the song of the paper lanterns which is reported by the narrator. The pertinent situation is a forbidden romance between Lizzie and Frank, who are walking the beach in the moonlight:

> They walked home by the lakeside way and out upon the water
> those gay paper lanterns, flashing, fleeting and careering, sang to
> them, sang a chorus of red and violet and green and gold, a song
> of mystic lands of the future (V, 10).

It is difficult to read this passage, or any of Crane's chorus sections, in literal terms. A figurative interpretation which regards the visual phenomenon as genuine sensory experience and the "song" as a narrative evocation of mood, of the budding romance and its possibilities, seems more viable. The narrator formulates the vague dreams of love in the two young people in terms of the soft light from the lanterns.

There is a similar passage at the beginning of Chapter 8 of *The Red Badge of Courage* after Henry has deserted and encountered the dead man in the forest with the ants running across his face:

> The trees began softly to sing a hymn of twilight. The sun sank
> until slanted bronze rays struck the forest. There was a lull in the
> noises of insects as if they had bowed their beaks and were
> making a devotional pause. There was silence save for the chanted
> chorus of the trees (II, 49).

Here again the chorus is reported by the narrator rather than rendered dramatically, and again it is difficult, even in the most Romantic context, to read the passage in the terms in which it is stated. It suggests the way in which Henry regards the evening breeze in the trees. After the most terrifying and confusing day in his life, Henry welcomes the solace of evening, which will diminish the fighting, hide him safely in the darkness, and allow him to rest. The narrator reports the significance of the experience to Henry without identifying the narrative restriction. The religious implications of the "hymn," the insects' "bowing" and "devotional pause," as well as the "chanted chorus" suggest the continuum of the "chapel" of trees in which he had viewed the dead man. In his flight from battle, Henry's agitated mind, filled with fear, remorse, and awe, perceives natural phenomena in religious terms, which the chorus passage communicates.

The use of the chorus to indicate the tonal and conceptual nature of thought is also present in *Active Service* in a scene in which the protagonist, Rufus Coleman, is subject to the seductions of the dark lady of the novel, Nora Black. Although he loves Marjory, the pure and virginal daughter of a college professor, Rufus goes to dinner in Nora's room, where she confronts him with quiet light, perfume, and black silk stockings. The narrator renders his thought process: "He was thinking. To go to the devil—to go to the devil—to go to the devil with this girl was not a bad fate—not a bad fate—not a bad fate" (III, 227). The narrator's projection of Rufus' mental flow reveals a fixation on the sexual prospects before him and disjointed and repetitious thoughts. Unlike the previous passages, however, this idea is repeated and identified by the narrator as a refrain a few paragraphs later, when the momentum of the seduction has become particularly acute:

> She left him again and his galloping thought pounded to the old refrain. To go to the devil—to go to the devil—to go to the devil with this girl was not a bad fate—not a bad fate—not a bad fate. When she returned he drank his glass of champagne (III, 229).

As for Lizzie and Frank and Henry Fleming, Rufus' mental refrain is a narrative revelation of thought rendered in stream of consciousness and revealing a disordered mental state.

In two of Crane's short stores, "A Man and Some Others" and "The Open Boat," the chorus technique pertains more directly to the underlying themes, especially those concerning death. In "A Man and Some Others," a story Crane wrote in the early months of 1896, less than a year before his filibustering adventure and the story based on it, there is a brief philosophical refrain, repeated twice. Bill, a shepherd, is threatened by a band of Mexicans who order him to leave the range, and a vicious gunfight ensues, witnessed by one of Crane's ubiquitous Eastern strangers. Just before the fight begins there is an ominous passage by a "fire chorus" relating to the insignificance of human life:

> Finally, when the great moon climbed the heavens and cast its ghastly radiance upon the bushes, it made a new and more brilliant crimson of the camp-fire, where the flames capered merrily through its mesquit branches, filling the silence with the fire chorus, an ancient melody which surely bears a message of the inconsequence of individual tragedy—a message that is in the boom of the sea, the sliver of the wind through the grass-blades, the silken clash of hemlock boughs (V, 60).

A few moments later, after Bill has killed one of the Mexicans, the narrator's attention returns to the fire and there is a repetition of the message of the chorus:

> The silence returned to the wilderness. The tired flames faintly
> illumined the blanketed thing and the flung corse of the marauder,
> and sang the fire chorus, the ancient melody which bears the mes-
> sage of the inconsequence of human tragedy (V, 62).

These passages function in the story in a complex way. For one thing,
they develop a statement of the insignificance of human life in the
midst of the Easterner's growing compassion and concern for Bill. In
one sense the story is a refutation of the chorus within it. Although
human life may be insignificant, it is of considerable value to people
who have empathetic capabilities. Indeed, the stranger comes to regard
Bill with "some deep form of idolatry" (V, 66). And unlike the *Active
Service* refrain, this one is generated in language deriving solely from
the mind of the narrator.

In "The Open Boat," however, the refrain is rendered as representing
the generalized thinking of the four men in the boat. Again the concern
for death is central to the thinking of the men, and once more this
preoccupation is set off against cosmic indifference. The narrator
introduces the refrain as an approximation of thought: "As for the
reflections of the men, there was a great deal of rage in them. Perchance
they might be formulated thus . . ." (V, 77). The narrator's projection
of these thoughts as mental flow provides the first and most complete
statement of the refrain:

> If I am going to be drowned—if I am going to be drowned—if I
> am going to be drowned, why, in the name of the seven mad gods
> who rule the sea, was I allowed to come thus far and contemplate
> sand and trees? Was I brought here merely to have my nose
> dragged away as I was about to nibble the sacred cheese of life? It
> is preposterous. If this old ninny-woman, Fate, cannot do better
> than this, she should be deprived of the management of men's
> fortunes. She is an old hen who knows not her intention. . . . The
> whole affair is absurd . . . (V, 77).

Implicit in the refrain is the men's preoccupation with danger, their
protest against what they consider to be an unjust Fate, their sense of
absurdity in human events, and their egotistical rage. The second appearance of the refrain is somewhat abbreviated but suggests the same
theme as does the third reiteration.

As in the other chorus examples in Crane's work, the refrain mode
here is a curious synthesis of stream-of-consciousness narration and
intrusive narrative projections. The device reveals thought formulated
by the narrator which provides a tentative interpretation of the action,
one later refuted by the events themselves. It is certainly not, as it has
sometimes been regarded, an omniscient passage that provides a reli-

able statement of the theme of the story. Rather, it reveals that the thinking of the men is cosmologically presumptive, assuming the malevolence of controlling agents in the universe. The first instance of the refrain occurs during an assessment of danger by the four men; the second, after it becomes clear that a man on shore waving his coat is not, as they had hoped, signaling the appearance of a rescue mission; and the third, during the night when the correspondent sees a shark.

It is at this point, the beginning of section six, that the narrative point of view leaves the collective consciousness to become associated almost exclusively with the mind of the correspondent, and as it does so the theme shifts from the concerns of action and danger to epistemology, a change that parallels the alteration in the view of nature from hostile to indifferent. The change in the correspondent's thinking develops from his protest to a new realization that "nature does not regard him as important," a view objectified by a distant star: "A high cold star on a winter's night is the word he feels that she says to him. Thereafter he knows the pathos of his situation" (V, 85). Later a similar realization follows the appearance of the tower on the beach:

> This tower was a giant, standing with its back to the plight of the ants. It represented in a degree, to the correspondent, the serenity of nature amid the struggles of the individual—nature in the wind, and nature in the vision of men. She did not seem cruel to him then, nor beneficient, nor treacherous, nor wise. But she was indifferent, flatly indifferent (V, 88).

Here, in this passage, are two of the most explicit Impressionistic themes in Crane's works: the recognition of a distinction between reality and what man perceives as reality, between "nature in the wind, and nature in the vision of men," and the development of a perception of nature as indifferent. What in "A Man and Some Others" is sung by the "fire chorus" is here embodied in a star and a tower and interpreted, finally, not by the narrator but by the protagonist.

There is a considerable diversity in Crane's handling of the unusual narrative method of the chorus-refrain. It varies from the narrator's projection of an interpretation of the events to his rendering of a quasi-Romantic statement by various elements of nature, to a stream-of-consciousness revelation of precognitive thought, to a generalized statement of what characters "must" be thinking.

The diversity of Stephen Crane's narrative methods suggests experimentation with a variety of modes and ideas. An exploration of the methods of his works reveals that rarely did he employ any of his strategies with absolute consistency and artistic integrity, although he was generally most consistent in what have come to be regarded, largely for other reasons, as his most important works. Although he dabbled in traditional first-person methods, and on occasion used omniscience, the tendency throughout his work is to restrict sources of information, to create countering points of view, to suggest ironically the limitation and erroneous interpretations of the principal characters.

On a more immediate level, what Crane was able to achieve, better than any previous writer in America, was the illusion of a sensory reality being apprehended by a character. His empirical intensity required the rendition of sharp but relatively brief units of sensation, the result for his fiction was a structure involving numerous episodes unified by continuities of theme and character. Often a single episode will begin with a sensorially descriptive passage rendered before the narrator moves into the portrait to record dialogue and describe action from within the scene. In the process, the narrative perspective often becomes identified with the mind of a single character, resulting in an immediate apprehensional awareness of the fictional world of the character. As Edwin Cady has remarked of Crane,

> the essence of his art was to give, in his characters, persons with eyes and to set them in turn within perspectives which would let readers see both very sharply and complexly around them. . . .[48]

The restriction to a third-person identification with the mind of a character, or even several characters, reveals the extent to which individual human beings comprehend only partial truths of the world about them, delude themselves about their knowledge, and live within a continuous matrix of distortion and self-serving reconstructions of data.[49]

The result of Crane's narrative methodology, as suggested by *The Red Badge of Courage*, is to present an Impressionistic epistemology of a world in which the appearance of reality is constantly in flux, a kinetic world of light and shadow, of sensory multiplicity, of confusion and uncertainty.[50] The reader's mind is first exposed to the narrator and then, as the narrator's perspective is fused with that of a character, identified with that character and drawn into his perspective. The resultant emphasis is on psychological reality, on a concern for the human receptor of sensory experience rather than external reality itself. This emphasis, among others, clearly distinguishes Crane's works from the standard Realistic fiction of his time.

To make a simple statement about an extremely intricate matter, Crane's narrative methods are a good deal more complex than has generally been assumed, especially by those readers who have regarded the narrators of his works as Crane himself. His narrative methods, almost without exception, portray a world that is "ephemeral, evanescent, constantly shifting its meaning and hence continually defying precise definition," a description Rodney O. Rogers uses to describe both Crane's works and French Impressionistic painting.[51] Narrative restriction, limitations of sensory data, distorted interpretations of information, modulations among differing points of view, these are Crane's basic methods of presentation. As a close analysis of the other dimensions of his art reveals, these narrative strategies are related to his episodic plots, sensory imagery, and epistemological themes involving perception and realization. Crane's methods of narration were diverse, innovative, and richly suggestive of a formulation of human reality remarkably modern and existential for the 1890s and fundamental to the central ideas and aesthetics of Literary Impressionism.

III

Theme: The Failure of Her Eye and the Wail of Despair

The basic themes in Stephen Crane's fiction derive from the isolation, delusion, and epistemological processes of his characters. If restrictive, ironic, and parallactic narration is the fundamental mode of Crane's fiction, its underlying meaning, the sum of its motifs and implications, resides in these Impressionistic ideas.[1] Crane's fiction suggests a situation in which the individual is basically insignificant, unable to comprehend or modify much beyond his own personal world. From this perspective, a character's view of life is necessarily solipsistic, perpetually tentative, unavoidably qualified by preoccupation and prejudice. As a result, reality is "complex, ambivalent, ambiguous, and elusive, as much a matter of the play of a peculiarity of mind as of a quality or character in the object itself."[2]

As the epistemological nature of Crane's narrative methods suggests, the truth is elusive and transient, and the search for it is likely to yield only momentary flashes of insight. If seen from several points of view, a portrait of life might enhance its verisimilitude without resolving the isolation and restriction of each of the viewers.[3] Isolation, delusion, cognitive restrictions, apprehensional difficulties, fantasies, and fears all qualify and restrict the potential for knowledge. Any progression from these limited states to a broader and more penetrating perception of things becomes a story of initiation, with its inherent pains of growth and qualified success; the counter story of cognitive stasis suggests perceptual blindness and the capacity of vanity and delusion to inspire human tragedy.

The language of vision is nearly inescapable in discussing Impressionistic themes because it metaphorically approximates conceptual states in terms of almost universal formulation. The development of visual themes suggests a concern for epistemological problems, human understanding, the restriction of knowledge, the conflict between truth and illusion,[4] all of which found a new role in American Impressionistic fiction following its appearance in the works of Nathaniel Hawthorne, Herman Melville, and other Romantic writers. As themes, the variables in the metaphor appear as visual limitation or blindness, as truth-illusion conflicts, or as epiphanies that bring the character to a new level of perception and deeper states of comprehension.

Crane's work is replete with these concepts in striking and often humorous formulations, especially those expressing limitations and blindness. Perhaps the simplest example of the interplay between the literal and figurative dimensions of the metaphor is a passage in Crane's early journalistic account of the parade of the Junior Order of United American Mechanics in Asbury Park:

> The bona fide Asbury Parker is a man to whom a dollar, when held close to his eye, often shuts out any impression he may have had that other people possess rights. He is apt to consider that men and women, especially city men and women, were created to be mulcted by him (VIII, 522).

If this comment suggests something of the moral blindness inherent in greed, the "cylinder of vision" Crane described in his "London Impressions" is perhaps indicative of the more common human circumstance in his fiction.[5] Because of this restriction, the acquisition of knowledge, or even basic sensory information, is severely limited and inspires a feeling of isolation, a sense of alienation from the physical world itself. The desire for a more comprehensive view, or the necessity for it, only intensifies the existential sense of limitation, as it does in *Active Service*: "Perhaps one of the first effects of war upon the mind is a new recognition and fear of the circumscribed ability of the eye, making all landscape seem inscrutable" (III, 173). The lack of a better view of things in this novel causes unnecessary fear and anxiety in Rufus Coleman; contrary to his assumption, there are no Turkish forces lurking in the brush waiting to attack him and his friends. This fact requires a definition of reality in Impressionistic, rather than Realistic, terms. Realism tends toward a description of external phenomena as they are commonly understood to be; Impressionism presents a simulation of sensory experience with little additional information. As a result, people perceive relatively little about the world around them, know less, distort the sensations they experience, and confuse the entire ontological process with the play of their own imaginations. Thus Henry Fleming runs from battle "like a blind man" in *The Red Badge*, fleeing not from external dangers so much as "all the horror of those things which he imagined" (II, 41).

Indeed the metaphors of perception generate the fundamental theme of *The Red Badge* in terms that explicitly link the novel to the development of Literary Impressionism in America. From the beginning of the novel Henry's most significant problem is his inability to formulate and sustain a realistic conception of himself and the conditions of war. Severely limited in experience, his mind resorts to fantasies of glory based on his reading about classical battles, and these conceptions compete for dominance with his fears of cowardice and death, his uncertainties about himself, his dread of the unknown. This mental conflict finds appropriate expression in his illusions of himself, restricted vision, and eventual perceptual growth.

Henry's underlying problem in the novel is not simply his effort to control his fear, as some critics have argued,[6] but rather to perceive and interpret himself and his situation with some degree of assurance. His insecurities are born of a need to understand himself. Since his father is dead, he has no role model to emulate; since war is unknown to him, he can only fantasize about it. Even Henry's fantasies and visions are essentially deductive, deriving from a heroic portrait of war. However, his attempts to understand himself and the specific circumstances of "his" war are basically empirical and inductive: "He saw that he would again be obliged to experiment as he had in early youth. He must accumulate information of himself . . ." (II, 10). His understanding must commence in total ignorance; early in the novel he is forced to the realization that "as far as war was concerned he knew nothing of himself" (II, 10).

Attempting to learn, Henry "tried to observe everything" (II, 23). When his regiment moved in the night, "he kept his eyes watchfully upon the darkness" (II, 21). When a skirmish began, "his eyes grew wide and busy with the action of the scene" (II, 28). His view is less than complete, however, presenting him with confused and incomplete data and inspiring in him a sense of isolation. This feeling, when mingled with his earlier heroic conceptions, casts him as a singular viewer of reality: "There was but one pair of eyes in the corps. He would step forth and make a speech. Shrill and passionate words came to his lips" (II, 25). As this passage suggests, Henry's attempts to see more clearly are compromised by his self-congratulatory illusions. Before he had left home, in thinking about the war "he had seen himself in many struggles. He had imagined peoples secure in the shadow of his eagle-eyed prowess" (II, 5), a fantasy that presents heroism in terms of vision. Now, actually confronting battle, he must also deal with an antithetical vision "of a thousand-tongued fear that would babble at his back and cause him to flee while others were going coolly about their country's business" (II, 20).

This conflict has its first manifestation in Henry's desertion. As the images of monsters and savage gods suggest, Henry's mind, driven by fear, has metamorphosed the enemy into "redoubtable dragons" and "red and green monster[s]"; his compatriots who stand their ground are certain to be "initial morsels for the dragons"; his brigade will be "gulped into the infernal mouth of the war-god" (II, 41–43). These visions so dominate his mind that it is impregnable, and he is cognitively "blind" when he runs. Later, the danger passed, he attempts to assess what has happened, and the pride of his earlier heroic notions replaces his fear. His blindness continues, but the obscuring thoughts are now complex rationalizations contending that he had acted more wisely than his comrades: "He, the enlightened man who looks afar in the dark, had fled because of his superior perceptions and knowledge" (II, 45). Pride, as well as delusion, is expressed in terms of vision, and his superiority over his fellows seems to him to indicate that they will not be able to comprehend his enlightened perspective: "Their density would not enable them to understand his sharper point of view" (II, 46).

If Henry's fear, which prompts him to perceive enemy forces as monsters and dragons, generates his impulse to flee, his continuing inability to see himself and battle clearly dominates the center of the novel. Henry is not alone in his problems: Jim Conklin had earlier rejoiced in a similar pride in his superior "prowess of perception" (II, 16) and now he was dead; Wilson, brash with confidence, had also believed in his own supreme perception: "He was sprightly, vigorous, fiery in his belief in success. He looked into the future with clear, proud eye" [sic] (II, 19). But Wilson had quavered in his resolve and, anticipating death, had given Henry an envelope to be returned to his parents.

Henry's experience with Wilson in the second half of the novel, beginning with Chapter 12, reveals that during Henry's absence from the regiment his "loud" comrade has undergone substantial growth. Wilson ministers to Henry's wounds with sensitivity and compassion, sacrificing his blanket at night, cooking for him in the morning. Henry is aware of Wilson's development:

> He was, no more, a loud young soldier. There was about him now a fine reliance. He showed a quiet belief in his purposes and his abilities. And this inward confidence evidently enabled him to be indifferent to little words of other men aimed at him (II, 82).

But the vehicle by which Wilson has achieved his sudden maturity is expressed in a metaphor of vision that expresses the theme of epiphany: Henry

> wondered where had been born these new eyes; when his comrade [Wilson] had made the great discovery that there were many men

>who would refuse to be subjected by him. Apparently, the other
>had now climbed a peak of wisdom from which he could perceive
>himself as a very wee thing (II, 82).

Wilson's "new eyes," which inspire humility and confidence and yet reveal to him his insignificance, are apparently the result of an epiphany born of the frantic activity of war which accelerates growth and allows significant character alterations within a short time. Henry's reflections indicate that the key to Wilson's transformation was the perspective from a "peak of wisdom" which revealed that he was one with his fellows.[7] It is significant that although he observes Wilson's development, this awareness does not, for some time at least, inspire a corresponding change in Henry himself.

In fact, although he rejoins his regiment after his desertion and walk with the wounded men, and after the death of Conklin and his own blow to the head, Henry persists in a self-serving rationale. He contemplates using the envelope to embarrass Wilson, despite his sense of Wilson's new humility (II, 85). He rejoices that "he had performed his mistakes in the dark" (II, 86) and never, until his subsequent appearance in "The Veteran," reveals the truth about what he did. As a new battle begins, his view again constricts: "Curtains of trees interfered with his ways of vision. He could see the low line of trenches but for a short distance" (II, 89). As he hears praise for his supposed bravery in the previous battle, however, he begins to change: "He became suddenly a modest person" (II, 91). This state of mind is temporary, for soon after, in the "chaos" of his mind, he begins to feel that "he had been a tremendous figure, no doubt" (II, 97).

As he moves into the key epiphanic episode, Chapter 18, his perceptual difficulties at first continue, his view "blurred by the hurlying smoke of the line" (II, 100). But in the rush of activity, Henry's perspective is suddenly transformed and he undergoes a maturing of self-awareness: Henry feels that "he had been made aged. New eyes were given to him. And the most startling thing was to learn suddenly that he was very insignificant" (II, 101). Henry's "recognition" improves his perception literally and figuratively. As the battle begins anew, his ability to perceive his environment is markedly improved:

>It seemed to the youth that he saw everything. Each blade of the
>green grass was bold and clear. He thought that he was aware of
>every change in the thin, transparent vapor that floated idly in
>sheets. The brown or grey trunks of the trees showed each rough-
>ness of their surfaces. And the men of the regiment . . . all were
>comprehended. His mind took mechanical but firm impressions, so
>that, afterward, everything was pictured and explained to him,
>save why he himself was there (II, 105).

Although it is significant that Henry has achieved a new level of insight, in accord with the psychological reality of the novel, perceptual growth is neither total nor invariable. Henry has seen, for the first time, the limitations of his importance, and he has begun to see his environment more clearly, yet the flux of life brings new circumstances. In a mad rush at the enemy, Henry charges with his eyes nearly closed and the scene becomes a "wild blur" to him (II, 108). Looking across a "clouded haze" to the battlefield, he must depend on his "misused ears" for information (II, 112). Later, in the heat of battle, smoke obscures the field and Henry "strained his vision to learn the accomplishment of the volley but the smoke hung before him" (II, 114).

For all of these difficulties, Henry's epiphany has brought a new awareness. As he surveys the battlefield after the conflict, he realizes that his emotional pitch during the action distorted his view: "Elfin thoughts must have exaggerated and enlarged everything, he said" (II, 117). His new confidence also allows moments of unimpaired vision, and he sees clearly the number and alignment of the troops (II, 122). In the final chapter, looking back upon his actions, Henry is capable of a more mature and balanced evaluation:

> His mind was under-going a subtle change. . . . Gradually his
> brain emerged from the clogged clouds and at last he was enabled
> to more closely comprehend himself and circumstance. . . . Later,
> he began to study his deeds—his failures and his achieve-
> ments. . . . At last, they marched before him clearly (II, 133).

This new visual capacity informs and qualifies the conclusion of the novel and gives meaning to its final image. Henry's eyes "open to some new ways," and in viewing his previous indiscretions he can "see them truly" and "despise" them. He has gained control of his fear; he has come to know and accept death: "He was a man." In the most telling comment in the novel, "it came to pass that as he trudged from the place of blood and wrath, his soul changed." Henry's epiphany has not been simply a matter of understanding battle: it has fundamentally altered him as a human being. As a result, the concluding image creates optimism: "Over the river a golden ray of sun came through the hosts of leaden rain clouds" (II, 135).

The story of Henry Fleming's growth in *The Red Badge of Courage* is no chronicle of confrontations with Deterministic forces, as a Naturalistic reading would require, nor even a Realistic account of combat. Rather, it is a record of Henry's progressive intensification of vision to a moment of epiphany in which he sees his world and himself in a larger perspective. The novel is basically a story of psychological adjustment to reality in which Henry achieves a reconciliation of his

romantic visions with his new awareness. He does not suddenly perceive all truth for all time, for such a conception, as Donald Pizer
suggests, would be reductive: "*The Red Badge* presents a vision of man
as a creature capable of advancing in some areas of knowledge and
power but forever imprisoned within the walls of certain inescapable
human and social limitations."[8] But the novel does document an
epistemological process in which a young boy makes gains in self-
knowledge, in his ability to perceive his environment, and in his
attempts to achieve a balance that keeps thought and emotion in con-
structive proportion. Even so, for Henry the "truth" is ultimately
tentative, relativistic, solipsistic, but as close to reality as a single
human being, insignificant yet egoistic, can ever come in an Impressionistic novel.

Another visual concept in Crane's works is the theme of illusion, of
faulty interpretation of experience. Illusion, as the distortion of either
apprehensive data or comprehensive analysis, is central to Impressionistic fiction and painting. Indeed, Maria Kronegger contends that
"since Flaubert, the essential tenet of all impressionist art is illusion."[9]
The difficulty of discussing illusion in Stephen Crane's fiction is that it
is everywhere. Almost every character expresses an interpretation of
reality that deviates to some degree from the "norm" the work itself
presents. From the Sullivan County tales to his last efforts, Crane's
stories develop a continuing record of the inability of the human mind
to interpret reality and to sustain a verifiable grasp of self. The disparity between illusions and realities, in fact, accounts for the basic
tone at the heart of his fiction. As James B. Colvert contends, "the
Crane story again and again interprets the human situation in terms of
the ironic tensions created in the contrast between man as he idealizes
himself in his inner thought and emotion and man as he actualizes
himself in the stress of experience."[10] Indeed, Colvert interprets "blinding delusion" to be central to Crane's fiction.

Illusions and deceptions exist on nearly all levels, from simple mis-
interpretations of empirical data to grand distortions of self-
perception. On the least complex level is the category of error represented by a scene in *Active Service* in which Rufus Coleman and his
endangered entourage are taken under protection by a Greek officer. In
the distance there are Greek horsemen appearing as "little black dots."
The scene is highly visual:

> The rise of ground was heavily clad with trees and over the tops
> of them appeared the cupola and part of the walls of a large
> white house and there were glimpses of huts near it as if a village
> was marked. The black specks seemed to be almost to it (III, 175).

The qualifying terms of uncertainty, "seemed" and "as if," indicate the illusion of proximity as the group draws nearer to the house; the concentration is clearly upon the deluding tricks of the eye:

> The white house grew larger and larger and they came nearly to the advance scouts who they could now see were not quite close to the village. There had been a deception of the eye precisely as occurs at sea (III, 175).

Visual phenomena are here characteristically problematic: the distortion of proximity from a distance, the diminution of the riders, the growth of the house, all suggest the unreliability of empirical data. Similar errors of sight and interpretation occur throughout Crane's fiction, from the tiny horses and riders Henry Fleming sees, to the erroneous interpretation of the American cruiser *St. Paul* as an enemy ship in "Chased by a Big 'Spanish Man-O-War'," to "The Lone Charge of William B. Perkins," in which a newspaper correspondent mounts an heroic offensive against what he thinks to be a "Spaniard in the bush." After an elaborate charge, he discovers that "his Spaniard was a bit of dried palm-branch" (VI, 117). In one sense or another, nearly every Crane character suffers from Perkins' problem.

But delusion in Crane's world affects both matters of fact and matters of judgment. These concerns are evident in *The Red Badge*, from Henry's empiricist assertion that "he must accumulate information of himself" (II, 10) to his later awareness that Jim Conklin could be in error in his self-estimate: "Still he thought that his comrade might be mistaken about himself . . ." (II, 13). Although direct experience is often incomplete and misleading, it is more reliable than any alternative method. As the soldiers discover in "Virtue in War," the study of books is an especially poor method: "Actually, there was not *anything* in the world which turned out to be as books describe it" (VI, 186). Indeed, the Swede's distorted view of the West in "The Blue Hotel" is thought by the Easterner to be the direct result of reading dime novels. And the Easterner himself, who seems consistently urbane and literate in the many stories in which he appears, derives no special claim to wisdom from his cultural sophistication. Further, reliable data are difficult to find in Crane's works and reliable interpretation of data even more rare. Save for those few instances in *The Red Badge*, "The Open Boat," and other works in which the character experiences a moment of epiphany, there is very little accurate "perception." Misinterpretation, distortion, misplaced emphasis, illusion dominate human understanding.

Perhaps one reason there is little accuracy of perception is the interference of self-deluding pride, a problem that blinds nearly all of the important characters. In Crane's work, pride exhibits itself not as confidence or self-assurance, but in the most egregious form of *hubris*, an assumption of worth and capability grossly irreconcilable with even the most generous assessment. If pride in such characters as Uncle Jake and Scratchy Wilson seems a harmless and even charming distortion, its role in the death of the Swede in "The Blue Hotel" and Bill in "A Man and Some Others" reveals its destructive potential. A somewhat less dramatic utilization of the same point runs throughout the Sullivan County tales, especially in the posturing of the little man in such works as "Four Men in a Cave," "The Octopush," and "A Ghoul's Accountant," each of which turns on the deflation of ego and diminution of stature for the central figure. A related epistemological matter derives from the fact that the little man's pride is such a distortion that it becomes problematic as to whether he can be considered to reside in reality at all. It is perhaps a telling point that throughout the Sullivan County tales, stories of deflation are intermingled with stories of hyperbolic distortion. As the narrator says in the opening of "The Way in Sullivan County," "wherever the wild deer boundeth and the shaggy bear waddleth, there does the liar thrive and multiply" (VIII, 220).

If the truth-illusion disparity is a continuing issue throughout the Sullivan County tales, it is equally important in almost any other grouping of Crane's stories. Uncle Jake is confounded by reality at the beginning of Crane's career and The O'Ruddy at the end of it. Throughout, reality is elusive, shifting, impenetrable. Illusion is universal. The children in Whilomville, playing out their interpretation of adult behavior, indulge in fantasy almost continuously. If the children reveal the social pretensions of their parents through their imitative fancy, so do they portray the common illusions of adult life.

The most significant development of self-deluding pride in the Crane canon, even more important than Henry's posturing in the first half of *The Red Badge,* is the perceptual distortion of pride in *Maggie.* As Colvert has pointed out, "like 'the little man,' the people in *Maggie* entertain false images of self which lead them into moral error." As well as a motivational device, distorted self-estimate, born of pride, suggests a thematic statement: "That human incompetency—comic in the Sullivan County sketches, tragic in *Maggie*—finds its source in vanity, delusion, and ignorance of self."[11]

The novel opens with an appropriately ironic event:

> A very little boy stood upon a heap of gravel for the honor of
> Rum Alley. He was throwing stones at howling urchins from
> Devil's Row who were circling madly about the heap and pelting
> him (I, 7).

Nearly every aspect of this passage points to the disparity between Jimmie's sense of mission and the reality of the scene. That he is very small, that he is defending a "heap of gravel" for "Rum Alley," are details discordant with the concept of "honor." His battle with "howling urchins from Devil's Row" conducted with primitive "thrown stones" further suggests that the participants conceive of their conflict as a fight for honor to shield from themselves the petty nature of their degraded scuffle.[12] The narrative irony derives from the projected views of the children, a device that underscores the extent to which their perceptions are inconsistent with their lives. That chivalric rhetoric is used to describe the action indicates the irony of the narrator's description of it. The distortions of the opening of the novel cast the characters in heroic roles in a grand social conflict, a post that disguises the degrading societal ambience and the violence and pretension of the Johnson family. As Donald Pizer has said, "the novel is not so much about the slums as a physical reality as about what people believe in the slums and how their beliefs are both false to their experience and yet function as operative forces in their lives."[13]

The irony of the opening scene persists throughout the novel with tragic results. Pete is introduced as a character whose true stature is hidden from him:

> Down the avenue came boastfully sauntering a lad of sixteen
> years, although the chronic sneer of an ideal manhood already sat
> upon his lips. His hat was tipped over his eye with an air of
> challenge. Between his teeth, a cigar stump was tilted at the angle
> of defiance. He walked with a certain swing of the shoulders
> which appalled the timid (I, 8).

His actions exemplify his character: he strikes one of the younger fighters in the back of the head. For Pete, as for Jimmie, delusion is part of his environment and a contributory force to the perpetuation of the status quo. The narrator's revelation of Jimmie's values serve as well for Pete: "He and his order were kings. . . . He was afraid of nothing. . . . After a time his sneer grew so that it turned its glare upon all things. He became so sharp that he believed in nothing" (I, 21). Jimmie and Pete are the products of a society that admires violence and arrogance and requires self-delusion to sustain its view of itself.

Such delusion has many facets: a false image of self, a distorted view of other people, a blindness to moral responsibility. Sexual relationships serve as dramatic manifestations of the social effects of this state. Jimmie is sufficiently romantic to murmur of a "star-lit evening," " 'D' moon looks like hell, don't it?' " (I, 23). At the same time, his sexual conquests represent an inconvenience: "Two women in different parts of the city, and entirely unknown to each other, caused him considerable annoyance by breaking forth, simultaneously, at fateful intervals, into wailings about marriage and support and infants" (I, 23). Maggie also participates in delusion, blindness, and distorted perspective. Moreover, she is sensitive and compassionate and in other ways ill-suited to survive in her environment. Her innocence is destructive, her compassion a weakness, and her naive perspective a block to an assessment of reality. Perhaps the focal point of her blindness is her perception of Pete, the Bowery tough become bartender and suitor. Maggie is impressed by his clothes, his aggressiveness, his "aristocratic person." The narrator reveals her limited perspective:

> Maggie perceived that here was the ideal man. Her dim thoughts
> were often searching for far away lands where, as God says, the
> little hills sing together in the morning. Under the trees of her
> dream-gardens there had always walked a lover (I, 26).

Indeed, the point stressed about Maggie throughout the novel is not her economic depravity, not her sensuality, not even the social influences on her behavior, but rather her inability to correctly perceive the world she lives in and to come to a personal judgment about how to behave within it.

For example, when Pete takes her to a neighborhood tavern, displaying the while his boorish and aggressive manner, Maggie sees only his cultured sophistication: "Maggie perceived that Pete brought forth all his elegance and all his knowledge of high-class customs for her benefit. Her heart warmed as she reflected upon his condescension" (I, 31). In fact, the courtship section of the novel emphasizes the disparity between Maggie's limited perception of life and the paltry reality itself. As Maggie is deceived by a ventriloquist, so is she generally guilty of accepting illusion for substance.[14] When she sees a melodrama at the local theater, she is similarly confused: "To Maggie and the rest of the audience this was transcendental realism" (I, 36).

It is in the context of Maggie's pathetic inadequacy to perceive her world that she is seduced by Pete. A contributory element is the attitude of Maggie's mother, who has become increasingly absorbed in her alcoholism: her physical appearance suggests insanity, and her attitude is one of suspicion and hostility. When Pete calls on Maggie in the central episode, Mrs. Johnson reveals that she believes Pete and Maggie have already begun their affair:

> "Yeh've gone t' d' devil, Mag Johnson, yehs knows yehs have
> gone t' d' devil. Yer a disgrace t' yer people, damn yeh. . . .
> Go t' hell wid him, damn yeh, an' a good riddance. Go t' hell an'
> see how yeh likes it" (I, 41).

Her mother's abuse influences Maggie to go with Pete, who offers tender consolation.

Mrs. Johnson's erroneous perception of her daughter is part of the history of causality of Maggie's eventual suicide. That the mother continues to perceive her daughter's "fall" as the betrayal of a respectable family is the dominant ironic motif of the second half of the novel. Mrs. Johnson's speech to Jimmie reveals her construction of the situation:

> "Ah, who could t'ink such a bad girl could grow up in our fambly, Jimmie, me son. Many d' hour I've spent in talk wid dat girl an' tol' her if she ever went on d' streets I'd see her damned. An' after all her bringin' up an' what I tol' her and talked wid her, she goes t' d' bad, like a duck t' water" (I, 43).

Beyond the obvious irony of her ranting, this conversation with Jimmie reveals another important point: a young lady named Sadie MacMallister has been "sent to the devil" by her young man. Jimmie's comment, " 'Ah, dat's anudder story,' " suggests that *he* is responsible (I, 44). Both Jimmie and his mother are pictured as morally blind: she does not perceive her complicity in her daughter's actions, and he, accepting the ethic of his society, adopts a double standard that frees him from responsibility in his relationships with women. As a consequence, his subsequent affectation of moral outrage at Maggie's "ruin" and his fight with Pete are revealed as shallow posings, as dimly perceived obligations with no real psychological force.

For her part, Maggie views her circumstances favorably. Against a threatening environment, she has the protection of Pete's strength; against her poverty and dreary job in the collar and cuff factory, she has his "wealth"; against an unknown future, she believes in one that is "rose-tinted" (I, 52). Maggie lives in a more secure and comfortable world than ever before, and her situation develops its own ethic: "She did not feel like a bad woman. To her knowledge she had never seen any better" (I, 52). Indeed, her sense of social stature has improved considerably, despite the fact that she is a "kept woman." She retains her sense of social respectability and virtue, sometimes with ironic implications, as when she leaves the tavern with Pete: "As they went out Maggie perceived two women seated at a table with some men. They were painted and their cheeks had lost their roundness. As she passed them the girl, with a shrinking movement, drew back her skirts" (I, 53). The passage indicates Maggie's assumption of virtue, the disparity between her view of self and her obvious similarity to the painted women, and the continuing theme of ironic delusion.

Maggie's lack of vision contributes to her downfall in the concluding chapters of the novel. In her innocence and submissiveness, she seems undesirable to Pete when compared to the more worldly-wise and assertive Nellie, and Pete soon leaves Maggie to her own devices. Abandoned by Pete, she is soon rejected by everyone else, including her family, to whom she appeals for help. From her mother she gets nothing but "scoffing laughter." Another mother in the same tenement snatches away her child before it can touch Maggie's dress. From the point of view of bourgeois morality, the very code Maggie had embraced, she has now become a pariah. Her family feels that she alone is responsible for her plight, whereas Pete takes the position that her mother and brother are at fault. His rejection of her is ironically an appeal to respectability: if people see Maggie associating with him, his job and reputation will be jeopardized. What is evident in the lives of Pete and the other characters is that there is so much delusion and moral uncertainty that the notion of respectability has become a destructive norm.[15] Even the clergyman maintains his moral pose by refusing to help Maggie: "His beaming, chubby face was a picture of benevolence and kind-heartedness. His eyes shone good-will. . . . But as the girl timidly accosted him, he made a convulsive movement and saved his respectability by a vigorous side-step. He did not risk it to save a soul" (I, 67). In addition to Maggie's innocent perspective, there is an important contributory pattern of causation based on a self-congratulatory respectability, which the characters value above their moral and personal commitments to one another.

Maggie's suicide is not the result of an unsuccessful venture into prostitution, for in fact she has a "handsome cloak" and "well-shod feet" even the night she dies, indicating that she has done well financially. Rather, it is the result of a progressive psychological and moral degeneration suggested by the decline in the stature of the men from whom she solicits on her final night. But the ultimate irony of self-deluding vision derives from the mother's reaction to the death of her daughter. Here again the central response is not genuine emotion or thought but a fulfillment of societal expectation. Mrs. Johnson is eating "like a fat monk in a picture" when she hears of her daughter's death, and the delay in her reaction defines her priorities: "She continued her meal. When she finished her coffee she began to weep" (I, 75). Her laments are filled with religious bromides and with melodramatic sentimentality: she weeps over Maggie's baby shoes. A woman in the background comes forward to plead that she forgive her daughter, which she refuses to do until others join in the appeal. Finally the mother says " 'Oh, yes, I'll fergive her!' "(I, 77). Even with regard to her daughter's death, Mrs. Johnson is more concerned with her shallow ethic than with genuine feeling. As R. W. Stallman says, "the grotesque buffoonery of this mock lamentation is comic enough, but underlying it is the tragic theme that all is false, even between mother and daughter."[16]

The novel ends ironically with the pretense of a heartbroken and wronged mother whose compassionate nature allows her to forgive this crime against her complacency. Pride, respectability, the church, middle-class morality, all have become agents that promote and sustain delusions of self. Tragically, the falsity of this approach to life also deprives them of genuine emotion, of compassion, of familial affection, and of a sense of responsibility in the conduct of their lives. These perversions of insight and perspective constitute the major causes of Maggie's tragedy, not an abstract "fate," economic or social Determinism, or even chance.

Such a reading of *Maggie* is obviously at odds with the more common Naturalistic assessment of the underlying themes of the novel. It is also at variance with Crane's inscription on the copies of *Maggie* he presented to Hamlin Garland, the Reverend Thomas Dixon, and Dr. Lucius L. Button, although not necessarily with the book he wrote. Crane's inscription read:

> It is inevitable that you will be greatly shocked by this book but continue please with all possible courage to the end. For it tries to show that environment is a tremendous thing in the world and frequently shapes lives regardless. If one proves that theory one makes room in Heaven for all sorts of souls (notably an occasional street girl) who are not confidently expected to be there by many excellent people.[17]

If this comment is read as a statement supporting the view that Maggie's death is the result of social and economic forces on her life, then it raises several problematic issues. It is possible that Crane's comment, although several times repeated, was an inadequate and misleading indication of his own views of the novel; it is possible that, as with nearly everything else he wrote, it is ironic and at least half in jest; it is also possible that the comment was sincere and yet not the best interpretation of the motivating factors of the novel. For one thing, of all the characters of the novel, Maggie, the girl who blossomed in a mud puddle, is less a product of her environment than nearly anyone else. Indeed, her worldly innocence and compassion mark her as singularly free of the influences around her.[18] For another, if societal pressures are a determining factor within her world, they are curiously selective in their application: Nellie, another young woman who is exposed to the same environment, and who has apparently had an affair with Pete, is certainly not subject to the destructive influences that presumably affect Maggie.

Maggie's death is tragic, in a modern sense, but it is clearly not the result of necessitarian forces, as such Naturalistic readings as that of Malcolm Cowley would have it. Cowley argues that "Maggie, the victim of environment, was no more to blame for her transgression than McTeague, the victim of hereditary evil. Nobody was to blame in this world where men and women are subject to the laws of things. . . . "[19] Cowley's interpretation seems inadequate: the environment does not pervade this girl who blossomed within it, who had "none of the dirt of Rum Alley . . . in her veins" (I, 24). Nor is Maggie driven by heredity: she little resembles her family and especially not her mother, who is violent and domineering, given to brutality and "sentimental self-pity."[20] Maggie dies as the result of a need for compassion, of her romantic dreams, of her dependency, and perhaps most of all, of her simplistic and distorted view of life. The major external contributory factors in her death are also false estimates of reality by Pete, Jimmie, and Mrs. Johnson. Maggie's death is the result of the epistemological problems of perception and interpretation and not of deterministic forces beyond the control of the characters.

Nellie's fortunes clearly imply this interpretation. Her confidence and dominance show on all levels: her attitude, her conversation, her fine clothes, her behavior with men. She uses and discards Freddie, her "mere boy," and following Maggie's suicide she manipulates and exploits Pete, who is drunk. She finally takes his money and treats him with dehumanizing patronage. She forsakes Pete, unconscious on the floor, and leaves the tavern in search of other opportunities. She is clearly not subject to destructive Deterministic forces, and thus the environment of the Bowery cannot be seen as requiring any particular destiny or role for the women in it. In its broadest context, *Maggie* is not thematically a work of literary Naturalism. Only in its setting does the novel exhibit Naturalistic tendencies. Its narrative irony and limited point of view, its brevity and structural balance, its stress on delusion and moral responsibility, and its fundamental meaning exceed the limits of Naturalistic Determinism.

These epistemological themes, directly related to Impressionistic methods of narration, are common in Crane's fiction. Within the variables of blindness and epiphany, nearly all of Crane's major works find their underlying meaning. Beyond the blindness of Maggie, the opacity of the Swede and the Cowboy in "The Blue Hotel," Scratchy's difficulties in comprehending the "new estate" in "The Bride Comes to Yellow Sky," and the pathetic limitations of Mrs. Kelcey in *George's Mother* and Henry Johnson in *The Monster*, there is a compensating epiphanic pattern of growth throughout the fiction which parallels that of Henry Fleming in *The Red Badge*. This continuing emphasis on moments of "new vision," with both apprehensive and cognitive implications, frequently results in a crucial modification of a character's assessment of his significance.

Such is the case for Rufus Coleman in *Active Service* when, in the central chapter of the novel, he is brought to a startling realization:

> Now when he saw the truth it seemed to bring him back to his common life and he saw himself suddenly as not being frantically superior in any way to those other young men. The more closely he looked at this last fact the more convinced he was of its truth. . . . He saw his proud position lower itself to be a pawn in the game (III, 211).

As for Henry, the experience of war accelerates the process of growth, and Rufus attains a new level of awareness. This concern for an altered perspective also plays a central role in "An Episode of War," in which the vehicle of epiphany is the wound the lieutenant receives.

In this brief story the protagonist is a lieutenant who, at the opening, is very much a creature of his status as soldier. He is first portrayed dividing a pile of coffee on a rubber blanket with his sword, a weapon he handles with appropriate dexterity, dividing the coffee into heaps "astoundingly equal in size" (VI, 89). As he is wounded in the arm, he undergoes a change of role, no longer displaying his prowess of swordsmanship:

> The officer had, of course, been compelled to take his sword at once into his left hand. He did not hold it by the hilt. He gripped it at the middle of the blade, awkwardly. . . . [He] seemed puzzled as to what to do with it, where to put it (VI, 89).

Sensitive to this alteration, his companions no longer regard him as a military superior; he has become simply a wounded man to them. But beyond this modification, there is a corresponding development in the lieutenant's perceptual capabilities: "As the wounded officer passed from the line of battle, he was enabled to see many things which as a participant in the fight were unknown to him" (VI, 90). What this view reveals is significant: as Maggie had encountered men in descending social order as she made her way to the river, the lieutenant confronts military personnel in descending rank but in increasing perceptual ability. He first sees a general attempting to survey a field whose view is obscured by a "green woods which veiled his problems." Around him is his staff, and beyond them a supportive group composed of orderlies, a bugler, and a standard bearer. Then the lieutenant comes upon a battery "swirling" behind the lines in an exchange with an unseen enemy. All the men actively engaged in battle are visually restricted:

"He saw the smoke rolling upward and saw crowds of men who ran and cheered, or stood and blazed away at the inscrutable distance" (III, 91). It is not until he encounters the stragglers behind the lines that he is able to get any information about the location of the hospital:

> He came upon some stragglers and they told him how to find the field hospital. They described its exact location. In fact these men, no longer having part in the battle, knew more of it than others. They told the performance of every corps, every division, the opinion of every general (VI, 91).

Beyond the irony of the inversion of knowledge relative to rank there is also a suggestion that preoccupation with battle precludes the acquisition of knowledge. The lieutenant develops a larger view of things once he has relinquished his position of leadership; the other officers are too close to the battle to perceive and comprehend its parts; the stragglers are in a position not only to see but to reflect upon the events about them. The wound has also initiated feelings of inadequacy for the lieutenant, and he fears that he does not know "how to be correctly wounded" when the stragglers bind his arm and when the surgeon later complains of his dressing. This is the basic attitude that continues to the conclusion of the story, which reveals the amputation of the lieutenant's arm and his ironic comment to his family that " 'I don't suppose it matters so much as all that' " (VI, 93).

What is consistent throughout Crane's work in moments of epiphany, when "new eyes" are suddenly given to a character, is the sensation of insignificance, of a deflationary self-estimate born of a larger view of circumstance. This continuing theme in Crane's works has led critics to regard his fiction as Naturalistic without making a distinction between pessimistic Determinism as a condition in stasis and the epiphanic phenomenon that records the recognition of insignificance as an awakening. Naturalistic protagonists are portrayed as being insignificant without cognition of that fact, without realizing anything beyond the pathetic misery of their lives imposed upon them without justification or meaning. Ordinarily, Impressionistic protagonists experience the feeling of insignificance as a stage in their growth. They customarily go on to a moment of reflection of such depth and sensitivity that these moments alone imply a refutation of their lack of importance.

These epiphanic moments are frequent in Crane's fiction, especially in his finest works. Wilson and Henry Fleming both experience this sensation in *The Red Badge* and subsequently go on to a more aware existence. The experience of Billie Dempster in "The Little Regiment" follows a similar pattern. After a scene revealing his ambivalent feelings for his brother, Billie contemplates the sound of surrounding guns and realizes something of his worth:

> The terrible voices from the hills told him that in this wide conflict his life was an insignificant fact, and that his death would be an insignificant fact. They portended the whirlwind to which he would be as necessary as a waved butterfly's wing (VI, 7).

But the implications of insignificance are countered by the unspoken affection between the two brothers, by their fear for one another, and by their developing realizations.

The insignificance of human life is repeatedly asserted by the fire chorus in "A Man and Some Others" in "an ancient melody which surely bears a message of the inconsequence of individual tragedy . . ." (V, 60). As in "The Open Boat," the inconsequence of human tragedy is set in the context of the indifference of nature, which is oblivious to human events. This sensation is more important in "The Open Boat" because feelings of indifference and insignificance replace the personal worth that the men, especially the correspondent, had previously assumed. As long as they can believe in the hostility of nature, or the perversity of Fate (the "old ninny-woman" against whom they rail in the refrain), then they can sustain a conception of themselves as important to supernatural forces.

In the early parts of the story, the sea is perceived as hostile, as the imagery implies in "the snarling of the crests" of the waves. The characters' thoughts, as revealed in the refrain, vary among passive states: " 'If I am going to be drowned' " suggests hostility on the part of undesignated forces. The phrase " 'If she [Fate] has decided to drown me' " objectifies the antagonist but still implies that a mystical force is concentrated on them (V, 77). But the unaltered activity of the gulls, clouds, and other elements of nature suggests a simple lack of concern. As the correspondent contemplates the distant star, he begins to realize that "nature does not regard him as important" (V, 84). When the boat heads for the beach, and as he thinks about the tower "standing with its back to the plight of the ants," he has a more direct realization:

> It [the tower] represented in a degree, to the correspondent, the serenity of nature amid the struggles of the individual—nature in the wind, and nature in the vision of men. She did not seem cruel to him then, nor beneficient, nor treacherous, nor wise. But she was indifferent, flatly indifferent (V, 88).

This passage, in addition to the explicit recognition of the distinction between reality and reality perceived, relates to two developments. The first is the correspondent's feeling of identification and compassion for other, fictional, people. This growth is revealed in his thinking about the "soldier of the Legion" in the poem "Bingen on the Rhine," which Crane condenses in the correspondent's memory. Having read this poem as a child, he has never regarded the plight of the soldier as having the slightest import. Now, sensing an analogy between his attitude toward the soldier and nature's toward the men in the boat, to him the poem becomes "a human, living thing. . . . It was an actuality—stern, mournful, and fine" (V, 85). The second development relates to the reflection of the men once they are safely on shore. When they contemplated the sea at night, the "wind brought the sound of the great sea's voice to the men on shore, and they felt that they could then be interpreters" (V, 92). In both of these instances there is a subtle modification of the theme of insignificance. If human beings are unimportant to the universe, they can nevertheless be vitally important to themselves in their thoughts and feelings.

Peza's experience in "Death and the Child" is remarkably similar. In this story set in the Greco-Turkish war, the narrator conceives of the scene as viewed from the vantage point of a bird, a perspective that makes the human agony of war insignificant: "The sea, the sky, and the hills combined in their grandeur to term this misery inconsequent" (V, 121). As the story progresses, and Peza is exposed to the war, he develops compassion: "Peza was alive with despair for these men who looked at him with such doleful, quiet eyes." His sympathy for the soldiers is, as it was for the correspondent, coupled with a sense of personal insignificance:

> In the moment some portion of egotism left him, and he modestly wondered if the universe took cognizance of him to an important degree. This theatre for slaughter, built by the inscrutable needs of the earth, was an enormous affair, and he reflected that the accidental destruction of an individual, Peza by name, would perhaps be nothing at all (V, 126).

This recognition reverberates throughout the story and is echoed in the concluding paragraph:

> Peza gasped in the manner of a fish. Palsied, windless, and abject, he confronted the primitive courage, the sovereign child, the brother of the mountains, the sky and the sea, and he knew that the definition of his misery could be written on a wee grass-blade (V, 141).

Among all the other concerns of the story—war, death, growth, multiple perspective, and fear—the unifying and most important theme is the development in Peza of a compassion born of a new perspective that reveals his insignificance.

The theme of insignificance, in its various formulations, is wide-spread in Crane's fiction, ranging from *The Red Badge* and "The Open Boat" to *The O'Ruddy*,[21] "An Experiment in Luxury," and "The Reluctant Voyagers," an early Crane story in which the "freckled man," adrift at sea, mutters, " 'I feel like a molecule' " (V, 20). This comment places Crane in the development of an idea in American literature spelled out in Naturalistic terms by Hamlin Garland and Frank Norris. As Lars Åhnebrink has said,

> Viewed . . . against the vastness and infinity of the universe, man was but an atom, a gnat, incapable of playing a significant role in the world at large. Even his little rebellions against the uni-verse were doomed to fail, for he could not change or disturb the laws that regulated life; on the contrary he was entirely subservient to them.[22]

Naturalistic fiction tends to stress the impotence of human beings, their lack of stature, the hopelessness of their condition, and the futility of their reactions to their circumstances. Impressionistic works, espe-cially those by Crane, develop a modified version of this concept based on perceptual isolation. Since reality is in flux, is perceived differently by each individual, and reveals only fragments of its complexity, human knowledge is inadequate in confronting the problems of the world. But the stress is not only on individual insignificance but also on how this perceptual separation engenders a sense of isolation and alienation. Crane's works have their closest associations not with the concurrent Naturalistic novels, which they superficially resemble, but with the existential elements of later works by Ernest Hemingway, William Faulkner, and James Joyce.

The theme of an indifferent universe, sometimes stated as "Nature," is dramatically articulated in one of Crane's poems:

> A man said to the universe:
> "Sir, I exist!"
> "However," replied the universe,
> "The fact has not created in me
> A sense of obligation" (X, 57).

If the corollary of indifference is a sense of personal insignificance, its humanistic expression is alienation. Any empirical art form suggests alienation by virtue of its record of individual sense experiences, but Crane's works go beyond this point to a dramatic revelation of isola-tion on the part of a character, as in the early story "The Octopush." What is comic in this story of drunken fishermen is serious in much of

Crane's work, in which there are seldom close ties among people and very little communication. The men in "The Open Boat" develop a mutual respect of sorts, but their "brotherhood" is quickly shattered when they reach the heavy surf. Henry Fleming loses his closest friend in *The Red Badge*, but even before Conklin's death Henry had deserted, alone, into an isolated existence. Throughout the *Bowery Tales* the members of families exist in psychological isolation, sharing little beyond physical space, as in *Maggie* and *George's Mother*. Contrary to Romantic solipsism, in which the individual is often ennobled through isolation, in Crane's works he is most often impoverished by his alienation and driven to desperate acts.[23]

In *The Poetry of Stephen Crane*, Daniel G. Hoffman said that "only in Poe, in Bierce, and in Hemingway among American writers is the sense of the individual's isolation as overwhelming as it is in Crane."[24] This isolation is not only reconcilable with Impressionistic concepts but is, in many ways, intrinsic to them. The adherence to restricted narrative modes, the focus on individual perspective, the concern for empirical data, all stress the isolation of the individual, his uniqueness, the quality of his sensations and mental reflections rather than his relationships with other people. For writers whose works exhibit Impressionistic tendencies, for example Bierce and Hemingway, there is understandably a heavy stress on individual consciousness, on the quality of mental and emotional activity. If the empirical edge of this concern relates to apprehensive states, the reflective limits involve emotional balance. It is not surprising, therefore, that Crane's works, as do those of Hemingway and Bierce, contain numerous characters who experience various states of mental pathology.

Isolation, alienation, and fear prompt aberrant psychological states, especially when these conditions are exacerbated by stress, as in war or other circumstances of danger. "The Sergeant's Private Madhouse," one of the most overt studies of insanity in Crane's works, is a story in which a young soldier, isolated on point duty, becomes so afraid of the unknown dangers that confront him that he loses control of his mind (VI, 172–79). His isolation is further increased by the fact that no one understands his condition: his comrades simply assume that he has been drinking. Similar situations develop in the war stories of Bierce and Hemingway, especially in Bierce's *Tales of Soldiers and Civilians* and in such Hemingway stories as "A Way You'll Never Be" and "Big Two-Hearted River." Crane's other works about war also touch on this theme: Henry Fleming is nearly mad with fear before he deserts in *The Red Badge*, and his isolation contributes to his imbalance. Even Crane's early Sullivan County stories contain these ideas, especially

"The Octopush," in which a sense of isolation drives the little man to weeping. As the four fishermen are left, each fishing from his own stump, they simultaneously develop a common sensation: "Suddenly it struck each that he was alone, separated from humanity by impassable gulfs" (VIII, 232). Their isolation and fear, combined with their drink, serve to distort the sights and sounds about them into ominous threats; the imagery of "grave-yards," "crypts," and "caskets" conveys their interpretive distortion and their sense of danger. Finally the little man's mind entirely succumbs to his imagination, and he believes that the stump he is on is actually an "octopush" and he is sitting on its mouth. Other stories, "A Ghoul's Accountant," "The Squire's Madness," "An Illusion in Red and White," "A Tale of Mere Chance," all contain significant problems of interpreting reality. In some instances, as in "A Tale of Mere Chance," there seems to be particularized psychological pathology, but most often in Crane these mental distortions develop from an acute sense of human isolation and remoteness.

The anguish of alienation and hopelessness is formulated in Crane's works in a startling motif, the wail of protest. Perhaps the most dramatic and sentient of these, although there are many examples, is in "An Experiment in Misery" when a "fellow off in a gloomy corner" begins to wail like a "hound." The imagery of the scene is of death and disease: the sleeping room is described as a "place of tombstones, where men lay like the dead." The narrator then expresses the meaning of this wail to the protagonist:

> The sound, in its high piercing beginnings that dwindled to final melancholy moans, expressed a red and grim tragedy of the unfathomable possibilities of the man's dreams. But to the youth these were not merely the shrieks of a vision pierced man. They were an utterance of the meaning of the room and its occupants. It was to him the protest of the wretch who feels the touch of the imperturbable granite wheels and who then cries with an impersonal eloquence, with a strength not from him, giving voice to the wail of a whole section, a class, a people (VIII, 288–89).

There are similar cries of agony throughout Crane's works, from the wail of the "unknown" that expresses the "trees' song of loneliness, and the lay of isolation of the mountain-grass" in "The Cry of a Huckleberry Pudding" (VIII, 255), to the death song in "The Black Dog" (VIII, 246), to the cry of the girl in "An Eloquence of Grief" (VIII, 383). Perhaps the most moving, because it is presented in what may be Crane's most optimistic work, is the sound of the wind in the trees in "Mr. Bink's Day Off." In this simple story of familial love there is a passage of natural beauty and universal sorrow:

From the night, approaching in the east, came a wind. The trees
of the mountain raised plaintive voices, bending toward the faded
splendors of the day.

This song of the trees arose in low, sighing melody into the
still air. It was filled with an infinite sorrow—a sorrow for birth,
slavery, death. It was a wail telling the griefs, the pains of all
ages. It was the symbol of agonies. It celebrated all suffering. Each
man finds in this sound the expression of his own grief. It is the
universal voice raised in lamentations (VIII, 312–13).

If this almost totally ignored story contains a general statement of
existential woe, there are numerous other examples of a more limited
despair, from the wail of the wounded Cuban in "The Price of the
Harness" (VI, 101), to the pathetic cry of the dog in "Ghosts on the
Jersey Coast" who rescues his owner from a shipwreck only to discover
that he is dead when they reach the shore:

The dog hauled the body out of reach of the water and then went
to whine and sniff at the dead man's hand. He wagged his tail
expectantly. At last he settled, shivering, back upon his haunches
and gave vent to a long howl, a dog's cry of death and despair
and fear, that cry that is in the most indescribable key of woe
(VIII, 641–42).

If these are lyric expressions of the anguish of the human condition,
Crane also made similarly direct statements in his journalism. A com-
parison of two such passages illustrates the continuity of this motif. In
"Stephen Crane's Own Story," the journalistic account that preceded
"The Open Boat" by some months, there is a remarkable passage on
the sinking of the ship:

Now the whistle of the *Commodore* had been turned loose, and if
there ever was a voice of despair and death it was in the voice of
this whistle. It had gained a new tone. It was as if its throat was
already choked by the water, and this cry on the sea at night, with
a wind blowing the spray over the ship, and the waves roaring
over the bow, and swirling white along the decks, was to each of
us probably a song of man's end (IX, 91).

But the sound of the whistle in this passage is remarkably similar to the
bugle in "A Soldier's Burial That Made a Native Holiday":

The sad, sad, slow voice of the bugle called out over the grave, a
soul appealing to the sky, a call of earthly anguish and heavenly
tranquillity, a solemn heart-breaking song. But if this farewell of
the soldier to the sky, the flowers, the bees and all life was heard
by the natives their manner did not betray it (IX, 176).

The expression of the human condition in these passages is remarkably "modern" for the 1890s and explicitly links Crane's works with twentieth-century existentialism. In another sense, this wail of protest represents the extension of basic Impressionistic concepts to their ultimate negativistic potential. Unlike Naturalistic figures, who seldom realize much about their pointless lives, or Realistic characters, whose anguish often derives from ethical conflict, Impressionist protagonists sense the isolation of their empirical solipsism, the indifference of the universe, and their irreducible alienation from other people. It is these moments that express the most profound feelings of Impressionistic fiction and that impel the deepest despair of its characters. As Maria Kronegger has said, "Impressionist protagonists often feel helpless, hopeless; they feel a crippling of the will power and a fruitlessness of all effort."[25] It was no small element of Crane's art that he expressed these concepts in lyric passages of a wail of despair.

One implication of the laments in Crane's work is a sense of protest against the conditions that life has meted out. Whether the controlling agent in this circumstance is perceived as Fate, chance, Deterministic social and economic forces, or the vagaries of genetic accident, the individual is helpless before them and can only express his rage in a baleful wail. This condition is often described by Naturalistic critics as the central element in Crane's work.[26] In fact, although Crane's themes are most often Impressionistic, there is some justification for this view in numerous statements in his journalism and fiction that suggest Deterministic concepts.

Perhaps the most direct of these comes in the "Telegraphic News" of the *Pike County Puzzle,* that curious newspaper that Crane and Louis C. Senger, Jr. got out in August of 1894. In it the Brothers of Anarchy pass a resolution:

> Whereas, We recognize the futility of human effort, the temporary element in human construction and general uncertainty of human plans, we hereby vest all power and control of this society in a more formidable being.
>
> Resolved, That the president of this society, in whom all power and control is now vested, shall be Wicked Wickham (VIII, 620).

Despite the undergraduate cleverness of the piece, with its personification of a malevolent Determinism, it sets the tone for a number of similar expressions in Crane's work, especially that before the book publication of *The Red Badge of Courage* in 1895.[27] For example, in "Nebraska's Bitter Fight for Life," which Crane wrote on the western trip that was ultimately to produce "The Blue Hotel," he reflected on the plight of farmers at the mercy of hostile nature:

> The farmers helpless, with no weapon against this terrible and
> inscrutable wrath of nature, were spectators at the strangling of their
> hopes, their ambitions, all that they could look to from their labor.
> It was as if upon the massive altar of the earth, their homes and their
> families were being offered in sacrifice to the wrath of some blind
> and pitiless deity (VIII, 410).

Here again there are statements of Naturalistic themes, of the antipathy
of natural forces expressed in religious imagery. There are many more of
these Naturalistic assertions, from the observation that "if a man is not
given a fair opportunity to be virtuous, if his environment chokes his
moral aspirations, I say that he has got the one important cause of
complaint and rebellion against society" in "The Mexican Lower
Classes" (VIII, 437), to the protest against fate in the refrain of the early
sections of the "The Open Boat," to the war-as-machine business in
"The Price of the Harness," to the general sense of social alienation the
revelers feel in *George's Mother* (I, 129).

But the crux of the matter does not depend upon Crane's inscriptions
or journalism for resolution, nor even upon expository assertions of
Determinism in some of the fiction. The ultimate decision as to the
viability of a Deterministic interpretation of Crane's fiction rests on an
assessment of the dramatic and narrative action of the stories and novels.
It is finally a judgment as to whether the death of the Swede and the oiler,
the desertion of Henry, and the trauma of *The Monster* and "An Episode
of War" are the result of necessitarian forces external to the wills of the
characters or whether they are the product of self-manipulated
delusions, perceptions, and actions which have their impetus within the
characters themselves. The crucial work for this assessment, because of
its complexity, is *Maggie*.

Many critics, Malcolm Cowley and Charles C. Walcutt among them,
have regarded Crane's comment to Garland about the force of environment to be an essentially reliable indicator of the underlying themes of
the novel.[28] Cowley is especially direct in asserting that Maggie was the
"victim of environment" and that the characters are not culpable for
their behavior in a world controlled by the "laws of things." Indeed,
there are some Deterministic indicators throughout *Maggie*, most
notably in the atavistic overtones of the boys "fighting in the modes of
four thousand years ago," in Pete's empathetic admiration of the aggressive monkey at the Menagerie, and in the almost continual imagery
of depravity that runs throughout.[29] But these matters do not mitigate
the individual responsibility of the characters for their pretensions to
bourgeois respectability, for their illusions of stature, for their choices
among alternatives of action. No force compels Maggie's seduction: she
chooses Pete as an escape from the sordid depravity of her family. Pete

is not driven by animal lust: he desires Maggie for her beauty and for the preservation of his pride in not being played for a "duffer." Nor are Jimmie or Mrs. Johnson or any of the other characters cast as helpless pawns at the hands of overwhelming Deterministic elements. The tragedy of *Maggie* is not the result of inexorable doom or impersonal forces but the more poignant result of numerous choices freely made on the basis of naiveté, confusion, and self-deluding pride. The melodramatic sentimentality of the milieu, its hypocrisy and violence, result not from inescapable forces beyond the characters but from weaknesses within them, from their lack of compassion and courage, from their ill-considered sense of themselves and their responsibilities. Ultimately Maggie is the victim of her pretensions and her longings, of her simplistic interpretations of others, and of the inadequacy of her view of life. As Milne Holton has said, *"Maggie* is about the fall of a Bowery sparrow, but it is also about the failure of her eye."[30]

Indeed, a theme far more important in Crane's works than pessimistic Determinism is its ethical antithesis, the freedom of each character to make moral choices. Crane's work derives much of its force from the confluence of the inadequacy of vision of the characters, their limitations and illusions, and yet their responsibility for their conduct deriving from these interpretations. Marston La France has given this situation a particularly acute formulation:

> Life is meaningful, morally significant, because every individual has the power to choose what is morally right for himself within whatever scope of awareness he possesses, and thus he can maintain his moral world intact as his awareness increases.[31]

It is this sense in Crane's work that further suggests its existential qualities and accounts for its decidedly modernistic tone.

Inadequacy of view does not relieve an individual of responsibility, does not shift blame to external forces, does not mitigate free choice among alternatives. Crane's characters anguish over their responsibility for their actions, however dimly perceived, and wrestle with feelings of guilt. Jimmie stares out the blurred glass of his window contemplating his role in his sister's demise, Henry Fleming searches frantically for some plausible rationale for his desertion, and the Easterner meditates aloud to the cowboy about the responsibility for the death of the Swede. "A Tale of Mere Chance" is expressly a story of guilt manifested in the protagonists's fantasy that the blood-stained tiles are tormenting him. Indeed nearly every important story contains an implication of individual moral choice. Certainly one dimension of *The Monster*, especially the conclusion, rests on the social ostracism the family must bear for Dr. Trescott's decision to care for the mutilated and deranged Henry Johnson. It is such moral themes that pervade the conclusions of *George's Mother*, "An Experiment in Misery," *Maggie*, and "The Clan of No-Name," and not implications of Deterministic forces that would relieve the characters of responsibility.

A number of other themes run throughout Crane's work but all, including Determinism and moral responsibility, are finally secondary to the fundamental epistemological concerns. One of these is social in nature, ranging from the benign dilemma of class stratification as a deterrent to romance, a complexity in *The Third Violet, Active Service*, and *The O'Ruddy*, to the devastating squalor and misery of many of the Bowery tales. Even the metonymous childhood traumas of the Whilomville tales contain serious social implications, especially in such stories as "The Stove," in which social hatred, pretense, and snobbery are all deflated by the burning turnips that disperse the assemblage of "a small picked company of latent enemies." Pretension receives a more substantial treatment in "A Night at the Millionaire's Club," in which the members of the organization extol their isolation from the "grimy vandals" of the lower classes, and in "An Experiment in Luxury," which explores more subtly the moral consequences of wealth. The most dramatically telling of the social pieces are, however, the Bowery tales, especially "The Men in the Storm," which focuses on derelicts at the mercy of Nature's rage and society's indifference, and "An Experiment in Misery," one of Crane's finest works. In these stories, and others, social stratification is a matter of survival, of devastatingly impoverished self-views, of diminished expectations. There is an element of social reform in these works, perhaps derived from Crane's interest in Jacob Riis as well as from his own experience, but in essence these themes provide a secondary level of concern in the fiction, one subordinate by some degree to individualistic, solipsistic, and ontological concerns.

Other themes invest Crane's works with fascinating ideas. Nature as fact and concept is a complex topic. The perception of it as hostile or benevolent or indifferent is often an indicator of important philosophical issues. Nature is often the innocent victim of human war, and the destruction of trees and animals is continual in *The Red Badge, Wounds in the Rain*, and *The Little Regiment*. Pastoral and mythic suggestions in the wilderness give a Romantic cast to some sections of *The Red Badge*, to the Sullivan County tales, and to such pieces as "Lynx-Hunting," in which the children feel the voice of Nature speaking to them in the silence (VII, 139). But most often Nature is beautiful and serene amid the calamities of human strife, a motif especially poignant when contrasted to the destruction of war, which is generally portrayed as the product of political ineptitude, as mindless hostility, or as an inscrutable condition in which an individual soldier must probe his identity and personal values. The concept of heroism in war is most often given satiric treatment, save for those instances, as in "A Mystery of Heroism," in which benevolent risk becomes admirable and vaguely heroic. These matters, and such other concerns as religion, courtship, death, the American West, and the role of women, are all themes of interest but are not finally central to the sustaining and the informing issues of Crane's work.

Viewed as a coherent body of literature, Crane's novels and short stories have as their underlying themes the concepts of empiricism, epistemology, and evanescent reality central to Impressionism. Part of the genius of Crane's creative talent was his ability to expand these basic notions to embrace congruent implications. His treatment of empirical processes suggests both limitations of knowledge and the potentiality for sudden flashes of insight in moments of recognition or epiphany. That these moments are expressed metaphorically in visual terms is philosophically effective: knowledge is vision; ignorance is blindness. Perhaps Crane's most significant implementation of these ideas was to press them beyond apprehensional states to psychological conditions. In addition to extraordinary instances of mental pathology, Crane's works explore the cognitive process of forming generalizations about life from isolated experiences, the problems of comprehending inadequately perceived phenomena, the enigma of formulating a sense of reality or self on the basis of experiences that have become mingled with fantasies, dreams, and fears which distort memory and impair perception.

To the extent that all of these ideas are related to Impressionism, Crane gave them artistic expression in fiction that attempts to define reality as viewed by a central character and narrative center of intelligence. What distinguishes Crane's work from the dominant Realism of his time is that he chose to emphasize not the nature of an external reality but the problems of perceiving it. Only a few of Crane's works suggest the pessimistic Determinism of Naturalistic fiction, and these are less than convincing. His stress is on the freedom of characters to form their own identities and to define their own realities. The moral responsibility of characters to choose among imperfectly understood alternatives evokes a uniquely modernistic and existential ideology for the 1890s, as does the sense of relativism, isolation, insignificance, and remoteness that Crane's characters often experience. Although in a richly complex body of literature such as the Crane canon there are certain to be variations of motifs and ideological contradictions, his fiction is remarkably consistent in stressing the fundamental ontological issues of Impressionism and in suggesting their humanistic consequences. If this condition leads to empirical solipsism, a sense of an indifferent universe, and a wail of despair at the human condition, it also suggests the need for tentative judgments, for a recognition of moral responsibility for behavior, and for compassion at the center of personal and societal attitudes. Crane's works are unique in the development of these themes within the philosophic and artistic norms of Literary Impressionism, which places severe limits on the expository development of theme and the range of aesthetic devices. The dramatic evocation of these themes, and the artistic integrity of his finest works, testify to the literary greatness of a writer who, more than any other of his age, created the fictional impressions of actual life.

IV

Characterization, Structure, Imagery

Characterization: descriptive epithets and shadowy protagonists

Stephen Crane's methods of characterization have not been explored with the vigor of studies of other dimensions of his art. Indeed, the method and "meaning" of his characters have been described in reductive terms by both his contemporary critics and modern scholars. As an example of the former, A. G. Sedgwick's comment in the *Nation* in 1896 is typical:

> His types are mainly human beings of the order which makes us regret the power of literature to portray them. Not merely are they low, but there is little that is interesting in them. We resent the sense that we must at certain points resemble them.[1]

Sedgwick's review of *The Red Badge of Courage*, in which he describes Crane's presentation of characters as "animalism," is provocative, as is the suggestion that in using "types" Crane presented characters from within a narrow range. That Sedgwick does not find the characters interesting is curious, for Crane had written by 1896 not only his war novel, in which Henry, Mrs. Fleming, Jim Conklin, and Wilson emerge as people of considerable variation and individuality, but also *Maggie: A Girl of the Streets*, which presents some of the most dramatic characters in American literature, and *George's Mother*, in which character definition plays a fundamental role. Sedgwick's acknowledgment that Crane's characters resemble actual life, and that he is made uncomfortable by them, suggests that Crane was innovative not only in presenting his figures but also in their conception. What Sedgwick stops short of saying, but what literary history reveals, is that the American reading public had never before experienced in fiction anything like the cast of characters Stephen Crane presented.

Harold Frederic, whose own fiction had earned international recognition by 1896, reviewed *The Red Badge* with a great deal more perception. He wrote that

it is more vehemently alive and heaving with dramatic human action than any other book of our time. The people are all strangers
to us, but the sight of them stirs the profoundest emotions of
interest in our breasts.[2]

Besides his appreciation of the novel and his empathetic reaction to its
characters, Frederic offers some valuable observations:

One barely knows the name of the hero; it is only dimly sketched
in that he was a farm boy and had a mother when he enlisted.
These facts recur to him once or twice, they play no larger part in
the reader's mind. Only two other characters are mentioned by
name—Jim Conklin and Wilson; more often even they are spoken
of as the tall soldier and the loud soldier. Not a word is expended
on telling where they come from, or who they are. They pass
across the picture, or shift from one posture to another in
its moving composition, with the impersonality of one's chance
fellow-passengers in a railroad car.

The dramatic revelation of the characters, as opposed to the expository
description of them, the narrator's use of tag names to identify them,
and their emergence from a kinetic portrait are all techniques central to
Crane's methods of characterization. Such methods of rendering character are also basic to Literary Impressionism.

The empirical and relativistic ideas at the core of Impressionism
have a direct bearing on the kinds of characters portrayed and on the
way in which they are presented. Restrictions of knowledge within the
center of intelligence require that long passages of background be eliminated. What remains is dramatic presentation through action or
dialogue. Unless they form a narrative center, thus revealing their
thoughts, the characters are described from the outside. Because of the
restriction of narrative data, the narrator must adopt a stance in which
he has no prior knowledge of the character, often not even of his name,
until that information emerges internally. Some characters are identified by rank; other figures characterized by region, especially the
ubiquitous Easterner; many known by occupation (the gambler, the
cowboy, the cook, the oiler, the correspondent); some hardly known at
all (the stranger); and hosts of figures make brief appearances but do
not remain in focus long enough for even cursory analysis. In short, to
present characters without prior knowledge, and on the basis of dramatic revelation, is to sharply limit the depth of all but major figures.
This practice, however, does not represent a conceptual weakness so
much as an adherence to restricted narrative modes.

Impressionistic methods develop a good deal more depth for protagonists, for the narrative identification with these characters allows the presentation of thought as well as action and dialogue. The reader has access not only to Henry Fleming's movements but to his heroic conceptions of himself, his fear and insecurity, and his memories of his mother and the seminary. As the novel progresses, a great deal is revealed about Henry through indirection. For example, it is clear that he has had some exposure to Greek literature in that he frequently conceives of war in classical terms; he is disappointed, for example, that his mother makes no mention of his "returning with his shield or on it" (II, 6). Furthermore, his growth is not stated in narrative assertions but implied by the alteration in the way Henry perceives himself and the world around him. Indeed, Henry's perceptual changes reveal his development as a human being.

As the characterization of Henry Fleming suggests, Impressionistic protagonists are frequently initiates engaged in unfamiliar actions and realizations. Organic change is best measured against a fixed point of reference; hence, often the development of an initiate is offset by the stable position of another, as Jack Potter's acceptance of a more "civilized" West is contrasted to Scratchy Wilson's inability to comprehend the "new estate" in "The Bride Comes to Yellow Sky." Within Impressionistic fiction "positive" characters are generally those who grow, who develop new realizations; these characters are often set against more "negative" characters, who are morally or cognitively blind and unreceptive to experience. As a result, there are many young people, even children, in Crane's works; most of the adults are engaged in experiences that have the potential for change; most of the characters who come to tragic ends (Maggie, for instance) do so as a consequence of their naiveté, blindness, or unyielding distortions of reality.

The central terms of Impressionistic characterization are objective, dramatic methods of presenting people who respond to experience. In these matters it is difficult to distinguish Impressionistic characters from Realistic ones, although it is somewhat more important in Realism to establish the backgrounds of key figures. An example of a typical Realistic protagonist is Silas Lapham, in William Dean Howells' novel, who is introduced "objectively" through the technique of his sitting for an interview for a newspaper series on distinguished Boston citizens. The basic facts of his "rise" are here established, and they provide the context in which to view his ensuing conflict. But Impressionistic protagonists generally face cognitive rather than moral dilemmas, and it is less essential to establish their histories. Their innocence is easily observable in their initial actions, and very little else is essential. This distinction aside, there are only minor differences between Realistic and Impressionistic characters: both modes present common individuals of free will and limited knowledge, revealed objectively, within a dramatic context.

The characters in Romantic fiction are distinct from Impressionistic ones in that Romantic figures are often symbolic. As a result, the mimetic constraints on Romantic writers are greatly diffused, and they can present figures who have almost no literal function at all. In "My Kinsman, Major Molineux," for example, Robin is a fairly realistic character who also represents universal innocence in his allegorical confrontations with sex, political upheaval, and maturation. He is an initiate who suggests planes of initiation beyond those he encounters. In general, Romantic characters also have a tendency to be one-dimensional, as are Dimmesdale, Chillingworth, Ahab, and Billy Budd, and to undergo little fundamental alteration. In methodological terms, they are described expositorially in narrative digressions that establish their referential values. Since their stories often involve postulations about universals, they frequently become associated with supernatural events. And as their lives before the event portrayed are generally known, so the narrator customarily reveals the rest of their stories in a concluding chapter, as Hawthorne does for Hester in *The Scarlet Letter* and Herman Melville for Captain Vere in *Billy Budd*. In method of presentation, function, verisimilitude, and continuity, Romantic characterizations are clearly distinguishable from those of Realism and Impressionism.

As Romanticism and Naturalism share narrative methods, so they share a tendency for expository character development and symbolic function. A Naturalistic figure is likely to be representative of a type, to be unindividualized. These characters exist to demonstrate the compelling nature of Deterministic forces, whether genetic or environmental, and their individual capabilities and limitations have little effect on their destinies. Since economic and social conditions affect most dramatically the lower class, Naturalistic characters tend to come from this group. Ethical choices, for people trapped by compelling forces, are essentially irreconcilable with the themes of their stories. Matters of cognitive growth too are of little significance for them. Their individualizing traits allow for sympathy, but in general these characters represent generalized conditions. Thus in both role and method they are not difficult to distinguish from Realistic and Impressionistic characters.[3]

Crane's adherence to Impressionistic narration compels a number of devices that distinguish his methods of characterization from the other modes. One of these is the use of descriptive epithets for identifying characters. This device caused a good deal of confusion among his contemporary reviewers, even those responding to his finest works. In assessing *The Red Badge*, a reviewer in the *National Observer* complained that

> none of the characters have any names—or if they have them are permitted to use them—and are designated throughout by descriptive titles such as "the youth," "the tall soldier," "the loud one," "the lieutenant," "the tattered man," "the friend." This is a trick which we find particularly aggravating and meaningless.[4]

The reviewer implies not simply that Crane should give his characters names but that he should narrate from a different set of assumptions. The narrator of *The Red Badge* is perceptive and yet does not possess preknowledge of the situation, the characters, or the meaning of events. He must identify people on the basis of their size, age, appearance, voice. As a result the "loud," "youthful," "tall" soldiers dominate the opening of the novel undescribed by personal names until they appear in dialogue. Others are described in terms of rank (the "lieutenant," the "colonel"), and still others, especially the wounded behind the lines, for whom rank is meaningless, appear as the "spectre of a soldier," "tattered soldier," or "cheery-voiced stranger." In narrative terms, descriptive epithets result from the restriction of knowledge to what a person newly introduced to the scene would be able to perceive about the people and circumstances.[5]

The "humanizing" function of this perspective extends beyond character description to the projection of war as seen from the point of view of a common soldier, one who knows nothing of strategy, deceptive maneuvers, or developments beyond his vision. As a result, rumors dominate the thoughts of the men, partial views are generalized into broad interpretations, speculation abounds. The novel presents little beyond what Henry can see and hear in battle, and his impressions are obscured by darkness and distance and distorted by fear and fantasy. Crane's use of epithets, far from being a weakness of his method, is thus a logical part of an epistemologically Impressionistic method of narration that made *The Red Badge of Courage* the finest American novel of the Civil War.

Crane's descriptive epithets suggest an immediate exposure to the surface of character, a tendency throughout his brief career. In the first draft of *Maggie*, for example, none of the characters had names; they were simply called "the girl" or "the girl's mother."[6] *The Red Badge of Courage* used personal names in the first draft, but Crane changed these to descriptive epithets in his revision, clearly indicating his concern for this method.[7] From such minor pieces as "The Reluctant Voyagers" (VII, 14–23), in which Ted is called the "freckled man" and

Tom Sharp the "tall man," to "The Open Boat" and "The Blue Hotel," Crane used tag names to imply initial apprehensions of character. At times, especially for ethnic minorities, there is a tendency for stereotyping, as there is with the Swede in such works as "The Blue Hotel" and "The Veteran." But most often the epithets reveal dominant traits which have a thematic function. The brash confidence of Wilson as the "loud" soldier is shown to be artifice when he confides his insecurities to Henry. The ubiquitous "little man" of such Sullivan County tales as "Four Men in a Cave," "The Octopush," and "A Ghoul's Accountant" exhibits outrageous egotism and self-confidence to mask his underlying uncertainty. In "The Open Boat" the epithets relate to both occupation and psychological preoccupation, as the opening paragraphs establish (V, 68–69).

The cook and the oiler are both concerned with the threat of the sea to their small craft, the cook passively, the oiler actively as he strains the oar in steering the boat. The correspondent and the captain, however, have responses more closely related to their occupations. The correspondent, who "watched the waves and wondered why he was there," is a reflective man who needs to search for the meaning of things in the course of his work. Later, it is he who will lead the thinking about the soldier of the legion, about fate, about the irony of their circumstances. Since he is never named, his epithet is important in suggesting his formulative powers and philosophical frame of reference. It is also significant that the fourth man in the boat is not simply an injured man but the captain, for he bears responsibility for the loss of the ship, a matter that affects him throughout the story. His occupation accounts for his "dejection and indifference" and his authority in commanding the boat. In his mind there lingers the image of the mast of his sinking ship; in his voice there is a "quality beyond oration or tears." All of these concerns are in some degree inherent in the descriptive epithets with which the characters are introduced. Crane was often able to present important concepts of role, personality, and thematic function through this device. No one before had done so much in suggesting depth of character with descriptive epithets.

The use of tag names implies a judgment rendered by the narrator based on observable traits. A more organic method is to allow characters to establish themselves through action and dialogue. This method, the most purely Impressionistic and objective, requires significant reader response to establish characters since they have no prehistory, little initial definition, and no reference beyond their specific actions and statements. They are highly individualistic, if only partially developed; they seem suggestive of real human beings, and yet their method of revelation, for all but major characters, precludes full development. As a result, there is some justification in John Berryman's contention that

> Crane scarcely made a type in all his work. At the same time, he scarcely made any characters. His people, *in* their stories, stay in your mind; but they have no existence outside. No life is strongly imaginable for them save what he lets you see.[8]

Berryman's complaint, which echoes Conrad's, has some bearing on the empiricist methodology and the philosophical condition Impressionism generally implies. Berryman's judgment, however, is more applicable to minor characters than to such protagonists as Maggie, Henry Fleming, Rufus Coleman, and The O'Ruddy.

Crane's method of description for even his minor characters is essentially consistent with the norms of Impressionism. When a more general observation of character is required, Crane found means to provide it in terms of what characters on the scene could observe. Thus the narrator functions as a generalizing formulator of the experience of several characters, as he is in projecting the refrain in "The Open Boat." A corollary of that method is the means of describing Pop in "The Wise Men." In this story the protagonists, the "kids" from New York and San Francisco, are established by exposition:

> They were youths of subtle mind. They were very wicked according to report, and yet they managed to have it reflect credit upon them. . . . Their smooth infantile faces looked bright and fresh . . . (V, 26).

The narrative method here suggests omniscience and exposition, except that these facts were established by "report," that is, that someone within the scene is recording these details from previous conversations. More typical of Crane's methods is the description of Pop, who is to run a race against the Mexican favorite. The kids, who bet heavily on Pop, have an understandable interest in analyzing his physique:

> The kids set down their glasses suddenly and looked at him. . . . Pop was tall and graceful and magnificent in manner, but he did not display those qualities of form which mean speed in the animal. His hair was grey; his face was round and fat from much living (V, 28).

The narrator is active as a formulator of the observations of the two kids, but the details he presents are external.

A similar function is given to the narrator of "The Silver Pageant," one of Crane's sketches of 1894. In this brief story, Grief, Wrinkles, and other aspiring artists bewail the lassitude of their friend Gaunt, who "never saw anything excepting that which transpired across a mystic wide sea" (VIII, 76). The basic description of Gaunt, as this passage suggests, is an assessment of his intellectual and emotional attitudes derived from judgments made by the other characters: "It was understood that Gaunt was very good to tolerate the presence of the universe, which was noisy and interested in itself" (VIII, 76). When Gaunt is found dead on the floor, having expired just as he was about to paint his obsessive vision, it is this sense of character which evokes the dual motifs of man's arrogance in an indifferent universe and the vanity of human wishes.

If the virtue of Impressionistic characterization is objectivity, its weakness is a limitation of scope. Consistent with the democratic tendencies of Impressionism in America, Crane's figures are common, limited, mimetic. They have little potential to become representatitives of universal strivings or transcendent philosophies. For this reason, many of Crane's sympathetic readers have perceived his fiction as being slight. Although Joseph Conrad wrote to Crane in 1897 to state his immense admiration of Crane's stories, saying "you are a complete impressionist. The illusions of life come out of your hand without a flaw," he also wrote to Edward Garnett later expressing somewhat more qualified praise:

> He certainly is *the* impressionist and his temperament is curiously unique. His thought is concise, connected, never very deep—yet often startling. . . . I could not explain why my enthusiasm withers as soon as I close the book. . . . It is as if he had gripped you with greased fingers.[9]

Conrad's disappointment in Crane's lack of depth can be explained in Impressionistic terms: by representing the sensory surface of human life, Crane's works become no more dramatically memorable or shocking than life itself. In terms of characterization, Crane's people approximate actual personalities drawn from the outside as they could be known within a brief period of time.

Modern scholarship has tended to echo both Conrad's enthusiasm and reservations. As Frank Bergon contends, none of Crane's characters have the mythic potential of Ahab or Gatsby; if Crane's people are memorable, it is not because they embody transcendent, mythical traits but because the process of their minds, the way in which they apprehend reality, closely approximates common human experience. Their portraits contain all the distortions, reactions, and limitations needed to make them seem real.[10] In this, Crane's psychological representations form part of the tendency of the fiction of the time to portray "organically linked mental states requiring representational emphasis on the nature of the sequential process" of thought.[11] This conception obviated representative characters whose depths result from extensive analysis of a single psychological state. Crane's people live in a condition of flux and development, changing subtly and incessantly as they move through experience. The Maggie who commits suicide, the Henry Fleming who seizes the flag, the George Kelcey who sees crabs on the wall as he watches his mother die, are all fundamentally different personalities from what they were at the beginning of their stories. Thomas A. Gullason's remark that "though they are given names—Maggie, Henry Fleming, and George Kelcey—these vague, shadowy protagonists are all one and the same symbol" is surely ill-conceived.[12] Not only are none of these characters symbols, but they respond to life quite differently from one another: Maggie distorts experience to conform to her limited view, Henry reconstructs it on the basis of his fears and fantasies, and George views it from the norms of his peer group, whose values are an alternative to those of his mother.

Crane's characters and his methods of characterization are essentially congruent with the basic concepts of Impressionism. His methods are objective, dramatic, descriptive; his characters are sentient, reflective, actively involved in the process of defining themselves and their world. In a sense, the least presumptive recorders of sensation make the best Impressionistic protagonists, and Crane's major figures tend to be innocents: Henry Fleming, Maggie, George Kelcey, and others are initiates into a world beyond their comprehension. Perhaps for this reason, Crane's works exhibit a predilection for employing children as characters. Despite considerable range and variation, the constant factor is the stress on the innocence of the children and on their sensations, which provide an inductive means to knowledge. For example, Tommy, who appears in "An Ominous Baby," "A Dark Brown Dog," and the early chapters of *Maggie,* is exposed to the bewildering violence and depravity of the Bowery, but the stress is not so much on his environment as on the growth of his awareness. "Tommy, with his preconventionalized consciousness, responds directly to appearances and in doing so provides a model for how the mind may work in conditions of free psychic flow, outside the rational patterns of received culture."[13] Crane's other important stories about children, including "Death and the Child" and the Whilomville tales, all focus on the process of interpreting experience, but at times, especially in the Whilomville stories, Crane shows how even a child's mind is conditioned by societal norms and is ultimately prone to distortion and misinterpretation. As Milne Holton maintains, "the Whilomville stories . . . are centrally concerned with how distortions of apprehension are engendered and enforced by a child's relationships with his peers and with his parents."[14]

In a sense, Crane's major works are finally stories of character, narratives in which the unique psychology of individual personalities, and the ways in which they perceive reality, is the central issue. As a result his characters tend to be organic and receptive to experience and his stories a record of the process of change. The growth of insight and self-awareness of Henry Fleming is a prime example, but the correspondent in "The Open Boat," the Easterner in "The Blue Hotel," the lieutenant in "An Episode of War," and many others undergo a similar transformation of perspective.[15] None of Crane's protagonists is truly "heroic" in a Romantic sense; his figures are modernistic in their isolation, in their uncertainty, and in their struggles to comprehend themselves and the world they live in. It is these qualities of characterization which have prolonged interest in Crane's works, which create the psychological depth of his portrayals, and which most closely link his figures to the tradition of Literary Impressionism.

Structure: vistazo *and symmetry*

Of all the aesthetic elements of Impressionistic fiction, structural organization serves as the most graphic indication of its unique characteristics. As in painting and music, the basic unit is a single moment of experience, what the French painters termed a *vistazo*, a "flash of perception," and what Ravel and Debussy transformed into abbreviated musical compositions.[16] In fiction, this idea results in fragmentary episodes, brief scenes that require unique organization to give the total work a satisfying artistic order. If episodic progression is the controlling idea, the juxtaposition of scenes for emphasis and the arrangement of episodes into patterns provide strategies for variations of design. In short, the two informing principles are the demand for episodic units and the artistic arrangement of these fragmentary experiences into an aesthetically satisfying conception.

Structural considerations of the work of Stephen Crane have produced widely divergent reactions from his readers, the majority of them negative. The most positive statement about his handling of structure has come from Ernest Hemingway, whose works are remarkably similar to Crane's and who is reported to have said that *The Red Badge of Courage* "is all as much one piece as a great poem is."[17] But most readers have found little to praise. H. L. Mencken reflected, with some insight, that Crane's

> superlative skill lay in the handling of isolated situations; he knew
> exactly how to depict them with a dazzling brilliance, and he
> knew, too, how to analyze them with penetrating insight, but be-

yond that he was rather at a loss: he lacked the pedestrian talent for linking one situation to another.[18]

John Berryman echoed Mencken's caveat in saying that Crane "threw away, thoughtfully, plot; outlawed juggling and arrangement of material. . . ."[19] And a host of others have admired Crane's work in general but have criticized its want of form, including R. W. Stallman, H. G. Wells, and Carl Van Doren. Such readers have admired the precision of Crane's episodes, with their sharp sensory descriptions, without acknowledging the theoretical basis for using brief scenes and without comprehending the ways in which these units are organized into larger patterns of considerable balance and control.

Perhaps as a result of his newspaper experience, Crane's fictional predilection was clearly for brief episodes closely resembling the length of the journalistic sketch. One implication of this method is epistemological: the effect is to portray the fragmentary nature of experience as it occurs in the consciousness of a character. Life consists of episodes: psychologically realistic fiction must portray events as abbreviated units of apprehension rather than, as in Naturalism or Romanticism, a continuum of action that reveals a unified meaning about the universe.[20]

As a result, his works consist of brief scenes that record the impressions of the center of consciousness. *The Red Badge of Courage* is episodic because Henry Fleming's experiences of war are fragmentary, discontinuous, and often confusing. Even Crane's briefest stories, such as "The Bride Comes to Yellow Sky," are composed of numbered sections, complete sketches within themselves, which depict discrete moments linked in meaningful progression.[21] The succession of episodes is not always teleological: there is a tendency for periphrasis, for digressive episodes of only tangential relation to the central plot. Often, however, these scenes provide important juxtapositions of events and ideas.

In "The Bride," for example, the first section deals with Jack Potter and wife on the Pullman. The newlyweds are rustics, comically out of place in a milieu of Eastern sophistication. The worldly-wise porters provide a perspective that contrasts sharply with the newlyweds' view of themselves. Both the serious and the humorous implications of the scene result from cultural displacement, from the situational naiveté of characters out of their normal environment. The same theme is present in the second section of the story, which retreats in time to cover the same moments in another setting, the Weary Gentleman saloon. As Jack and the bride were comically innocent on the Pullman, so the Eastern drummer is here humorously out of his element. He does not realize the significance of Scratchy Wilson's rampage, which brings a "chapel-like gloom" to the bar. His innocence serves as a counterpoint to that of Jack Potter.

The first two episodes derive humor from geographic dislocation; the third, which focuses on Scratchy, develops the more subtle comedy of temporal displacement. Wilson is in the right place for a desperado of the wild west but not at the right time: he has grown too old for these exploits and, poignantly, time has passed him by. Civilization is moving westward, leaving him a comic anachronism. These ideas form the confrontation in the final episode, which resumes the time scheme of the opening, and in which the living remnant of the old West confronts the embodiment of the new estate: the wife of the town marshal. That Potter can take a wife is incomprehensible to Scratchy, who is described as a "creature allowed a glimpse of another world." The humor of Potter's naiveté in the first section, and of the drummer's in the second, is now addressed to Wilson, "a simple child of the earlier plains" (V, 120). Jack and his wife have just come from a ride into the future; now they must deal with a relic of the past. Scratchy is undone by the bride, and the seemingly inevitable duel in the streets is deflated by his confusion and uncertainty. Thus one unifying theme of the four episodes is the infringement of the values of the East on the last vestiges of the old West. Seen from its conclusion, the story is a model of unity: it combines two antithetical lines of action, focused on a common idea in four episodes, to form a confrontation of great, if comic, intensity. The result was one of the finest works Crane ever wrote and one of the most memorable pieces of fiction in American literature.

As "The Bride Comes to Yellow Sky" indicates, there is a great deal of evidence that Crane was deeply concerned, even meticulous, about the arrangement of fiction. It is known, for example, that he and Joseph Conrad would talk far into the night about matters of form and content in fiction.[22] Ford Madox Ford has recalled similar conversations during the 1890s in which structural methods, especially *progression d'effet*, were the central concern.[23] What seems to have developed as Crane's principle of organization is in a sense paradoxical: an adherence to the episode as the basic unit of fiction and yet a unity of detail, imagery, and theme that fuses separate units into an artistic whole. As his works reveal, he achieved sophistication of design through a number of patterns: a balanced plot, especially in the novels, which divides physically and thematically into halves; an envelope device, used primarily in short stories, which encloses disparate scenes between opening and closing sections of related content; and the use of details, events, and images to unify and give coherence to an episodic story.

Perhaps the most dramatic evidence of Crane's meticulous craftsmanship is the fact that many of his major works, including *The Red Badge of Courage, Maggie, George's Mother,* and *The Monster,* are basically symmetrical in structure. *The Red Badge,* in fact, is organizationally a duplication of Nathaniel Hawthorne's *The Scarlet Letter,* which not only divides its twenty-four chapters at the center but mirrors the second half with the first in matters of character, theme, and action. None of Crane's other works are arranged in exactly this pattern, but *Maggie* divides in half at the point of her seduction, *George's Mother* balances around the crucial drunk scene, and *The Monster* devotes twelve of its twenty-four chapters to showing how Henry Johnson was transformed into a monster and twelve more to depicting the resultant monstrosity of the community. The design of each of these works is rich and complex and deserves detailed comment.[24]

The Red Badge of Courage is almost a perfect model of novelistic symmetry. Its twenty-four chapters divide neatly in half, the first twelve treating the causes and effects of Henry's desertion, the second twelve dealing with his reunion with his regiment and with his developing realizations. Each half is also balanced, so that Henry's desertion comes in the middle of the first half and his epiphany in the center of the second half. The first half of the novel concerns Henry's pride and heroic illusion, his flight from battle, his shock at the death of Jim Conklin, and his own wound in Chapter 12. The movement is toward isolation and fear, disillusionment and despair. The second half reunites him with his comrades and focuses on his growing courage, his increasing knowledge of himself, and his sense of manhood at the conclusion. There is a psychological progression for Henry toward a realistic view of his place in the universe, toward an understanding of his military role, and toward an acceptance of himself, cowardice and fear included, while at the same time recognizing his limitations.[25]

The first six chapters of the novel, leading to Henry's desertion, stress his uncertainty about himself and his confusion about the nature of war. At times he thinks of himself in heroic terms as facing "Greeklike" struggles and "Homeric" battle; more often he is concerned with his fear, with his mother's admonition that he "must never do no shirking," and with his attempts to "mathematically prove to himself that he would not run from a battle." The alternation between these two lines of thought informs the central conflict of the opening chapters: his struggle is internal; the physical battle is at a distance until Chapter 5, when Henry confronts the "phantoms" who oppose him. By the next chapter he feels that he is against "redoubtable dragons" and "monsters" who seek to devour him, and in a moment of panic he runs: "On his face was all the horror of those things which he imagined" (II, 41). The irony is that Henry runs from himself, from his fear, distortions, anxiety; his comrades, who stayed to confront the opposing troops, hold the line without difficulty.

The next six chapters, leading to the exact center of the novel, focus on a new level of psychological complexity: Henry's attempts to justify his desertion and to diminish the stature of his comrades who did not flee. The vagaries of his mind run full circle, from his conviction that "he, the enlightened man who looks afar in the dark, had fled because of his superior perceptions and knowledge" (II, 45), to his subsequent self-hatred, following the death of Conklin, when he wishes he were dead (II, 62, 64, 67). It is at this point that he receives his wound, his ironic red badge of courage, and is led by the "cheery-voiced" stranger back to his regiment. The first half of the novel traces Henry's progression from pride to panic, flight, and guilt; from his group status to isolation and back to his comrades; from uncertainty and projection to the beginning of an ability to confront reality.

The second half of the novel begins with the regiment in essentially the same position it was in at the beginning; what has altered is Henry's psychological state.[26] He is sympathetically received by his comrades and gently attended by Wilson, suggesting some mitigation of his alienation from the group. Even more remarkable, however, is the transformation in Wilson, whose earlier fears and uncertainty had made him the "loud soldier."

> There was about him now a fine reliance. He showed a quiet
> belief in his purposes and his abilities. And this inward confidence
> evidently enabled him to be indifferent to little words of other
> men aimed at him (II, 82).

Wilson's confidence is the product of "new eyes" which allow him to perceive his insignificance and yet accept himself. These matters in Chapter 14 indicate not only Wilson's growth but the direction of Henry's development, which culminates in Chapter 18, the center of the second half of the novel. Despite his desertion, Henry retains the capacity to become what Wilson already is.[27] When Henry and Wilson overhear their officers discussing the dangers of the upcoming battle, Henry feels that "he had been made aged. New eyes were given to him. And the most startling thing was to learn suddenly that he was very insignificant" (II, 101). He has reached an important point in his development in a revelation of insight parallel to Wilson's. As the first quarter of the novel records the psychological causes of Henry's desertion, the second quarter the effects, so the third quarter has brought him to an awareness that informs the conclusion of the novel.

The final six chapters document Henry's transformation in direct counterpoint to the opening of the novel. He now functions as an integral part of his unit; he controls his fear; he no longer entertains heroic delusions of stature. Earlier he was perceptually and cognitively impaired, seeing little and comprehending even less; now "he saw everything" and in the details of battle "all were comprehended" (II, 105). In harmony with the other men of his regiment, he subordinates his personal fears to collective action, and the group is victorious in a skirmish: "They gazed about them with looks of uplifted pride, feeling new trust in the grim, always-confident weapons in their hands. And they were men" (II, 115). The change in the regiment is analogous to Henry's development, as is Wilson's. Henry has found a new "self-confidence," his vision is now "unmolested," and "he was enabled to more closely comprehend himself and circumstance" (II, 133). By the final chapter Henry has grown a great deal, largely on the basis of his "new eyes." He is now able to comprehend his earlier actions; "his soul changed," and "he had rid himself of the red sickness of battle" (II, 135).

The final chapter serves to unify the novel artistically and thematically. It concludes the action, character development, and patterns of imagery of the earlier sections, and it brings a coherent meaning to the psychological changes Henry has experienced. There are no indications that Henry's personality has become fixed and every reason to assume that just as the war has not ended, Henry's maturation is not as yet complete. But he has undergone significant development from the first chapter, when he questioned himself and doubted his bravery. Ultimately *The Red Badge* is not a book about the Civil War so much as a study of psychological conflict and change. From a structural point of view, it is impressive that Crane could fashion a narrative of this magnitude working with Impressionistic episodes arranged in a symmetrical design. It is this careful arrangement that gives coherence to the disparate episodes of the novel and that may have led Hemingway to marvel at its poetic unity.

Maggie is also a structurally balanced novel. Its plot turns on the seduction of Maggie, which takes place in the center, and its use of juxtapositions and corroborative scenes give the narrative a unified design. Stated briefly, the nineteen chapters of the novel are arranged in six groups of roughly three chapters each. The central event, Maggie's seduction, occurs between chapters 9 and 10. In a sense, the first half of the novel documents the causes of Maggie's seduction, the second half the effects. The first three chapters are largely background. They establish the degradation of the Johnson family, the hostility of the environment, and Maggie's personal gentleness, compassion, and need of human warmth. The next two chapters take place after a number of years and demonstrate the effects of this background on the lives of the Johnson children. Tommie has died and was buried with a stolen flower in his hand; the father has also died, leaving the violent and alcoholic Mrs. Johnson in control; Jimmie has become an arrogant and aggressive truck driver, "so sharp that he believed in nothing" (I, 21). Only Maggie seems untouched by the more degrading aspects of her environment. The narrator is explicit in describing her beauty, her freedom from the taint of the Bowery, and her discontent with the condition of her life. Maggie's weakness is in her innocence and in her need for close human contacts: "Under the trees of her dream-gardens there had always walked a lover" (I, 26). The next four chapters trace the courtship of Maggie and Pete, stressing her perception of him as a knight and her desire to escape the drudgery of the factory. Throughout these chapters Maggie's view of Pete as the means of romantic fulfillment in her life is contrasted to the tawdry reality of the Johnson family. All of these factors contribute to the unique vulnerability of Maggie in her needs, her dreams, her desire to escape from the judgmental dominance of her mother.

It is at this point that the seduction takes place, during a period after the culmination of Chapter 9 and before the beginning of Chapter 10. The next three chapters deal with the effects of that event: Mrs. Johnson condemns Maggie; Jimmie seeks to avenge the family name by fighting Pete (just as he had fought for "honor" in the opening of the novel); Pete has grown in self-estimate ("He could appear to strut even while sitting still . . ." [I, 51]); and Maggie has become dependent on Pete, devoid of all self-reliance. The vindictiveness and melodramatic righteousness of these sections lead to a pattern of rejection in the next three chapters. At the center of the second half of the novel, Maggie is abandoned by Pete, rejected by her mother and brother, and ignored by a clergyman more concerned with his respectability than with helping the people of his parish. The final three chapters take place after several months and document the culmination of all of these factors. Maggie has apparently succeeded financially as a prostitute, for she is well-dressed; however, the progressively more decrepit series of men she encounters, ending with the "ragged being with shifting, blood-shot eyes and grimy hands," suggests a figurative decline in Maggie's sense of stature and self-respect.[28] This decline leads to her suicide in the river, a matter, as was her seduction, suggested indirectly by surrounding events. Pete comes to a parallel end as he is played for a "duffer" by Nellie and abandoned drunk in the saloon. The novel concludes ironically with the mother's forgiveness, which epitomizes the false morality, trivialized sentiment, and figurative blindness that were part of Maggie's world from the beginning.

Structurally, *Maggie* is a marvel of organization and unity. The plot turns on a central event; each half has its own pivotal action; the conclusion reveals the natural consequences of previous acts by each of the characters. The novel as a whole has a balanced design despite the highly fragmented nature of the Impressionistic vignettes comprising it. No episode runs for more than a page or two, and yet the novel seems to portray a coherent series of events in a montage of Bowery life.[29]

George's Mother is not the novel that *Maggie* is, despite Crane's comment in a letter to Hamlin Garland that "I have just completed a New York book that leaves Maggie at the post. It is my best thing."[30] In a sense the two books are of a single conception: they both take place in the Bowery, many of the scenes in the same tenement; some characters, Maggie and Pete, for example, appear in each; there is a similar concern for the destructive potential of bourgeois respectability; and both are modeled on a structural design with the key motivational event in the center of the novel. As does *Maggie*, the novel develops from background scenes through a definition of character and conflict to a central axis, the drinking party, and unfolds in reverse to a tragically ironic resolution. The seventeen chapters of the novel, each basically an Impressionistic episode, are symmetrically arranged. The first three establish the Bowery milieu and the personalities of George and his mother; the next four chapters trace George's growing attraction to the saloon and his uneasiness with his mother's temperance morality. Underneath there is a more subtle conflict between the mother's gratifying illusion that she is an ideal parent of a sterling son and her growing awareness that George is no better than his fellow Bowery toughs. As in nearly all of Crane's works, self-delusion, forced into contact with actual life, becomes a destructive force.

The precipitating event for this confrontation comes in the central chapters, eight through ten, in the party at Bleecker's at which George becomes drunk. The following four chapters, balancing the four before the party, deepen the conflict between George's new life and the values of the church, to which the mother adheres. In this section George intensifies his involvement with his group just as his mother discovers the truth about his activities. This discovery leads directly to the final three chapters, which involve a direct confrontation between mother and son, the loss of his job, and the mother's final illness and death. The two halves of the novel thus mirror one another in organization around the central party; the conflicts introduced in the first half are systematically resolved in the second. Once again, in *George's Mother* as in *Maggie* and *The Red Badge,* all of which were composed during the same period, Crane used Impressionistic vignettes to construct a symmetrical novel of considerable thematic force.[31]

The Monster is structurally identical to *The Red Badge* in that it has twenty-four chapters which turn on a central event, in this case the disfiguration of Henry Johnson in a fire and Dr. Trescott's decision to care for him despite the hostility of the community. In a sense, Crane was giving novelistic form to the conflict Henrik Ibsen explored in *An Enemy of the People,* which was produced in the United States in 1895: the antagonism between individual moral responsibility and an unassailable communal will which, in Crane's novel, isolates Dr. Trescott and his family and threatens to destroy them socially and financially. The resultant theme is what James B. Colvert has termed "the malice of self-righteous respectability."[32] The structure of the novel strengthens this conflict. The first twelve chapters trace a series of events that show how Johnson, the black stable-hand of the Trescott family, is physically and mentally deformed by his attempt to save Jimmie from a fire; the last twelve show how the community of Whilomville is transformed into a moral monstrosity by its reactions to this situation. As in *Maggie, The Red Badge,* and *George's Mother,* there is a cause and effect pattern: half of the novel explains the cause, half the effects.[33] But the central point for an Impressionistic reading of these novels is that all four provide ample evidence that Crane not only worked with brief, fragmentary episodes in the construction of his fiction, but that he organized them into precise units of action which turn on a central axis and which give artistic design to the whole.

Beyond the use of Impressionistic episodes and the arrangement of chapters into symmetrically patterned novels, there are a number of other structural devices that Crane used effectively in his works. One of these is the envelope technique, restricted almost exclusively to the short stories, in which opening and closing episodes frame sections devoted to other matters, or, in a variable pattern, passages of Impressionistic description begin and end the story. Crane employed this device in many of his finest stories. Perhaps the subtlety of his organizational patterns is attested to by the fact that very few of his readers over the decades have realized how tightly ordered his fiction actually is.

The prototype of the frame technique is "The Clan of No-Name," a neglected story of considerable merit which uses an envelope with themes analogous to those of the sections within. The story begins with a unique device, a seven-line poem that invites both exegesis and comparison to the story that follows:

Unwind my riddle.
Cruel as hawks the hours fly,
Wounded men seldom come home to die,
The hard waves see an arm flung high,
Scorn hits strong because of a lie,
Yet there exists a mystic tie.
Unwind my riddle (VI, 119).

Presumably the solution of the riddle is to be found in the ensuing narrative, although the relationships between poem and story are somewhat oblique. The poem does suggest some levels of correspondence in its theme of the transience of life, in the reference to "wounded men," and in its concern for a lie. The intriguing matter of the "mystic tie" implies two levels of concern: the relationship between the story and the poem and that between the narrative frame involving Margharita's courtship and the central war episodes in which Manolo is killed.

The poem itself has an envelope structure in the repeated invocation to "unwind my riddle." The frame for the story consists of sections one and nine, both of which focus on courtship. In the first, Margharita, in her garden in Florida, delays her flirtation with Mr. Smith long enough to receive an envelope containing a photograph from her secret love, Manolo, who is going off to war in Cuba. That Margharita clutches the envelope desperately suggests her affection for the young man, and his photograph, along with the one she has given to him, becomes another device for establishing internal unity. The central seven sections dealing with the war are complex: they move forward and backward in time and are related from varying narrative persectives.

In section two a Spaniard guarding a blockhouse is hit in the chest and killed. The action is reported, as is the entire story, with emotional detachment; there is insufficient context to understand the meaning of the events. The context is provided later by a flashback of several sections concerning the Cuban revolutionaries, for whom Manolo fights, before returning in section eight to the Spanish soldiers once again. The two scenes concerning the Spanish blockhouse thus become a frame within a frame. The main development of the "Cuban" sections, three through seven, is the death of Manolo. As the action progresses it becomes clear that the mission is to move supplies through the Spanish lines and past the blockhouse, an endeavor led by the Cuban *practicos*. Manolo is a second lieutenant who becomes inadvertently involved in this action. Section five brings those activities up to the time when the

Spanish sergeant was shot; it also reveals that the insurgents attacking the blockhouse are about to be separated from the main force. Manolo is dispatched to this group to inform them of their condition and to tell them they must hold their position at all costs. In attempting to hold ground, Manolo is first wounded (at which point he thinks of the photograph in his pocket) and then killed by a Spanish soldier in a grisly scene:

> His negro face was not an eminently ferocious one in its lines, but now it was lit with an illimitable blood-greed. He and the young lieutenant exchanged a singular glance; then he came stepping eagerly down. The young lieutenant closed his eyes, for he did not want to see the flash of the machete (VI, 132).

The repeated emphasis on the youth of Manolo underscores the tragedy of his death, which is of no consequence in the battle. His death is further degraded in the following section, when the Spaniard lies about it. When he produces the photograph that Manolo carried, he says "I took this from the body of an officer whom I killed machete to machete" (VI, 133). On the back of the photograph is written " 'one lesson in English I will give you—this: I love you, Margharita.' "

As a result, when the conclusion of the story returns to the garden in Tampa, the courtship has a new level of meaning. Margharita sustains her composure during her mother's insensitive remarks about Manolo's death and then accepts the proposal from Smith. Her final act is to burn the photograph she had given Manolo, which has somehow been returned to her. The story ends with a poetic statement on duty by the narrator:

> For the word is clear only to the kind who on peak or plain, from dark northern ice-fields to the hot wet jungles, through all wine and want, through lies and unfamiliar truth, dark or light, are governed by the unknown gods, and though each man knows the law no man may give tongue to it (VI, 136).

This enigmatic conclusion suggests both Manolo's reflections on his obligations and the perplexing riddle with which the story began. Manolo is clearly among those who are governed by the "unknown gods" and to whom the "word is clear." The "mystic tie" of the riddle would seem to unite the war and the courtship, both of which are conducted according to ritualized codes of behavior that are essentially corrupt: the needless death of Manolo and the falsification of the report of it obviate concerns for honor and bravery; Margharita's acceptance of Smith is equally false. There is no indication that she loves him and a good deal to suggest that her motives, as well as those of her mother, are economic. The ultimate implications of the story relate to those of *The Red Badge*, "A Mystery of Heroism," and "The Veteran" in suggesting that idealized conduct in war is untrue to reality. "The Clan of No-Name" is thus doubly framed: the war action is enclosed by the romantic concerns of the garden in Tampa, and the scenes involving Manolo are encased in two episodes dealing with the Spanish troops.

There are many other examples of Crane's use of the envelope structure, a few of which deserve specific comment. Perhaps the best of these is "An Experiment in Misery," a story originally published in the New York *Press* in 1894, which begins and concludes with the protagonist in reflective isolation in New York. The story is cyclical in this respect, but the contrast of his attitudes in the two scenes suggests moral and psychological growth from his experience. The story ends with emphasis on his newly realized compassion for the destitute and his commensurate social guilt.[34] "The Men in the Storm" starts and ends with passages of Impressionistic description which serve as a frame for the section within. Indeed, there is a cinematic quality to the structure of the story: it begins with an establishing shot seen from a distance, moves in for a series of tight shots, and concludes with a wide-angle portrait from the original distance. Similar Impressionistic passages open and close other stories, including "The Veteran," "A Man and Some Others," "The Fire," and "Queenstown."

The most frequent design for Crane's stories, however, is a modification of the frame concept, which begins a work with sensory description and concludes it with an ironic event or comment. The sensory evocation of scene at the beginning of a story has the effect of making the reader part of the scene by presenting the impressions that a person on the location would have. The lack of background information, the absence of explanations of the motivation or meaning of the initial scene, has the effect of intensifying interest in sensory details, from which such understandings must be derived. The abrupt introduction of empirical data reflects the fragmentary nature of life with its discontinuous units of experience. The ironic endings often provide a center of meaning for the preceding events. For example, the cowboy's ironic comment at the end of "The Blue Hotel" forces the Easterner's earlier statements into a unique perspective. The irony of the mother's comment that concludes *Maggie* dramatically underscores the themes of delusion and bourgeois respectability which inform that novel. The deflation of the little man at the conclusion of nearly all the Sullivan County tales emphasizes his illusion of stature and the futility and ignominious defeat at the center of his life. This sense of insignificance and loss, similar to many of Anton Chekhov's endings, ironically presented, is the tonal corollary of Crane's basic themes and a nearly perfect method of conclusion for most of his stories.[35]

Another of Crane's methods of giving fragmentary scenes a sense of unity is the use of repeated events and details. The most unique of these is the refrain, a device Crane employed effectively in such stories as "The Open Boat" and "A Man and Some Others." But more often the unifying elements are less extraordinary. In "A Mystery of Heroism" the episodes are unified by key details: the white duck trousers of the battery, the desire for water, the horses, the house and barn in the distance. In "Four Men in a Cave" a statement made by one of the men early in the story is reiterated to ironic effect at the end. In *Maggie* a single motion is repeated three times: early in the novel Maggie lifts her skirts when leaving the tavern to avoid contact with the scarlet women; later, after her seduction, other women repeat the gesture to avoid contact with her; and finally, just before her suicide, a clergyman snatches back his cloak when Maggie attempts to seek help from him. The pretension in all of these scenes underscores the irony at the heart of the novel. The three violets help unify the sections of *The Third Violet* as does the macabre countenance of the dead man in "The Upturned Face."

A reading of "The Veteran" (VI, 82–86) demonstrates how Crane could use casual details to unify a story. It begins with a characteristic passage of Impressionistic description:

> Out of the low window could be seen three hickory trees placed irregularly in a meadow that was resplendent in spring-time green. Further away, the old dismal belfry of the village church loomed over the pines. A horse meditating in the shade of one of the hickories lazily swished his tail. The warm sunshine made an oblong of vivid yellow on the floor of the grocery.

The scene is carefully described. The view is from inside a building looking through a window. In the foreground is the green meadow with its hickories. In the distance, giving depth to the portrait, a church rises over the pines. Closer to the viewer is a horse, standing in the shade. Back inside the grocery, the sunshine makes an oblong on the floor. The viewer is taken from inside to the meadow, beyond to the church, back to the meadow, and again inside the store. The portrait has depth, color, motion, light and shade, and a frame. The kinetic and synaesthetic image of the horse that "swishes" his tail provides further sensory evocations of an already vivid scene. Many of the details of this paragraph recur throughout the story, unifying its sections with the opening. The concern for horses is one of them: there are references to Sickle's colt, which Henry Fleming mentions to turn Jimmie's thoughts away from his grandfather's admission of fear, to the mare and workhorses Fleming gets out of the burning barn, to the two colts he dies attempting to save. The belfry of the church, a visual image in the opening, becomes auditory near the end as the bell is rung to announce the fire. The yellow of the sunshine in the opening becomes the yellow of the flames, the "wild banner," as Henry opens the doors to the barn. These details not only give the story a vivid, cinematic quality but establish a pattern of internal references that create a sense of unity.

As this story indicates, the general effect of Crane's use of unifying details is to give coherence to the basic fragmentary units that comprise his fiction. Another important implication is that Crane's stories were hardly "thrown together," as Hamlin Garland once said, but that they exhibit organizational patterns, unifying references, juxtapositions, and an impressive aesthetic balance that attest to Crane's artistic control and support Hemingway's admiration of his ability to create fiction with poetic unity.

Imagery: patterns and evocations

Another important unifying device in Crane's fiction is imagery, especially imagistic clusters or patterns. These imagistic groups occur frequently and produce a variety of effects from gratuitous humor, to ironic contrast, to significant thematic suggestions. For example, the torture and death images in "Making an Orator" not only stress what agony it is for Jimmie Trescott to speak in front of an audience but link his fate to that of the men in Tennyson's "The Charge of the Light Brigade," which he is forced to recite. Unable to complete the poem, Jimmie is sent to his seat in a state imagistically "after death" in which he is a "spirit" free from the "travail of our earthly lives" (VII, 162). In similar fashion, contrasting patterns of imagery generate the most amusing levels of "The Angel-Child" (VII, 129–37) in that religious images underscore the reverential affection of the parents for Cora and pagan images suggest, hyperbolically, the true nature of her activities. In contrast to the parents' view of their "angel," the narrator describes her as a begum, a Moslem woman ruler, who presides over the "less heavenly children" who pay her "homage." As the children enter a candy store, the comic imagery intensifies, the children becoming "drunken revelling soldiers" attending an "orgy" who soon look as though they had been "dragged at the tail of a chariot." This playful imagery provides the principal source of humor in a story involving only mildly comic events.

As these examples demonstrate, Crane's imagistic patterns are important in that they suggest levels of meaning not always inherent in the action of the story, create ironic contrasts, or support themes with rhetorical figures. In "One Dash—Horses" the images of assassins, tombs, corpses, graves, blood, and impending disaster express Richardson's fears of the Mexicans who attempt to kill him. The religious imagery of "A Great Mistake" supports Tommie's reverence for fruit and "worship" of the man who owns the fruit stand. Throughout, the man is described in terms of divinity, the fruit as a "feast of gods," and Tommie as a "simple worshipper at this golden shrine" (VIII, 51). In Crane's *Reports of War*, as James B. Colvert has pointed out, "a long strain of pastoral imagery—purling streams, shepherds, fair fields, sparkling skies—plays dramatically against a contrary strain of demonic imagery—monsters, sinister shadows, serpents of the night,"[36] indicating the indifference of nature and the psychological savagery of war. Similar images of primitive battle have a comic effect in "The Lover and the Tell-Tale" as Jimmie prepares to fight his school-mates. The images of torture, the references to scaffolds and dungeons and whips, suggest the exaggerated remorse of the boys, who are confronted by an elderly Henry Fleming in "Lynx-Hunting" after they have mistakenly shot his cow. Henry sees them as "three martyrs being dragged toward the stake" (VII, 143).

Among Crane's imagistic patterns, those involving animals and battle occur with greatest frequency, especially when used to describe behavior lacking compassion. In "The Little Regiment" the shells scream "with panther-like noises at the houses," the men resemble "leashed animals, eager, ferocious, daunting at nothing," and when they charge, "the line, galloping, scrambling, plunging like a herd of wounded horses, went over a field that was sown with corpses, the records of other charges" (VI, 15–17). The imagery is notable: it implies the predation of artillery, the impatience of men anticipating conflict, the destruction and maiming of battle. The figure of a "field that was sown with corpses" antedates T. S. Eliot's use of planted corpses in *The Waste Land* and the sardonic and hopeless sowing of the dead. These imagistic clusters invest Crane's fiction with important values that define roles, suggest psychological states, and imply fundamental themes. At times Crane is self-conscious about using them. In "War Memories" he describes the artillery shells from the *Dolphin* as "dogs" that drive the Spanish "birds" out of cover; he adds, "Yes, they were the birds, but I doubt if they would sympathize with my metaphors" (VI, 232–33).

If animal imagery dominates the stories of war, battle imagery is more common in domestic settings. For example, when old Henry Fleming charges into the burning barn to save the horses in "The

Veteran," the action is described in images of war: the flame waves like a "banner"; Henry plunges into the smoke, knife in hand, much as he did in *The Red Badge of Courage;* he is even wounded, receiving a true badge of courage, when a horse smashes his hip (VI, 85–86). Henry, who witnessed the gruesome damage to the horses in the Civil War, and who has just lost stature in the eyes of his grandson for confessing his desertion, fights his most heroic battle attempting to save his animals, especially the colts that Jimmie loves. The battle imagery in "An Ominous Baby," part of the Tommie series, is heroic in vehicle and degrading in tenor. The child is described in images of chivalric honor: his clothing suggests "the chain-shirt of a warrior"; his dirty and scratched face resembles one covered with "scars and powder smoke"; he looks like a "battler in a war" (VIII, 47–50). The implication is that for this child life in the Bowery is a continuous fight for survival conducted on a level for which chivalric imagery is grossly inappropriate. This story, in which Tommie steals a toy fire engine from another child, reveals that constant struggle has made him stronger than other children, more capable of surviving relentless conflicts, but hardly heroic.

In many stories the imagistic patterns are more complex and require more elaborate exegesis. The figures in "An Experiment in Misery," for example, do a great deal to extend the meaning of the action. As the young man, Willie, goes into the slum section of New York, the imagery becomes ominous, with shoes leaving "scar-like" impressions in the mud and with the elevated train described as a "crab squatting over the street" (VIII, 284). The door of the saloon has "ravenous lips" and it "smacks" as it gorges itself with "plump men." The suggestion is that the environment kills and devours human beings, an idea that explains the death-images in the scene that follows. Willie is led to the flop-house by his new friend, the assassin, who gives him his first real look at the poor. As soon as he enters the building he encounters "unspeakable odors" that seem like "malignant diseases with wings" (VIII, 287). These images suggest a sociological pathology that is soon expressed in images of death. Indeed the further implication is that living under these conditions is itself a kind of death. Willie's locker is like a "tombstone" and the men around him lie on their cots in "death-like silence" and snore like "stabbed fish." The youth's bed feels like a "slab" and the man next to him sleeps "corpse-like": "The man did not move once through the night, but lay in this stillness as of death, like a body stretched out, expectant of the surgeon's knife" (VIII, 288). The man is passive, receptive to the destructive will of external forces. Other sleeping men, sprawled out along the "tombstones," are "statuesque, carven, dead" in a room that resembles a "graveyard."

The imagery describing the men in the morning, however, is remarkably positive and suggests an important theme. Parading about the room naked, the men show themselves to have "brawn" and skin that is "clear and ruddy." Some of them "took splendid poses, standing massively, like chiefs." The effect, one very important for Willie's "experiment in misery," is to establish a dichotomy between these men as they are "naturally" and as they are perceived in social context.[37] The disease, the living death, is a social phenomenon, not the result of any inherent depravity in the men. The underlying theme of social protest, crucial to a sense of Willie's anguish and guilt at the end of the story, is established through imagistic patterns of pathology and death, which corroborate the physical action of the story.[38]

The figures in *Maggie: A Girl of the Streets* repeat many of these images. Fundamentally, the imagery that describes the environment is rich in suggestions of degradation, rubble, appalling social conditions, brutalized human relations. The implications are of dehumanization and primitive behavior. For example, the opening scene portrays prisoners as a "worm" of convicts that "crawls" along the river, the boys as "swearing in barbaric trebles," and the victorious Devil's Row gang as yelling "songs of triumphant savagery" (I, 7–8). Such images establish early the level and tone of life in Maggie's neighborhood. Beyond these images, and there are a lot of them, the dominant imagistic patterns, all supportive of the dehumanizing portrait of the society, are those of animals, war, and religion, which is treated ironically. The animal imagery helps reinforce the sense of a savage milieu in which only the wary can survive. Early in the novel Maggie is portrayed as eating "like a small pursued tigress," and Jimmie comes into the tenement "with the caution of an invader of a panther den" (I, 14, 18). Later, when he has matured into an aggressive truck driver, he views the slower street cars as "intent bugs" and pedestrians as "mere pestering flies." Fire engines, which violently race through traffic, he admires with a "dog-like devotion" (I, 22–23). The implications are clear: Jimmie has the perspective of an animal; to establish any sense of social elevation, he must perceive others as insects.

This imagistic strain is especially telling in the scene in which Jimmie goes to Pete's bar seeking retribution for Maggie's seduction. Jimmie perceives this as a noble venture, preserving the honor of a morally outraged family. The imagery betrays the true level of his quest. He snarls at Pete "like a wild animal"; Pete glares back like a "panther"; they bristle like "roosters"; Jimmie moves like a "cat" (I, 47–48). In short, their petty scuffle is devoid of honor and continues the same level of brutalized conflict that began the novel. Other animal images portray the true nature of other roles. Three weeks after her seduction, Maggie attempts to retain her respectability, but she has developed a "spaniel-like dependence" on Pete that makes her less intriguing, and he soon leaves her for the allure of Nellie (I, 57). Later, as Maggie approaches the river in her final degradation, and immediately before her death, the last man she confronts in her solicitations is the "huge fat man" whose body shakes like a "dead jelly fish."[39] Maggie has reached the bottom of her animal kingdom; the death image prefigures her destiny.

The war and religious images are equally significant. Basically, the war images underscore the climate of unrelenting conflict in the Bowery and define the psychological and moral temper of its life. The imagery surrounding Jimmie is replete with suggestions of war and soldiers. Pete's shoes look like "weapons," and the Johnson home is more like a battlefield than a domestic retreat. As these images approach suggestions of chivalric honor, they become ironic and bitter. Pete assumes the attitude of a "supreme warrior" and Maggie views him as a "knight," indicating her unrealistic view of him, her blindness to his true role (I, 27, 28). The religious imagery is even more ironic in that it underscores the bromidic and empty values that spiritual concepts provide for the Johnson family. Nearly all the characters are at some point described in religious figures: Jimmie is compared to a monk, Pete to a priest, the mother to a "fat monk." These images do not attribute religious significance to these characters, as some readers would have it. Rather, they point to the fact that in a world of role-playing and illusion, religion too is a sham and a deception. The reality is that life is Hell for them and religion has little value in their lives, as is most dramatically established by the failure of the clergyman to respond to Maggie's plea for help.[40] All the characters subscribe to religious homilies as a means of elevating their conceptions of themselves and justifying their behavior. Thus the imagistic patterns reinforce the basic themes of moral blindness, self-deception, and degrading conflict that inform the action of the novel.[41]

George's Mother is also rich in pertinent imagery, particularly that of battle. As the original title of the novel, *A Woman Without Weapons*, indicated, this is a story about conflict in which the mother is vulnerable to the attacks of her son. As Joseph X. Brennan has demonstrated, the central dispute is between conflicting religions described in the language of medieval romance. The mother adheres to the idealism of fundamental Christianity; the son devotes himself to a new creed of humanistic fellowship, which he finds in the saloon.[42] As is predictable in Crane's stories of the Bowery, the tragedy of the novel results from self-deluding pride, romantic illusions, and an inability to face the realities of life in both mother and son. The imagery of the novel establishes these points.

When George is introduced, he is depicted as moving through a chivalric world of "castles and fortresses" in which there are "mighty hosts" and "banners" and a good deal of "pageantry" (I, 115). In contrast, the mother is portrayed as engaged in a more mundane struggle in a world of violence and urban rubble. She handles kitchen implements as though they were "weapons," her broom is a "lance," her voice expresses "a shout of battle and defiance," and she attacks her stove as though it were a "dragon." As the imagery portrayed George's heroic view of his surroundings, so it reveals the mother's world as a place of conflict and strife, occasioned in this instance by the fact that George is late in returning home from work. In both cases the imagery reveals the mental states of the characters and suggests the fundamental conflicts at the center of their lives: the mother's battle to preserve her son within a tradition of Christian piety; George's attraction to the secular world of the Bowery. This imagistic line of development concludes after the drinking scene when the mother, like a "soldier," fights a "battle" to arouse him and is vanquished by his swearing, by his loss of a job, by his affection for alcohol.

> She went about with a gray, impassive face. It was as if she had survived a massacre in which all that she loved had been torn from her by the brutality of savages (I, 167).

George, on the other hand, is the "acknowledged victor" who wishes to be an "emperor." He has won the battle, but he has destroyed his mother's sustaining delusions of stature and she quickly weakens and dies.

There are other strains of imagery as well, much of it thematically significant. For example, in George's conflict between church and tavern, the church is imagistically associated with isolation and alienation and the saloon with fellowship, cameraderie, and brotherhood.[43] This fact suggests that the key event in George's life is not his drinking in the Bowery but the death of his father and four brothers (I, 117). The fellowship of the saloon fulfills an important emotional need in George, one to which the mother is blind. For the mother's part, there are images of chivalric love which imply that George fills the roles of son and lover in her life: "The wrinkled, yellow face frequently warmed into a smile of the kind that a maiden bestows upon him who to her is first and perhaps last" (I, 133). She dies not only a mother whose authority has been overthrown but a victim of unrequited love. And there are numerous other imagistic touches as well, including the anthropomorphic imagery of the door of the saloon as a mouth, a figure Crane used throughout his Bowery tales. The "swaggering" clock appears twice in the early part of the novel and returns at the end when the mother is on her deathbed. Significantly, the clock no longer swaggers, suggesting some loss of illusion of stature for George. Most important in the final scene, however, is the evocative image of the "brown roses" of the wall-paper that George feels to be "hideous crabs crawling upon his brain." With Crane's method of narrative restraint, which eschews expository comment, George's expression of guilt and remorse, the full weight of his role in the precipitating conflict, are expressed solely within this image. It is a device that Crane used on several occasions, and it demonstrates a sophistication of imagistic treatment uncommon in American fiction.

As even this brief survey reveals, Crane used patterns of imagery to give his fiction internal coherence as well as to suggest layers of meaning. As the "crab" image from *George's Mother* indicates, his individual figures are sometimes deceptively complex and function in ways not adequately described by conventional critical terminology. They are often ironic, projecting a character's erroneous interpretation of events, and they rarely function in the manner of traditional images. To treat them as such leads to serious interpretive misdirections, as in James Trammel Cox's assessment of the religious imagery of "The Blue Hotel" as a religious allegory with the stove as the "symbolic center of the story" and the Swede as an ironic Christ figure.[44] The error here is to regard these images as serious and traditional, invoking external meanings in a conventional way. But Crane often used imagery in a manner which is "evocative," which comments on external matters rather than drawing associations into the narrative. For example, when Jimmie runs from his mother "shrieking like a monk in an earthquake," the image does not cast Jimmie in the role of a cleric but rather suggests the shallow faith of monks, the self-deception of their proclaimed belief in a benevolent deity, the superficiality of their conviction.

Nearly all of Crane's religious imagery, and certainly that of "The Blue Hotel," works in this way, outward rather than inward. John Berryman encountered similar hermeneutic problems in his study of Crane by regarding the horse as a symbol of violence and Crane's interest in older women as an indication of an Oedipus complex. The trenchant comment by A. J. Liebling on this interpretation is instructive:

> It had not occurred to Berryman that a man whose "idea of happiness" is a saddle might just like horses, or that if a man is much with horses, rides horses, covets horses, and thinks a good

deal about horses, a high percentage of the images in his prose
and verse are likely to be horse images. Or that most very young
men spend a lot of time thinking about women older than they
are, because the women younger than they are are still children.
. . . [45]

Such interpretive problems are common. Crane's imagery is complex
and evades simplistic or programmatic exegesis. As Edwin H. Cady has
remarked, "Crane's imagery has obviously only begun to be
comprehended."[46]

Crane's own comments do little to guide interpretations of his figures, although they indicate that he was conscious of his devices and
often thought about them. For example, in "Death and the Child" the
narrator comments that the child weeping on a boulder is a "powerful
symbol"; Rufus Coleman regards a scene as "uncanny symbolism" in
Active Service; in "Patriot Shrine of Texas" Crane remarks that San
Antonio "seemed to symbolize . . . the poetry of life in Texas"; and in
"War Memories" he refers to one of his figures as a metaphor. In the
same work he recalls seeing a man in a Panama hat with a walking
stick strolling about the front lines: "That was the strangest sight of my
life—that symbol, that quaint figure of Mars" (VI, 244).

But beyond establishing a critical literacy for Crane, such passages
do little to guide an understanding of his images. Indeed sometimes, as
in his use of the term "symbolism," they contribute to the difficulties of
understanding how his images actually function. His broad range of
innovative figures, however, is impressive, and it includes what must
surely be one of the most atrocious images in fiction. In *Active Service*
Crane writes that "Coleman took the dilemma by its beard" (III, 257).
Crane was also capable, on rare occasions, of forming classical figures,
such as when a personified "Reason" is driven away in an emotional
moment in "The Broken-Down Van," the earliest of the New York
City sketches (VIII, 275). In "Stephen Crane in Texas" he used personification to pit Nature against Tradition (VIII, 470). In "The King's
Favor" he used zeugma:

> The lives of all musicians do not glide on in a quiet flow of
> melody and unpaid music bills. It is popularly supposed that a
> musician is a long-haired individual who does nothing more ex-
> citing than fall in love with his loveliest pupil, [and] dine on
> mutton chops and misery all his life . . . (VIII, 569).

Beyond such conventional devices, some of Crane's imagery is
anthropomorphic, animating buildings, machines, and weapons of
war with human characteristics. This is especially common in the
Bowery tales, in which tenements and saloons often have the ghoulish

appearance of devouring people. And occasionally, especially in works involving fear and guilt, there are surrealistic images, as in Henry's views of artillery shells as having "rows of cruel teeth that grinned at him" (II, 42). A similar usage occurs in "A Tale of Mere Chance," in which the protagonist reflects on the tiles stained by the blood of the man he murdered: "At night I think they flew in a long high flock like pigeons. In the day, little mad things, they murmured on my trail like frothy-mouthed weazels" (VIII, 102).

Given the wide variety of Crane's figures and the diversity of their effects, it is difficult to posit a single artistic ideology that explains them all. Contrary to prevailing critical doctrine, which assumes that Crane was a Naturalist who used "symbols" throughout his works, the most revealing approach to the figures is from an Impressionistic perspective. Such an interpretation, congruent with restrictive narrative methods, explains much of the source and meaning of the sensory imagery that pervades Crane's works, including the color images. Further, it suggests that few if any of Crane's figures are genuinely "symbols" that derive their values from established associations. More often these devices are better understood as images and metaphors which project a character's psychological state, express feelings undramatized in action, and objectivize meaning and mood in the manner of Imagistic poetry. Since all of these matters are complex and elusive, it is perhaps best to consider them individually.

Crane's fiction derives from a narrator's projection in language of the thoughts and sensory experiences of a principal character. These are "impressions" in a fundamental sense, and they reveal the limitations of the center of intelligence and the psychological "reality" of his experience. As a result, these images evoke a sense of "realism" in the reader, who is able to experience visual, auditory, tactile, olfactory, and kinaesthetic sensations on the same level as the experiential character. This appeal to the senses naturally results in a good deal of synaesthetic imagery in Crane's prose as well as in his verse. The first paragraph of "A Ghoul's Accountant" serves as an example: "In a wilderness sunlight is noise. Darkness is a great, tremendous silence, accented by small and distant sounds" (VIII, 240). Here the light as sound transference is so complete that by the end of the passage it is not clear if the phenomena described are lights in the distance or muted sounds.

In a sense, Crane's handling of impressions is nearly identical to that involved in Impressionistic painting and music. His works are alive with verbal evocations of experience at nearly every level; the acuity or obscurity of the images defines the character's awareness and place him within a scene. The images of Crane's characteristic openings, such as the first paragraph of *The Red Badge,* involve the reader in the sensations of a setting, especially visual ones. Almost every episode in Crane's fiction is sharp in its description of color, light, shadow, and movement. Sergio Perosa's demonstration of over six hundred verbs of vision in *The Red Badge of Courage* indicates the depth of this method and suggests that the novel is truly a record of Fleming's "vision" of war.[47] But virtually any passage from Crane's works would reveal a similar sensational vitality, especially a passage from the beginning of a story, as the opening of a scene in "The Fire" illustrates:

> We were walking on one of the shadowy side streets, west of Sixth avenue. The midnight silence and darkness was upon it save where at the point of intersection with the great avenue, there was a broad span of yellow light. From there came the steady monot-onous jingle of streetcar bells and the weary clatter of hoofs on the cobbles. While the houses in this street turned black and mys-tically silent with the night, the avenue continued its eternal movement and life, a great vein that never slept nor paused. The gorgeous orange-hued lamps of a saloon flared plainly, and the figures of some loungers could be seen as they stood on the cor-ner. Passing to and from, the tiny black figures of people made an ornamental border on this fabric of yellow light (VIII, 338–39).

Here there is light and shadow and color, a variety of sounds, the movement of streetcars and people, the passage of time expressed in the deepening darkness, and a sense of coherent design in the concluding metaphor, which forms the entire scene into a living yellow fabric with a black border of people. It is a brilliantly evocative Impressionistic passage, one indicative of Crane's descriptions at their best.

The intensification of sensory data, as the passage from "The Fire" indicates, results in a heavy emphasis on images of color. These images pervade Crane's work and contribute values from the purely descriptive to subtle evocations of mood. This dual aspect of Crane's color imagery was noted in a review of *The Red Badge* in 1895:

> In assembling the good qualities of the book, we must name also the quick eye for color which is shown on every page, and not for the mere externals of color alone, but for the inner significance of its relation to the events and emotions under hand. Metaphors and similes, too, abound in rich profusion, not strung on for effect, but living and actual as Homer's.[48]

This unknown critic called attention to an aspect of Crane's imagery that became a matter of curiosity in the 1890s, inspiring parodies and even a subgenre called the "Stephen Crane Joke," one of which ran: " 'I really believe that Stephen Crane is color blind,' said the girl who is given to cogitation. 'Why' asked the chorus. 'I just believe that all the red he sees is only greenness.' "[49] Crane's use of colors has remained an enigmatic subject ever since, one which may forever escape definitive analysis. Basically, however, these images fall into two categories: those related to the visual experience of the perceiving intelligence, and those which express in color the mood or mental state of the character.

The first of these relates directly to Crane's narrative method of presenting data drawn from the sensations of the characters. It is this aspect of his color imagery which has prompted numerous comparisons to the devices of the Impressionistic painters. Milne Holton, for example, has commented that

> color . . . occurs in quick, bold strokes. Usually the colors are primary, and they are carefully chosen in twos and threes for contrast and balance of composition. Whether or not Crane's painterly concern with colors is attributable to the influence of artists, the similarity to the paintings of the American impressionists has always been a striking one.[50]

Orm Øverland's remark that "Crane's use of color on many points bears close resemblance to the technique of the impressionist painters" is in fundamental agreement, and he goes on to demonstrate that Crane not only used color in the manner of a graphic artist but frequently made explicit comparisons between his descriptions and Impressionistic paintings, as in *George's Mother* and "One Dash—Horses."[51] These remarks in Crane's fiction, which generally refer to what people "denounce" or "condemn" in painting, indicating the still reluctant acceptance of Impressionism in the 1890s, suggest that whatever the efficacy of Crane's verbal implementation of graphic techniques, he thought of his colors in terms of painting.

Another direct link of Crane's colors with those of Impressionism in painting is his use of bold primary colors (red, blue, yellow) in a manner that resembles the Impressionistic law of compensatory color, which left the process of blending to the eye of the viewer, as in pointillism. Although R. W. Stallman may have gone too far in insisting that

> Crane paints with words "exactly" as the French impressionists paint with pigments: both use pure colors and contrasts of colors. Black clouds or dark smoke or masses of mist and vapor are surrounded by a luminous zone; or, conversely, specks of prismatic color are enclosed by a zone of shade[,][52]

there is no doubt that there is a painterly quality to his prose. In general, Crane's titles have a visual quality that recalls not only the titles of the paintings of the Impressionistic masters but also those of the musical compositions of Claude Debussy. It is evident in *The Red*

Badge of Courage, "The Blue Hotel," "The Silver Pageant," "An Illusion in Red and White," and it pervades Crane's fiction from the early sketches to the work just before his death. But colors are abundant beyond mere titles. Richard P. Adams has documented more than a hundred color images in "The Open Boat," for example, and Melvin Schoberlin has noted a similar density in *The Sullivan County Sketches.*[53] Virtually any of Crane's works would show a similar intensity of color.

To develop just one instance, "The Open Boat" establishes the slate color of the waves, with their white tops, in the first paragraph of the story, along with the observation that none of the characters "knew the color of the sky." Here the imagery not only evokes a visual sensation but reveals the limitation of the views of the men, their concern for the threatening waves, their intense concentration on survival. Significantly, later, when the men have better learned to maintain their balance, the "yellow tone" of the sky is described, indicating some relaxation of their concern. Still later,

> as darkness settled finally, the shine of the light, lifting from the sea in the south, changed to full gold. On the northern horizon a new light appeared, a small bluish gleam on the edge of the waters (V, 82).

Here is not only color and light but depth, revealing the enlarging perspectives of the men. These verbal paintings occur throughout the story, especially in passages that begin an episode:

> When the correspondent again opened his eyes, the sea and the sky were each of the gray hue of the dawning. Later, carmine and gold was painted upon the waters. The morning appeared finally, in its splendor, with a sky of pure blue, and the sunlight flamed on the tips of the waves (V, 87).

This word-picturing creates a vibrant portrait in which the action of the story takes place. It is also remarkably consistent with the theories of Impressionism of Jules Laforgue, who maintained that an Impressionist is "a modernist painter endowed with an uncommon sensibility of the eye." He went on to say that

> the Impressionist sees and renders nature as it is—that is, wholly in the vibration of color. No line, light, relief, perspective, or chiaroscuro, none of those childish classifications: all these are in reality converted into the vibration of color and must be obtained on canvas solely by the vibration of color.[54]

The kind of chromatic vibration that Laforgue describes in Impressionistic painting, Stephen Crane brought to his fiction in descriptive images.

But Crane used color images in ways that transcend their purely descriptive function and that seem to relate to Goethe's theory of color as expressed in *Farbenlehre* (1810). In this book, which was translated into English by Sir Charles Eastlake as *Goethe's Theory of Colors* (1840), Goethe explored the sensation and effect of colors on the human mind and posited a physiological connection between colors and emotions. As Robert L. Hough has explained, Goethe believed that

> emotional reactions to colors were caused by physiological changes in the eye which brought about changes in the mind. Thus one was physically conditioned to certain responses of color and light, not psychologically conditioned.[55]

As a result, particular colors invariably produced a given emotional state, and a skillful artist could manipulate his colors to produce the desired mood at each moment. The color red, in Goethe's view, produced a high state of energy and excitement in the viewer, one associated by both physiology and common experience with disturbing emotions and violence. Yellow, by contrast, produced a "warm and agreeable" sensation unless contaminated by other colors, which then provoke negative feelings of revulsion and impending calamity. In effect, Goethe was not only describing a phenomenon of physiological process but devising an aesthetic program of color implementation for writers and painters to use in the future. Some of his ideas were remarkably prescient. At one point he observes that

> color combinations have also the common quality of producing the intermediate color of our colorific circle by their union, a union which actually takes place if they are opposed to each other and seen from a distance. A surface covered with narrow blue and yellow stripes appears green at a certain distance.[56]

What Goethe described in 1810 became part of the doctrine of Impressionistic painting in the 1870s, especially that of the pointillists, who juxtaposed dots of pure color which the viewer's mind then blended.[57]

There is biographical evidence that Crane knew Goethe's theories and put them to use in this handling of color imagery. Frank W. Noxon wrote about this matter in a letter to Max J. Herzberg in 1926, saying that

> after the book [*The Red Badge of Courage*] appeared he [Crane] and I had somewhere a talk about color in literature. He told me that a passage in Goethe analyzed the effect which the several colors have upon the human mind. Upon Crane this had made a

profound impression and he had utilized the idea to produce his effects.[58]

The adoption of Goethe's theories by Crane would explain the function of those images which do not describe but rather relate colors to abstract qualities. As Hough points out, there are more than sixty "red" images in *The Red Badge*, most of them associated with fear, hatred, and destruction. The images of war as a "red animal," the reference to the "red sickness" of combat, Henry's "red rage," relate the tonal associations in the reader's mind with the color "red" to the situation depicted. In a method similar to that of objective correlative, Crane is able to provoke the mood in which the action should be perceived. For example, in *Maggie*, when the girls in the collar and cuff factory are described as sitting in "various shades of yellow discontent," the associations evoke the depravity of their condition, as do the descriptions of a "worm of yellow convicts," the "orchestra of yellow silk women and bald-headed men" in the tavern, the "yellow glare" of lights from a building and the "yellow glare" of the factory on the river just prior to Maggie's suicide. All of these images, according to Goethe's theory, would depend on a defilement of the color yellow to produce a sense of ugliness and impending disaster.[59] Similarly, Crane could use blue, green, grey, and variations of light and shadow throughout his works for tonal as well as visual effect. Although Crane's use of colors is not rigidly controlled by Goethe's theories, his fiction employs color images as part of an aesthetic of sensory detail which creates an empirical and emotional reality for reader and character alike in a maner suggestive of Goethe's theories of color and of the implementation of color by Impressionistic painters.[60]

Related to Crane's use of color images are figures often described as symbols but which actually function in a way similar to the objective correlative. As symbols generally point outside of a work to meanings established by historical precedent, Crane's figures, which might best be called "imagistic correlatives," express internal meanings drawn from the minds of the characters. These are individualized, associational meanings, pertaining to one experience only; the same image, used in another context, could have different values. The brown roses, which George Kelcey feels to be "hideous crabs crawling upon his brain" in *George's Mother*, derive their significance from George's guilt and remorse rather than from any historical meanings roses might have. Crane used this device often and with sufficient consistency to suggest a principle of imagery. For example, in *The Third Violet*, when Hawker is nearly overwhelmed by the revelation that Florinda loves him, his emotional reaction is objectified in an image:

"There was a little red lamp hanging on a pile of stones to warn people that the street was being repaired" (III, 85). The color image suggests Hawker's emotional agitation; the whole of the figure is related to the feeling and meaning of what has just happened, what the Imagist poets, especially Ezra Pound, regarded as the central function of an image: "An 'Image' is that which presents an intellectual and emotional complex in an instant of time."[61]

Crane's imagery displays remarkable fidelity to Pound's dictum, especially in that he used imagery rather than exposition to reveal the mental life of his characters and that his images encapsulate the full impact of a story, particularly in concluding paragraphs. For example, in "Lynx-Hunting," on what had been a bright, fine day, Jimmie Trescott mistakenly shoots Henry Fleming's cow. Jimmie and his friends "turned to flee; the land was black, as if it had been overshadowed suddenly with thick storm-clouds . . . (VII, 142). The passage obviously involves not a meteorological condition but an image revealing Jimmie's anxiety and trepidation. Crane also used this device in his journalism. In "Nebraska's Bitter Fight for Life," for instance, there is a passage that summarizes the anguish of the farmers and their vulnerability to the vagaries of nature:

> Then from the southern horizon came the scream of a wind hot as an oven's fury. Its valor was great in the presence of the sun. It came when the burning disc appeared in the east and it weakened when the blood-red, molten mass vanished in the west (VIII, 410).

This description, remarkably similar in method and content to the "red sun . . . pasted in the sky like a wafer" in *The Red Badge*, expresses layers of feeling and thought never directly stated in the essay.

Sometimes Crane used an imagistic correlative as a concluding image for an episode or work which focuses the meaning of the preceding action on a vivid, sensory figure. This device, often described as an Impressionistic technique of compression, occurs frequently in Crane's works. At the conclusion of *The Monster*, for example, as the full weight of Henry Johnson's sacrifice, Dr. Trescott's decision to tend him despite the community's revulsion at the idea, and the social ostracism of the Trescott family become clear, Crane provides a final descriptive passage to focus these thoughts and feelings:

> The wind was whining around the house and the snow beat aslant upon the windows. Sometimes the coal in the stove settled with a crumbling sound and the four panes of mica flushed a sudden new crimson. As he sat holding her head on his shoulder, Trescott found himself occasionally trying to count the cups. There were fifteen of them (VII, 65).

There is no other attempt to express how the Trescotts feel, what these events signify for the community, or what they suggest about human morality. A similar device concludes "The Bride Comes to Yellow Sky." After a tense moment when Scratchy Wilson threatens the new-lyweds with his gun, as he grapples with the incomprehensible marriage of the town marshal, and as the defeated Wilson turns and leaves, the story concludes with a single image: "His feet made funnel-shaped tracks in the heavy sand" (V, 120). Here the impact of the story is summarized in "an intellectual and emotional complex in an instant of time." The image contains the meaning of the story. Indeed the quotation of any of Crane's correlative images (the wafer, the tracks in the sand, the teacups, the "golden ray of sun" through the clouds) recalls for his readers the full impact of individual works.

An Impressionistic approach to Crane's fiction reveals a good deal about the function of his imagery, as a consideration of *The Red Badge of Courage* demonstrates. If the narrative method of the novel is perceived as rendering the experiences, thoughts, feelings, and fantasies of the protagonist, then the images within the novel become components of psychological revelation. They describe not only the way in which Henry perceives the external world but also the quality of his mind at a given moment. Most of the images reveal Fleming's fear, uncertainty, innocence, and growth as the novel progresses.

As Henry develops through the stages of the novel, imagistic patterns alter according to his psychological state. In the first six chapters, which portray Henry through his frantic desertion, the imagery reveals his grappling with reality, his confusion, and his sense of prescient doom. The infantile images of "armed men just born of the earth" and of Henry as a "babe" (II, 23) underscore the youth and the inexperience of the regiment and suggest that Henry must speculate about matters he does not fully understand. His fantasies project encouraging visions of heroic glory and dark forebodings of monsters, machines, and pagan gods, contrasting images that reveal Henry's confusion and anxiety. He is late of the seminary, his mother's guidance, the counsel of Christian teachings; confronted with battle, his mind formulates war as a pagan religion, destructive and sacrificial, a "blood-swollen god" in conflict with Christian ethics. Before he ever sees an enemy soldier, he struggles with these conflicting values within his mind.[62] Another polarity contrasts heroic images against those of monsters, indefatigable destroyers of human lives. Henry at times pictures himself as a warrior in a "Greek-like struggle" or in medieval combat involving "heavy crowns" and "high castles," but as he comes closer to actual combat he more often thinks of war in images that deflate heroic concepts and reveal him to be a fearful boy nearly overwhelmed by trepidation.

The narrator twice makes explicit the relationship between Henry's fear and the images of monsters. Alone in his tent, he has "visions of a thousand-tongued fear" that will force him to desert: "He admitted that he would not be able to cope with this monster" (II, 20). At the moment of his desertion, as he gazes through the smoke at what appear to be "redoubtable dragons" and a "red and green monster," he runs with an expression that reveals "all the horror of those things which he imagined" (II, 41). Clearly the monster within is more frightening than the enemy soldiers without, whom he seldom sees. Indeed the initial monster images reveal his view of his own troops, and the figures of "dragons" and "reptiles" describe Henry's mind rather than the Confederate soldiers. The monster imagery manifests his fear and his confused sense of reality; it also points to a conflict between domestic tranquility and national combat, between his need to be admired and comforted and his obligation to risk his life pursuing the destruction of others. This antithesis is supported by other strains of imagery: Nature is described as tranquil, serene, fertile, spiritual, in opposition to the savage rituals of war. Animal images further deflate his heroic conception of himself, especially when they involve domestic animals of slaughter: sheep, rabbits, and chickens. But nothing reveals more clearly the process of the projection of his mind than does the image of the artillery shells as having "rows of cruel teeth that grinned at him" (II, 42). All of these images are essentially vehicles of psychological revelation. They take the place of expository assertions of mental states and reveal indirectly the thoughts and feelings that lead to Henry's desertion and occupy his mind during it.

Following his desertion, and continuing to the center of the novel, Henry faces new problems: unyielding guilt for his desertion; remorse over the death of Jim Conklin; a wound from a blow to the head; his need to rejoin his regiment. The imagery of this section underscores these problems. For example, although he avoids acknowledging his guilt for his desertion, repeated references to shame and crime reveal his true feelings. Henry initially seeks relief from recrimination in the self-deception that he possesses superior knowledge, a "sharper point of view" than his comrades. Finding little consolation in these ideas, he seeks justification in nature, in the hasty retreat of the squirrel from a pine-cone, in the concept that nature is a "woman with a deep aversion to tragedy" (II, 46). Just as he consoles himself with this rationale, however, he confronts its refutation: death in the chapel of nature, the dead soldier lying under the pines.

The description of this scene is a visually sharp and shocking passage. It is an important experience for Henry, and the visual sensations of it are acute. The scene is recorded in precise detail: the tree and the overhanging branches form an enclosing frame; within the picture attention is drawn to progressively smaller details in cinematic close-up. At first the focus is large enough to reveal the entire body of the soldier seated against a tree; then it moves to his face; next it moves still closer to the eyes and the mouth; finally it reveals ants on the face, becoming almost microscopic in the picture of a single ant carrying a bundle along the lip of the dead man. The colors are ghastly: the faded blue of the uniform, the dull white of the man's eyes, the yellow of his mouth, the grey of his face (II, 47). Here Henry confronts death directly and must acknowledge that it too is part of nature. Through the vivid pictorial description, the reader is forced to confront the same experience.

Death dominates the next two chapters, culminating in the demise of Jim Conklin and the celebrated image of the sun as a wafer. As Henry joins the line of wounded men, images of death are all around him: in the doggerel of "twenty dead men baked in a—pie" to the "grey seal of death" on the face of the "spectre of a soldier" he does not recognize as his friend. It is significant that in this section the religious images of Conklin lurching "rite-like" in the manner of a "devotee of a mad religion" mock any consolations he might seek in doctrine. Indeed, the only nonsatiric imagery of religion in this section relates to nature, specifically to the "hymn of twilight" and the "chorus" sung by the trees (II, 49). This portrayal is reinforced by other patterns of imagery that stress the tranquility of nature amid the passion of war. The colors of nature, for example, are consistently soft and muted green, brown, gold, and bronze,[63] while war is described in violent colors, especially red.

The key image in this section, and one of the most disputed figures in American literature, is that which describes Henry's reaction to the death of Conklin: after a long and precarious march, Henry's friend succumbs to his wounds, collapsing and dying in front of Henry and the tattered soldier. Henry's response is only briefly stated:

> The youth turned, with sudden, livid rage, toward the battle-field. He shook his fist. He seemed about to deliver a philippic.
> "Hell—"
> The red sun was pasted in the sky like a wafer (II, 58).

Much of the controversy over this passage arose from R. W. Stallman's reading of the novel as a Christian allegory. Stallman's analysis, published in *Stephen Crane: An Omnibus, The Houses That James Built: And Other Literary Studies, The Stephen Crane Reader,* and elsewhere, contends that "symbolism" is the key to the novel, "particularly the religious symbols that radiate outwards from Jim Conklin."

> He is sometimes called the spectral soldier . . . and sometimes the
> tall soldier . . . , but there are unmistakable hints—in such descrip-
> tive details about him as his wound in the side, his torn body and
> his gory hand, and even in the initials of his name, Jim
> Conklin—that he is intended to represent Jesus Christ.[64]

Stallman goes on to say that

> I do not think it can be doubted that Crane intended to suggest
> here the sacrificial death celebrated in communion.
> . . . Henry partakes of the sacramental blood and body of Christ,
> and the process of his spiritual rebirth begins at the moment
> when the wafer-like sun appears in the sky. It is a symbol of sal-
> vation through death.

Following such logic, Stallman contends that the novel is an allegorical account of Henry's spiritual redemption through the sacrifice of
Conklin, a Civil War paradigm of the myth of Christ. As a symbol, the
figure needs both literal and extensional meaning. The literal reference
of the "wafer" is to a communion wafer, Stallman maintains; the
necessary association is with the story of the sacrifice of Christ.

This interpretation is fraught with difficulties on a number of levels,
thematic as well as literal, all generating from the initial supposition
that the wafer image functions as a symbol. This assumption, which
leads Stallman to the interpretation of the novel as a Christian allegory, similarly leads Edward Stone to regard the sun as a "symbol of a
celestial partisan, of an *enemy*, agent of man's misery and violent
ends," and Jean Cazemajou to regard it as a symbol of the Aztec practice of human sacrifice to the sun.[65] But the image is fundamentally *not*
a symbol, does not reach outward for planes of value, does not cast the
novel as an allegory or archetypal construct. Rather, it is another of
Crane's imagistic correlatives expressing a character's psychological
state. As in numerous other instances, the ultimate meaning of the
image is to be found within the narrative surrounding it and not outside in mythological structures.

Stallman assumed that the literal reference, the vehicle, of this figure
is dominated by the word "wafer." Since communion ritual also employs "wafers," he apparently felt that his interpretation had a factual
as well as thematic basis. However, as a number of critics have shown,
the literal wafer could be found in a number of other objects, all of
them more common to a war setting than communion wafers. Jean G.
Marlowe, for example, has shown that the wafer could easily be a
cannon primer wafer, a suitably round object related to death and
battle.[66] Scott C. Osborn posits yet another possibility: the "red wafer of
wax used to seal an envelope," which would serve equally well.[67] And

Marston La France argues that the "use of 'wafer' and 'pasted' implies the seal at the end of a legal document and thus suggests completion, [and] finality. . . ."[68]

All of these references provide literal "wafers" without depending upon elaborate allegorical constructs for support. Further, Crane's consistent treatment of Christian rituals throughout his works is ironic and satiric; nor is there any biographical data to suggest that as an adult, even when approaching death, Crane thought in terms of Christian redemption; and the rest of the novel does not support the notion of Henry's "redemption," Christian or otherwise, except in the most labored sense. As a result, there is no necessary eucharistic value to Crane's wafer.[69] That it is round is a function of the shape of the sun; that it is red reveals both its actual color and the passion that Henry feels; that it is pasted suggests its clarity against a background, a singular sight related to Henry's unique emotions. In other words, the image evokes Henry's feelings, expressing them imagistically. This is Crane's consistent methodology throughout the novel; the wafer image is yet another instance of it.

If there must be a nonartistic source for the wafer, it is most likely that of sealing wax, often red, customarily affixed to documents of the time. Furthermore, the literary precedent for associating the sun with a wax wafer goes back to another Impressionistic work, the *Journal* of the brothers Goncourt. In July of 1864 Edmond Goncourt recorded that "this evening the sun looks like a wafer of cherry-colored sealing wax, glued onto the sky over a pearl-colored sea." Years later, in 1885, in describing the painting of Delacroix, he wrote: "His reds are like the wax seals on the papers of bankrupt stationers. . . ."[70] These images predate the wafer figure in Rudyard Kipling's *The Light That Failed* (1891) that Osborn, James B. Colvert, and J. C. Levenson suggest could be the source of the metaphor. It is possible that Kipling derived the image from the Goncourt journal, for his passage is remarkably close to the earlier one. He wrote: "The fog was driven apart for a moment, and the sun shone, a blood-red wafer, on the water." Other references within Kipling's novel to the sun as a "wrathful red disk" and as a "savage red disk" suggest a possible link to Crane's early draft description of the sun as a "fierce wafer," an image that would hardly connote redemption.[71]

Other possible sources for the image include a number of paintings, chief among them Monet's *Impression, Setting Sun* (1872) in which a red, round sun is set distinctly against the sky. A related source might be an essay by Cecelia Waern entitled "Some Notes on French Impressionism" which appeared in the *Atlantic Monthly* in 1892 during the period when Crane was living with art students in New York. Waern's provocative discussion would surely have been of interest to Crane and his friends, and her stress on the recording of impressions may well have influenced him. Her comments on "les pointillistes" are of special interest for Crane's imagery in that she emphasizes that in their attempts to produce the same visual effects with paint that occur in nature, the Impressionists used

> an immense surface dotted with a multitude of little purplish or turquoise-blue, vermillion, and greenish-yellow wafers. You dimly see that they are arranged in forms, which seem to stand for curious representations of trees and grass and shadowy human beings, but the most conspicuous things about the pictures are the wafers.[72]

Crane could very well have developed his references to wafers and disks of color out of these comments. In any event, none of these sources, artistic, literary, military, or documentary, would suggest eucharistic associations, nor do similar images in Crane's other works.[73]

But there are also thematic reasons for rejecting Stallman's interpretation. If the death of Conklin redeems Henry, if the image is truly a Christian symbol, then some alteration of Henry's spiritual state should be evident in the text. No such evidence exists. Indeed, subsequent to Conklin's death Henry reaches his psychic depths. He wishes that he were dead; he wallows in self-hatred; he longs for the defeat of his own comrades to vindicate his desertion.[74] These sentiments are hardly indicative of his religious redemption. On a larger scale, there is little evidence that Conklin's death has deeply affected Henry. He mentions the fact only once, and that in passing to Wilson (II, 83), although the event occurs to him briefly once again as he reviews his experiences at the end of the novel (II, 134). Of far greater import are Henry's own wound, which serves as a vehicle for his acceptance back into his regiment, and his realization of his insignificance, which changes his orientation to war, to himself, and to others. In short, there is no reason to regard the wafer image as a symbol. Rather, it is another instance of Crane's use of imagistic correlative to express the emotions of a character and to conclude an important scene with an image that contains the meaning of what has preceded it.

The imagery from the death of Conklin to the center of the novel develops two important strains: narrative "picturing" and summary imagery. The picturing represents the narrator's description of Henry's fantasies, at once an effort to escape outside of himself, thus free from guilt, and to see himself objectively: "Swift pictures of himself, apart, yet in himself, came to him . . ." (II, 64). One fantasy portrays Henry at the moment of heroic death, another in a bold charge at the enemy; an opposing fantasy of accusation envisions his comrades placing "their defiant bodies before the spear of the yelling battle-fiend and as he saw their dripping corpses on an imagined field, he said that he was their murderer" (II, 67). These projections reveal Henry's struggle to understand the meaning of what is happening to him and to sort out for himself his proper role in the war, a process that culminates in his epiphany in Chapter 18.

The summary images of Chapter 12 pick up the major imagistic patterns of the first half of the novel and put them into focus, a function Chapter 24 serves for the last half of the novel. Here, once again, are images of infants to describe the men; of "dragons," a "blood-swollen god," and a "red animal" to reveal Henry's view of war; there is a brief passage of acute sensation after he is struck on the head in which he remembers his home. Henry, moreover, briefly resembles Conklin, once falling "tall soldier-fashion," and later fearing the traffic on the road. As the chapter ends, the sensory descriptions become especially vivid. There are voices to be heard as well as the "unspeakable jumble" of cavalry, and Henry looks into a world of color: yellow, blue, purple, black, brass, and orange tones paint a variegated portrait before him. All of the important images of the first half of the novel but the wafer and classical heroism are reiterated, paving the way for new imagistic patterns in the second half of the novel.

The images in the last half of the novel move from darkness to light, from blindness to vision, from youth to maturity, thus underscoring Henry's growth and development. Chapter 13 opens in the darkness of night, four hours after his desertion, with his senses "deadened" from his wound. The images are of "black shadows," of "black and monstrous" figures that move in the dim light of the fire, of "visages that loomed pallid and ghostly, lit with a phosphorescent glow" (II, 77). Added to the ominous suggestions of darkness are more explicit images of death: the men of Henry's regiment are colored in "corpse-like hues"; their bodies seem "pulseless and dead"; the trees seem to become a "charnel place," a "house of the dead" (II, 80). Although all of these images derive from genuine sensory experience, the interpretation of them results from Henry's "disordered mind," from the frightening context of his brush with death in the last few hours. To these interpretive distortions are added his perceptual limitations, the "vacancy of his eyes" (II, 96), the obscuring smoke of battle, the restriction of darkness.

But there are compensating images as well that portend a more optimistic destiny for Henry. Whereas in the first half of the novel he is described in images of passive acceptance, a creature to be devoured by agents of predation, now the images cast him as an active figure: a "wild cat," a "war-devil," a "barbarian," a "tremendous figure" who becomes, not without irony, a "knight" (II, 97). Opposed to the darkness of the opening of the section, there are recurring sun images which grow in frequency and significance, finally concluding with the last sentence of the novel. But most important are images of epiphany, of a sudden insight that alters perspective, attitude, and identity. These images first apply to Wilson, Henry's Doppelgänger in the second half of the novel. The formulation is visual: Henry senses that "new eyes" have been given to Wilson, that he has "climbed a peak of wisdom from which he could perceive himself as a very wee thing" (II, 82). Henry, by contrast, is still "blind," still struggling to perceive himself, still grappling with "trees [that] interfered with his ways of vision," still peering through a "blur" at the scene before him. In Chapter 18, however, "new eyes were given to him" and he realizes for the first time what Wilson has learned, that he is "insignificant" (II, 101). Here, at the end of the third quarter of the novel, the imagery suggests that Henry has moved out of darkness, away from illusion and distortion, toward humility and vision.

Underlying the theme of perceptual growth, visual images dominate the final six chapters of the novel. As Henry's epiphany has allowed him to reject fantasies and illusions about his role in battle, so it permits him to perceive reality in precise, sensory terms. The visual imagery, with its scores of references to "eyes," reveals the acuity of his new vision: "[H]e saw everything. Each blade of the green grass was bold and clear. . . . His mind took mechanical but firm impressions . . ." (II, 105). In battle, when smoke once again obscures the scene, he finds that his hearing is sharper than it had been. But soon the cloud of smoke clears and he can see the battle more completely than ever before (II, 123). Finally, it becomes evident that the perceptual implications of the visual images are only the surface of more important comprehensional values:

> Gradually his brain emerged from the clogged clouds and at last he was enabled to more closely comprehend himself and circumstance. . . . At last, they [his actions] marched before him clearly. . . . And at last his eyes seemed to open to some new ways (II, 133–35).

The visual images are the corollary of his cognitive growth, and they allow the narrator to suggest development of understanding with a minimum of expository rendering of precisely what that understanding is. Henry is seen to grow dramatically, through his perceptions, through the change of visual images from blindness to perception and reflection, to a mature awareness of himself.

The visual pattern is not the only cluster of images in the final section, but it is the most important one. The recurring image of the flag is yet another indicator of his growth. At first it is a remote objective for him, an enemy flag that evokes ambivalence: "It was a woman, red and white, hating and loving, that called him with the voice of his hopes" (II, 108). It is clear that the qualities attributed to the flag come from within Henry and reflect his own values. But as the flag images recur, they increasingly signify his loss of fear, his acceptance of danger, and his control of himself, until finally, the enemy flag captured, Henry, having become a flag-bearer, shares congratulations with Wilson.[75] Although there are many other isolated images throughout the final action, Chapter 24 concludes with an imagistic summary of the novel. Brief images evoke once again the tattered soldier, Conklin, the colors of battle, the "red sickness of battle," the peace of nature. The final sentence, "over the river a golden ray of sun came through the hosts of leaden rain clouds," concludes a pattern of sun images that reveal Henry's emotional state, and it is positive, optimistic, full of hope. But the most significant pattern is that of visual images that establish and support Henry's perceptual growth. As *Bildungsroman,* the novel shows Henry's discovery of reality from the turmoil of his confused vision of things, through his distorting projections, his blindness, his fear, to new vision, an acceptance of life, death, and human limitation. His story of initiation is nowhere as clearly established as in the gradually evolving images that move out of darkness and illusion to a perceptual epiphany in which he sees life clearly. This dimension of the novel alone makes it one of the truly memorable American novels of war.[76]

Crane used imagery in a variety of other ways as well. One of these was to establish character, a particular problem in Impressionistic fiction, in which direct expository comment is sharply limited. The qualification that an objective narrative stance imposes upon imagery is that the image is generally the product of perception and is hence potentially as unreliable as any other assertion by the narrator. The grand symbolism of an omniscient narrator in Naturalism is almost entirely absent. For example, the mother in "An Explosion of Seven Babies" is described in hostile, savage images not because she is necessarily a barbaric sort but because that is how she appears to the men, who are terrified of her (VIII, 264–68). Sometimes the images establish more reliable aspects of the role of a character, however temporary. For example, in *Active Service,* as Rufus Coleman and Coke compete for the attentions of Marjory, the imagery suggests differences in their suitability for her: Coke is described as an animal whereas Rufus is surrounded with the images of a gentleman, including a large gold watch (III, 232). At one point in the novel, when Coleman takes charge of the group, he is described as a "priest" raising his hands in "supplication" over them and as distributing chocolate in the manner "of the father of a church" (III, 200). The imagery ironically contrasts the saintly virtures of the clergy with the personality of Rufus, who is more at home in a bawdy house than in a house of worship, but it also reveals the extent to which he realizes and enjoys his artificially superior position. Royalty imagery is similarly used in "A Man and Some Others" to describe Bill's sense of himself as a bouncer, just before he is thoroughly deflated by being beaten in a fight (V, 57). Jack Potter's getting a coin out of his pocket for the porter in "The Bride" in the manner of a man "shoeing his first horse" is humorously appropriate and yet underscores the more serious theme of cultural dislocation (V, 112). And when Mr. Winter drives Dr. Trescott out of the house, Winter is described as "barking" at Trescott and "yelping" ("he was like a little dog"), which suggests his subhuman behavior as well as the implication that he is more sound than substance.

At times Crane's images are ironically inappropriate, as in his use of land images in sea stories and oceanic images in stories set in the arid plains and deserts of the American west. To mention only a few of these, in "The Open Boat," in which four men long desperately to escape the threat of the waves, the imagery is patently that of land. Presaged by a figure in an 1892 sketch, "The Captain," in which Crane wrote that "the wind is strong enough now to make the boat leap like a racehorse" (VIII, 13), in his later story he described the boat as a "bucking broncho," a "wild colt," and a leaping horse (V, 69). There are additional images of hills, prairie chickens, hens, and of a "mountain-cat." The counter pattern is equally ironic. As "The Open Boat" is filled with land imagery, "One Dash—Horses," which takes place in the Mexican desert, contains numerous images of the sea, particularly of the vastness of the ocean, of swimming, of a sinking ship, and of sailing. José, spurring his horse fanatically, "resembled a man on a sinking ship, who appeals to the ship" (V, 23). As Collins runs across the field of fire in "A Mystery of Heroism," he views the farmhouse "as a man submerged to the neck in a boiling surf might view the shore" (VI, 54). Scratchy Wilson picks up his "starboard" revolver at the end of "The Bride Comes to Yellow Sky." When the Swede leaves for the saloon in "The Blue Hotel," he "tacked across the face of the storm as if he carried sails" (V, 165). There is a good deal of this imagery in the stories, much of it gratuitous, but some of it underscoring the narrative detachment that allows for playful comment at the very moment of the characters' most desperate needs.

But these minor imagistic idiosyncrasies notwithstanding, the major thrust of Crane's imagery is Impressionistic. It is certainly not, as has been widely assumed, symbolic, especially not in the sense of referring to external values for significance. In common with the realists of the late nineteenth century, Crane avoided figures that would point to spiritual and supernatural planes for their meaning, or even to systems of mythology, as symbols often do.[77] Crane's images refer inward to meanings established by context, to moods evoked by color, to values generated by the thoughts and feelings of major characters. In essence, the nature of Crane's imagery is determined by his narrative methods: the device of identification with the consciousness of the central character evokes both sensational images and imagistic correlatives. The latter of these devices, the closest aspect of Crane's works to Expressionism, constitutes the most subtle of his methods of revealing psychological insights dramatically in a way consonant with his full artistic methodology. Other devices of imagery, word picturing, ironic images, imagistic juxtapositions, indicate the range of Crane's experimentation in fiction and the sophistication of his techniques. What a consideration of the imagery as manifestations of Impressionism ultimately reveals, beyond the standard critical approaches, is that Crane's imagery generates not from his mind but from the experiences and· reflections of his characters, that his figures are closer to objective correlatives than to traditional symbols,[78] that the effect of the imagery is to allow the reader to participate in the cognitive and sensational life of the character, and that an interpretive stance sensitive to Impressionistic methods is essential to an understanding of the method and meaning of his rich and varied images.

In characterization, structure, and imagery, Crane's works show tendencies for Impressionistic ideas and devices. In a sense, all of these derive from the central method of restricting information to the sensory experiences and associations of a central character. The use of descriptive epithets in characterization, the portrayal of naïve protagonists and characters in the process of changing their views of themselves and the world about them, further link his stories and novels to this movement. His structural predilections are especially significant in this regard. The tendency for fragmentary episodes of intense sensory experience recalls both Impressionistic painting and music, as does Crane's concern for order. His imagery, perhaps the most difficult of his devices to analyze definitively, is yet another dimension of his art to demonstrate this affinity, as it does in its vivid sensory evocations, psychological revelations, and internal references. In the details of these dimensions of his art, as well as in narrative method and theme, Stephen Crane's fiction reveals a decided and fundamental relationship to the central concepts of Impressionism.

V

Conclusion: Impressionist and Literary Chameleon

Literary Impressionism is more than an occasional tendency in Crane's fiction; it is the continuing and informing concept of both art and theme throughout his works. It has a direct bearing on his central themes and methods from his earliest stories through his major works to his final novel. The norms of Impressionism provide a context in which his narrative methods, themes, characterizations, images, and structural devices can be perceived as part of a holistic aesthetic behind nearly everything he wrote.

But Impressionism is not the only impulse visible in Crane's fiction. His work embraces a wide range of literary tendencies. The occasional use of personification as a device of characterization, and of zeugma as figure, reveal studied Classical tendencies. The suggestion of spiritualism in nature implies Romanticism and Transcendentalism, although Crane's use of this idea is decidedly limited. There are Genteel elements in the romance plots of *Active Service* and *The Third Violet* and some of the short stories, such as "The Grey Sleeve." Indeed, as Daniel G. Hoffman has said, "Crane was a literary chameleon, writing in almost every fashion then prevailing: naturalism, impressionism, psychological realism, local color, native humor."[1] But the only two movements, other than Impressionism, that have played a significant role in his fiction are Naturalism and Realism.

The extent to which Naturalism can be perceived as having influenced Crane's work depends on definition. If Naturalism is described as an historical period, as is sometimes the case, then Crane may be considered part of it, perhaps even the originator of it in American literature with the publication of *Maggie* in 1893. But pure historicism is surely not adequate to the task, for it fails to discriminate among concurrent movements and does not specify what aspects of Crane's works justify this classification. Nor do broad assumptions about an author's "vision" or "intentions" serve this matter well, op-

erating, as they do, on uncontrollable and nondiscursive methodologies. Ultimately, some comprehensive model must be constructed
which embraces specific and fundamental themes and artistic devices.
—If Naturalism consists of themes involving pessimistic determinism,
atavism, and evolutionary concepts with both genetic and socioeconomic implications, if omniscient narrative methods help generate
these themes, as do related and dominant symbols, then Naturalism
played a minor but undeniable role in Crane's fiction.

Although there is virtually nothing Naturalistic about *The Red
Badge of Courage* and most of Crane's other works, there are definite
Naturalistic tendencies in some of his stories, especially in the Bowery
tales. Crane's inscription in Hamlin Garland's copy of *Maggie* to the
effect that "environment is a tremendous thing in the world and frequently shapes lives regardless" expresses an awareness of sociological
determinism, although it inadequately describes the events of the
novel.[2] The boys of the opening chapter "fighting in the modes of four
thousand years ago" (I, 9) provide direct textual evidence of Naturalistic ideas, as do the Bowery setting of the novel, the degraded characters, the tone of their lives, and the generalized feeling that life is a
hopeless struggle.

These kinds of ideas appear in nearly all of the Bowery tales, sometimes with savage force. Surely "A Dark-Brown Dog," in which a
father throws his son's dog out a window to his death, develops a sense
of devastating degradation (VIII, 52–58). Other of these stories, including "An Ominous Baby" and "A Great Mistake," portray the debased
human condition of this environment. A largely ignored story, "The
Snake," contains a direct indication of genetic Darwinism. As a man
encounters a deadly snake in the wild, the narrator explains the man's
instinctive reaction: "In the man was all the wild strength of the terror
of his ancestors, his race, of his kind. A deadly repulsion had been
handed from man to man through long dim centuries" (VIII, 66).
Later, as he seizes a stick and smashes the snake to death, "the man
went sheer raving mad from the emotions of his fore-fathers and from
his own." The Bowery environment is a significant motivational
impulse in *George's Mother*, as it is in *Maggie*, especially if the term
"environment" means not only things and persons but attitudes and
ideas as well.

Of the stories with Naturalistic elements, perhaps the finest are "The
Men in the Storm" and "An Experiment in Misery." "The Men in the
Storm" portrays Nature as a cognitively hostile entity lashing out at
men who wait to enter a soup kitchen. The men are debased and
hopeless; social injustice and callousness have turned them into passive

sheep; their expressions suggest that they "were trying to perceive where they had failed, what they had lacked, to be thus vanquished in the race" (VIII, 317). "An Experiment in Misery" develops similar themes of social injustice, suggesting social pathology in the lives of derelicts who, stripped of clothing and other indicators of economic status, stand "massively, like chiefs." Their deficiencies do not emerge until they don their clothing and once again assume a definable role in society (VIII, 290).

If Naturalism plays a role in these stories in the portrayal of the lower classes, a hostile Nature, and genetic and economic determinism, it is ultimately inadequate as a term to describe Crane's works in general. Epistemological processes are far more important than deterministic forces, Nature is more often indifferent or inscrutable than hostile, free will plays a more important role than either chance or fate. Nearly every aspect of artistic methodology points toward Impressionism rather than Naturalism, even in the Bowery tales. Moreover, Crane's use of irony in all of his important works is patently discordant with Naturalism, which most often grinds on with steadfast seriousness toward the revelation of tragic inevitability.[3] Even those scholars who regard Crane as a Naturalist are forced to admit that the dominant unifying element in his work is not the exercise of inexorable destiny but the ironic and problematic disparity between truth and illusion, between "nature in the wind, and nature in the vision of men" (V, 88).

In Naturalism reality is stable, known, and analyzed to reveal its causal forces. There is no interpretive disparity to create a basis for irony. On the other hand, the uncertainties of Impressionism, its apprehensional difficulties and its stress on the relativity of points of view, create a constant ironic interplay of varying perceptions of reality. Given these polarities, Crane's works almost invariably belong in the Impressionistic ledger. As R. W. Stallman has said, "irony is Crane's chief technical instrument."[4] There is an ironic disparity at the heart of Crane's work, some distortion or paradox or misinterpretation that gives the narrative an ironic impulse beyond the bare structure of events.[5] The most frequent source of such irony is false estimate of self, a disproportional sense of stature that often leads to a climactic scene of diminution.[6] In effect, Crane's Impressionistic method makes ironic what in Naturalism would be tragic. In Crane's work deflation brings a character into confrontation with reality, however uncomfortable, and may equip the slighted character to better grapple with the world around him. In Naturalism deflation beneath the crushing forces of socioeconomic deprivation would be overwhelming, resulting in a totally defeated, defenseless character. In this sense *Maggie* and

George's Mother may contain elements of Naturalism, but *The Red Badge*, the Sullivan County tales, Crane's potboiler novels, and the bulk of the stories certainly do not.

Despite Alfred Kazin's contention that Crane was a Naturalist "by birth," and the tacit concurrence of Richard Chase, Harry Hartwick, R. W. Stallman, and Lars Åhnebrink among others, Crane's works are almost anti-Naturalistic, especially artistically.[7] Naturalism tends toward epic scope in length and focus; Crane's works consist of episodic units of extreme brevity. Naturalism employs an omniscient narrator who, in largely expository passages, analyzes the themes of the narrative; Crane's works utilize a restricted narrative stance which projects the interpretations of the characters and eschews authorial comment. Naturalism uses symbolization to enforce its main concerns; Crane uses sensory images and imagistic correlatives drawn from the minds of the characters to reveal not the narrator's "truth" but the psychological state of the characters. Naturalism builds, with straightforward sincerity, toward elevation and broad social significance; Crane's works tend ironically toward reduction and specificity, to individual human concerns.[8] Naturalism forces its characters into the common lot, into a condition shared by other members of the group; Crane's Impressionism, with its stress on unique sensory evocations and personal interpretation of experience, tends toward isolation, individuality, discrete human personalities. Any businessman could become George Hurstwood, any downtrodden farmer Sam Lewiston, but there will only be one Henry Fleming, one Professor Wainwright, one George Kelcey, one Maggie. For all of these reasons, Crane's works must ultimately be viewed as containing elements of Naturalism in selected works but also as having more significant attributes in both theme and technique which are directly counter to Naturalistic norms.

Realism plays a much more significant role in Crane's fiction on nearly all levels. One problem in determining the extent to which Realism functions in Crane's works is that it is difficult to postulate clear distinctions between it and Impressionism in many areas. For example, both movements employ similar characters, common folk drawn from middle-America and portrayed in everyday situations. If Crane's characters have this in common with Realism, there are also some aspects of his methods of characterization that have a different emphasis. Although both Realism and Impressionism use objective narrative methods, Realistic works have somewhat more access to information derived from sources beyond empirical data. As a result, a Realistic narrator is likely to know the names of the characters; an Impressionistic narrator often does not. Biographical background is more important in Realism than in Impressionism, and Realistic works often provide such information directly or devise a dramatic method for its revelation. But even here the methods and efforts can be similar. In *The Rise of Silas Lapham,* for instance, Howells provides an account of Silas' early financial rise through the strategy of having Bartley Hubbard interview him for the "Solid Man of Boston" series in *The Events.* The reader gets not only the facts of the case but Hubbard's cynical view of their stereotypic and melodramatic qualities as well. Crane deals with his character's previous life a bit more subtly in *The Red Badge* by placing Henry in a situation of uncertainty and stress in which he might naturally review the events that brought him into the war, especially if these memories recall a more secure period in his life (II, 5–9). As his regiment becomes more involved in the fighting, it becomes quite clear that Henry "wished without reserve that he was at home again" (II, 18). But there are not sharp disparities between these methodologies.

Differences in the roles the characters play, however, do offer some lines of determination. This point is not clear in simple "slice of life" Realism, which closely resembles Impressionism, but it is somewhat more distinct in Realistic works that culminate in moral crisis for the central character, as do *Silas Lapham, A Modern Instance,* and a host of other works by Howells, along with Twain's *Huckleberry Finn,* Cable's *The Grandissimes,* James' *The American,* and other proto-typical works. Such climactic scenes function in Realism because the protagonist understands reality well enough to be able to ponder a complex choice of alternatives. But ethical issues are incapable of reso-lution in Impressionistic works in which the central character is struggling to perceive reality and in which his grasp of circumstances is inchoate. Thus little drama is involved in his choice of one course of action over another. In such works, some alteration of perception is sufficient to provide a climax, a problem certainly anterior to any capacity for meaningful moral decisions. In this sense the themes and plots of Impressionism are more primitive, occur earlier in the epis-temological process, than those of Realism. The irreducible norm of Realism is that reality is known and recorded; this assumption is not certain in Impressionism. As a result, Realism concentrates more on determining what to do about reality, Impressionism more on attempt-ing to define and understand it.

Within these polarities, Crane's fiction is decidedly Impressionistic rather than Realistic. Although many of his works touch on various ethical matters, very few of them use a moral crisis as a climactic moment. Far more of them have as a central scene some key juncture in the growth of a character in which something is realized, perceived in a new way, or not perceived when it should have been. For example, in

"The Open Boat" the correspondent's realization that Nature is indifferent and that he is, as an individual, insignificant in the universe, provides the intellectual climax of the story, just as the arrival on shore constitutes a resolution of the adventure plot. The same kind of climax is at the crux of *The Red Badge, George's Mother, The Monster*, "The Blue Hotel" and "The Bride Comes to Yellow Sky," while *Maggie* offers a case in which much might have been realized by Maggie, her mother, Jimmie, and Pete, but is not. Here the perceptual themes culminate in vacuity, opacity, blindness; the central ethical questions are evaded rather than confronted by the characters.

There are also some structural distinctions between Realism and Impressionism which help place Crane in the latter category. There is no injunction for brevity in Realism; since reality is known, it can be represented as a continuum of experience, reasonably stable, certain, comprehensible. On the other hand, in Impressionism reality is in rapid flux; Claude Monet's haystacks are very different when viewed at varying times of the day, even when seen from the same perspective. To portray Impressionistic reality, therefore, episodes must be brief, capturing discrete moments of experience in which the world is perceived and internalized but not arrested, touched for an instant but not known for all time. In this regard Crane's works, with few exceptions, such as *The O'Ruddy*, are emphatically Impressionistic, tending toward aggregates of episodes rather than continuous action. There is little distinction here between the structural units of the short stories and these of the novels: both tend to be composed of episodes of a few pages strung together by continuities of character and place but not of action. There is rarely a story that proceeds from beginning to end with no lapses in chronology, no breaks between scenes. Nor does Crane characteristically provide expository links to explain what happened between episodes; scenes begin and end abruptly, often commencing with visual descriptions of the environment and concluding in the midst of action or dialogue. No attempt is made to circumscribe reality, to give it full definition.

If there is a sense in which Crane must be described as a Realist, beyond historic considerations, it is in his portrayal of the mental flow of his characters. Crane was not a psychological Realist in the Jamesean sense in that he did not portray with any sophistication the major psychological theories of the day, unique aberrations of thought or feeling, extraordinary psychic trauma. Indeed, what is compelling about the mental lives of his major figures is their normality. Fleming's guilt and fear, Maggie's romantic longings, George Kelcey's love-hate relationship with his mother, are all of the most ordinary sort. Crane's psychological "realism" is notable as an epistemological record of sensory experience, followed by internalization, reflection, fantasy. It is the very commonality of this process, the "truth " of it, which gives the sense of being real.

Certainly there is a dramatic psychological realism in *The Red Badge* which overpowers any dimension of historical scene. The Bowery of *Maggie* is somewhat more present in the rich description of saloon halls and grimy tenements, but it is ultimately the mental distortions of the principal characters that carry the most force. The same thing is true of Crane's portrayal of the West in "A Man and Some Others," "The Bride Comes to Yellow Sky," and "The Blue Hotel." "The Open Boat" eschews the realistic physical detail of the journalistic sketch "Stephen Crane's Own Story" to focus more intently on the thought and emotional development of the correspondent. Even Crane's journalism shows much more gift for psychological process than for descriptive detail.

Ultimately, then, Crane can be considered a Realist in only a qualified sense. His work shares with the norms of American Realism a rejection of many of the tendencies of Romanticism, including stylistic elevation, transcendental metaphysics and pantheism, symbolization, allegorical plots and characters, and a general inclination to represent people and events as emblematic of a significance beyond themselves. As did most realists, Crane portrayed ordinary people who spoke in the vernacular and confronted situations drawn from within a common range. But unlike the Realists, Crane depicted an unstable, changing world in the process of being perceived. Things "seem" to be a certain way in Crane; they "are" in Realism.

Viewed in totality, and with regard for both craft and meaning, Crane's fiction exceeds the limits of both Realism and Naturalism and ultimately must be described and interpreted as being essentially Impressionistic. When seen from this perspective, the Crane canon, and the major phases within his work, reveal a rather different writer, and a rather different contribution, than has generally been recorded in modern scholarship.

The Impressionistic tendencies in Crane's fiction are evident from the first of his artistic efforts to his last, with some indications of a growing dominance. Even the early stories such as "Uncle Jake and the Bell-Handle" and "The King's Favor" develop their force from a multiplicity of views of life, from a protagonist's uncertainty of what is truth and what is illusion, and from a pervasive irony. Sensory imagery, sensational descriptions of landscape, the stress on epistemological process, plots that culminate in an altered consciousness or perception of reality, all adumbrate the ideas and devices Crane would develop in his mature fiction. Similarly, the sketches in the

Sullivan County tales are more valuable for what they predict than for what they accomplish. In what John Berryman called "a series of queer stories" and Donald Gibson "wild fantasies,"[9] Crane again employed his characteristic devices: episodic scenes; sensory imagery, including that of color; shifts of narrative stance to stress the relativity of perspective; irony; and the perceptual distortions brought by fear. Structurally, these tales are models of Impressionistic fiction. They are brief stories composed of abbreviated moments of experience; they are often unified by an "envelope" of sensory description; they represent discontinuous episodes presented dramatically and without expository unity. The structural development of plot in each story ensures a dramatic irony: as the interpretive conflict develops, the central character moves into a progressively more limited view of circumstances while the reader's perspective, informed by multiple points of view, is systematically enlarged. The resolution of this ironic tension comes, on those occasions when it is relieved, in an epiphany that suddenly reveals to a character his diminished and absurd role in the situation. The conjoining of multiple perspective with verbal and situational irony forcefully reveals the delusion and vulnerability of the central characters. Throughout, the restriction of data to sensory experience reveals a world about which it is difficult to form generalizations. An assessment of reality must remain tentative, forever qualified by the perspective of the viewer. The world of Sullivan County is disordered; there is no explicit system of values; each experience, isolated in time and space, becomes its own momentary reality. As Orm Øverland has said, "the fundamental view of impressionism is that experience *consists* of fragments, therefore *is* these fragments. . . ."[10] The tone of these stories is one of apprehension born of isolation and uncertainty. The situation of the men in "The Octopush," stranded alone on isolated stumps in an environment they cannot comprehend but which seems to them vaguely hostile, is an emblem of the generic human condition in all of Crane's fiction.

At about the same period in his life when he was writing his Sullivan County sketches, Crane was also at work on what would become a more important and complex body of fiction, his tales of the Bowery. The most substantial of these works, *Maggie: A Girl of the Streets*, represents a significant advance beyond the earlier tales, but it also shares many of the same thematic and artistic traits that link Crane's fiction to Impressionism. The narrative is composed of abbreviated episodic units filled with sensory imagery. Although the threatening natural world of Sullivan County has become the abusive urban environment of New York, the ultimate human dilemma is much the same: uncertainty about reality, deflation of a tenuous pride, distorted views of life. As James B. Colvert has said,

> as in the Sullivan County stories, the motif of false self-estimate
> emerges everywhere—in gesture, statement, act, situation—weaves
> into structural units, and finally fuses into an implicit statement
> of theme: that human incompetency—comic in the Sullivan
> County sketches, tragic in *Maggie*—finds its source in vanity, delu-
> sion, and ignorance of self.[11]

The stress is on epistemological process, perception, blindness, self-
serving delusion, and the tragic consequences of worldly innocence
pressed into confrontation with reality. This point is established subtly
but effectively through Impressionistic narrative methods which present sensory data and thought but eschew expository judgments by the
narrator, a strategy directly counter to that of the Naturalism of Frank
Norris and Theodore Dreiser.

Crane embraces Impressionistic methods and ideas throughout the
Bowery tales, intertwined, at times, with other tendencies. But to over-
look the Impressionistic nature of these works is to ignore not only the
artistry of the stories but the underlying perceptual and interpretive
difficulties as well. Maggie's death comes not of economic or social
necessity but of her delimited ability to see and comprehend herself and
the world around her. A similar conceptual malaise invests the themes
of *George's Mother*, especially in the emphasis on the destructive capabilities of gratifying illusions. The other major stories of the Bowery,
"An Experiment in Misery" and "The Men in the Storm," contain
some aspects of Naturalistic social degradation and characterization,
but they also employ fundamentally Impressionistic artistic devices in
narration, imagery, and structure, as do the several score of lesser
works.

The Red Badge of Courage is Crane's major work and the first monumental Impressionistic novel in American literature. It is the finest
piece of extended fiction that Crane ever wrote and it depicts a far more
significant series of experiences than anything he had previously
written, but it is very much of the same impulse as the Sullivan County
sketches and the Bowery tales. It represents the artistic fruition of his
earlier work, not a distinct inspiration. Here his typical narrative
strategy, imagery, structure, characterization coalesce into a richly
satisfying aesthetic whole. The primary focus is still on epistemology;
the conflicts are psychological; their resolution comes in a more balanced integration of thought and feeling. Crane's sensory emphasis
makes reading the novel seem more a visual than a verbal experience,
one recorded as a series of related yet distinct episodes of intense perceptual acuity. Throughout, in addition to Henry's continuing experience, the artistic components of the novel, the carefully controlled
patterns of images, juxtaposed scenes, and tightly restricted experiential

data, give these isolated scenes a sense of wholeness, of aesthetic completion, that Henry's brief story does not of itself possess.

These traits are shared by nearly everything Crane wrote after *The
Red Badge*, although there are some variations. Certainly *The Third
Violet* and *Active Service* were influenced by the popularity of Genteel
novels of the trials of young love, which reveal their influence in artistry as well as in subject and plot. Crane's two novels are longer, less
tightly controlled, inclined more toward an omniscient narrative
stance than his characteristic, more serious, work. *The O'Ruddy* shares
many of these tendencies while affecting the norms of the picaresque in
a manner perhaps influenced by Crane's trip to Ireland with Harold
Frederic and by Frederic's own *The Return of the O'Mahony*. But even
in these works there are Crane's habitual irony, disparities among interpretations of reality, episodic development of plot, deflations of
pride, and other traits consistent throughout Crane's work.

But beyond these aberrations, Crane's fiction continued to utilize the
fundamental devices and themes of Impressionism to the end of his
career, from his tales of Whilomville, to those of the American west, to
his dramatic stories of war. The struggle for new realizations in "The
Bride Comes to Yellow Sky" and "The Little Regiment," the parallactic interplay of points of view in "Death and the Child" and "A Man
and Some Others," the extraordinarily restrictive data of "Three
Miraculous Soldiers," the epiphanies of "The Open Boat" and "The
Blue Hotel," the structural organization of "The Monster" and "The
Clan of No-Name," the sensory imagery of "The Veteran," and the
dramatically revealed characterizations, irony, restriction, and truth-
illusion disparity of nearly all of his fiction identify his work as Impressionistic. Crane's world is remarkably unsettled, tentative, inscrutable for his time, and his characters display the uncertainty, anguish,
and sense of isolation more common to the Modern sensibility than
that of the late nineteenth century.

Indeed, it is precisely Crane's Impressionistic tendencies which form
his most significant influence on the twentieth century and which
evoke the Modernistic tone of his fiction. His objective mode of presentation and ability to portray tragedy with understated emotion are a
dramatic foreshadowing of what would become hallmarks of the style
of Ernest Hemingway. A paragraph in "Crane at Velestino," one report in Crane's journalistic coverage of the Greco-Turkish war, is a
characteristic example:

> I noticed one lieutenant standing up in the rear of a trench rolling
> a cigarette, his legs wide apart. In this careless attitude a shot went
> through his neck. His servant came from the trench and knelt weep-

ing over the body, regardless of the battle. The men had to drag him in by the legs (IX, 21).

In style and tone and subject, this passage is remarkably similar to Hemingway's early sketches about war:

> They shot the six cabinet ministers at half-past six in the morning against the wall of a hospital. There were pools of water in the courtyard. There were wet dead leaves on the paving of the court-yard. It rained hard. All the shutters of the hospital were nailed shut. One of the ministers was sick with typhoid. Two soldiers carried him downstairs and out into the rain. They tried to hold him up against the wall but he sat down in a puddle of water. The other five stood very quietly against the wall. Finally the of-ficer told the soldiers it was no good trying to make him stand up. When they fired the first volley he was sitting down in the water with his head on his knees.[12]

Hemingway's technique in this passage recalls the detachment in de-scribing violence and tragedy that Crane displayed in such stories as "An Episode of War," "The Upturned Face," and "A Mystery of Heroism." The stress is on sensory data, those observable details of scene and action that a person could perceive as the action took place. There is no background, no expression of sympathy by the narrator, no moral opinion offered, no conclusions drawn. The events of the shooting are made the more forceful and compelling by having them thrust directly onto the reader with no intervening consciousness to soften the blow or suggest the reaction.

Crane shared these traits with few other writers during his own time. Hamlin Garland was the first important advocate of Impressionism in America, and he was close to Crane during the early years, but little of his fiction is truly consistent with the theory of composition he proposed. Henry James was, of course, a consummate artist who implemented Impressionistic ideas and techniques in both his theory and fiction. Harold Frederic, a close friend of Crane's during the English years, incorporated Impressionistic notions of perception and epiphany into his *The Damnation of Theron Ware*. Both Ambrose Bierce and Kate Chopin were writing stories in the Impressionistic mode during this period, as was, on occasion, William Dean Howells, in such stories as "Editha." In England, where Crane lived his last years, there were Joseph Conrad and Ford Madox Ford, two important Impressionistic writers, both of whom made major contributions in theory and practice.

But the most influential single work in American literature to grow out of the origins of Impressionism in the 1890s was clearly *The Red Badge of Courage*. It was the first American Impressionistic novel to attain widespread popular attention in both Europe and the United States. Although the reviews of it were mixed, partly out of confusion about its methodology, it quickly won critical acclaim. It was described variously as a battle painting, a montage of photographs, a verbal record that permitted the reader to "see" the action. Behind it were Crane's years as a struggling journalist with an eye for detail and an ear for irony, his experience with young painters in the Art Student's League, his untiring attempts to write true to his own vision and in his own style. From *The Red Badge* and the works surrounding it there radiates an enormous and generally misunderstood influence on American letters.

Crane wrote out of the Flaubertian style, not the Balzacian. His work is sparse, crisp, sensory; there is no authorial presence, little unobserved description and even less judgment, and few wasted words. The ultimate impact of his work is aesthetic. There is little call to social action, no program of economic reform, and rarely a word of popular social theory. Those scholars who would place him on the Naturalistic shelf with Frank Norris, Jack London, Theodore Dreiser, John O'Hara, and others, respond only to the surface of his work, to the environment of the Bowery tales. But Crane's fiction shares almost nothing with such writers and their expository novels. Rather, his line of influence leads to the economy of Imagist poetry, as Carl Sandburg acknowledged in his "Letters to Dead Imagists":

Stevie Crane:

War is kind and we never knew the kindness of war
    till you came;
Nor the black riders and clashes of spear and shield
    out of the sea,
Nor the mumblings and shots that rise from dreams on
    call.[13]

It also points to the brevity and sharpness of Hemingway, Sherwood Anderson, F. Scott Fitzgerald, Caroline Gordon, and to parts of John Steinbeck, William Faulkner, John Dos Passos, and a host of other writers who used Impressionistic themes and devices in their work. Crane is thus an important figure in the line of development of Impressionistic tendencies from Flaubert's fiction through the sensory images of the French Symbolist poets to such writers as George Moore and Virginia Woolf, the Norwegian Jacob Lie, and other writers in the decades around the turn of the century. The relativistic realities of Crane's Impressionism play a key role in the development of what came to be known as Modernism, especially in its sense of an indifferent and undefinable universe and a lack of individual significance. His evocative and surrealistic imagery predicts similar strategies in Expressionism. In his Impressionism, in its empirical isolation, are the seeds of Existential alienation and resultant despair and anguish; the interpretive uncertainties of his Impressionism foreshadow the absurdity of the French New Novel and much of Post-Modernism. The aesthetics of Crane's Impressionism, especially its anti-didacticism and art-for-art's sake implications, bear some similarities to such recent developments as Sur-Fiction in the United States. The recognition of Crane's role as an Impressionist is thus a crucial determinant of his place in cultural history.

The significance of Crane's achievement has not been totally ignored, even though it has been widely misinterpreted, by literary scholarship. Both Vernon Louis Parrington and Fred Lewis Pattee proclaimed him to be the genius of his decade.[14] Carl Van Doren, writing in 1924, maintained that Modern American literature began with the work of Crane.[15] Looking back in 1926, Joseph Conrad wrote that in Crane "we had an artist, a man not of experience but a man inspired, a seer with a gift for rendering the significant on the surface of things. . . ."[16] And Conrad was joined by Edward Garnett in declaring Crane to be the leading Impressionist of his time. The enthusiastic interest in Crane's fiction that emerged in the 1920s, and the enormous attention paid to his life and work in modern scholarship, attest to the continuing value of his contribution, a contribution that is fundamentally and inextricably part of the development of Literary Impressionism.

Notes

Chapter I

1. "A Man and Some Others" had appeared in *Century*, 53 (February, 1897), 601–07, and "The Open Boat" in *Scribner's Magazine*, 21 (June, 1897), 728–40.

2. Joseph Conrad to Stephen Crane, Dec. 1, 1897, Letter 210, *Stephen Crane: Letters*, eds. R. W. Stallman and Lillian Gilkes (New York: New York Univ. Press, 1960), p. 154. This volume hereafter cited as *Letters*.

3. Joseph Conrad to Edward Garnett, Dec. 5, 1897, Letter 213, *Letters*, p. 155.

4. My assessment here echoes that of R. W. Stallman, *Stephen Crane: A Biography* (New York: George Braziller, 1968), p. 443. Hereafter cited as *Biography*.

5. Edward Garnett, "Mr. Stephen Crane: An Appreciation," *Academy*, 55 (1898), 483–84. For another analysis of these comments, see my essay "Impressionism in 'The Open Boat' and 'A Man and Some Others,'" *Research Studies*, 43 (1975), 27–37.

6. *Stephen Crane: The Critical Heritage*, ed. Richard M. Weatherford (Boston: Routledge & Kegan Paul, 1973), p. 97. This volume hereafter cited as *Heritage*. Banks' review was originally published in *Bookman*, 2 (Nov., 1895), 217–20.

7. *Heritage*, pp. 109–10. Originally published in the *New Review*, 14 (Jan., 1896), 30–40.

8. *Heritage*, p. 111.

9. *Heritage*, p. 101. Originally published in *Saturday Review*, 81 (Jan. 11, 1896), 44–45.

10. *Heritage*, p. 164. Originally published in *Godey's Magazine*, 131 (Sept., 1896), 317–19.

11. *Heritage*, p. 122. Originally published in *Academy*, 49 (Feb. 1, 1896), 135.

12. *Heritage*, p. 126. Originally published in the New York *World* (Feb. 23, 1896), p. 18.

13. Stephen Crane to Nellie Crouse, Jan. 12, 1896, *Stephen Crane's Love Letters to Nellie Crouse*, eds. Edwin H. Cady and Lester G. Wells (Syracuse: Syracuse Univ. Press, 1954), p. 35.

14. *Heritage*, pp. 116, 119. Originally published in the New York *Times* (Jan. 26, 1896), p. 22.

15. *Heritage*, p. 149. Originally published in *Harper's Magazine*, 92 (May, 1896), 961–62.

16. *Heritage*, p. 215. Originally published in *Godey's Magazine*, 135 (Sept., 1897), 331.

17. *Heritage*, p. 286. Originally published in the New York *Times* (Nov. 10, 1900), pp. 766–67.

18. *Heritage*, p. 81. Originally published in *Bookman*, 13 (April, 1901), 148.

19. Edward Garnett's essay is reprinted in *Friday Nights: Literary Criticim and Appreciations* (New York: Alfred A. Knopf, 1922), pp. 201–17. See, especially, pp. 206–10.

20. Quoted from *Stephen Crane's Career: Perspectives and Evaluations*, ed. Thomas A. Gullason (New York: New York Univ. Press, 1972), pp. 127, 130, 133. This volume hereafter cited as *Career*. Wells' essay was originally published as "Stephen Crane: From An English Standpoint," *The North American Review*, 171 (Aug., 1900), 233–42.

21. Hamlin Garland, *Crumbling Idols: Twelve Essays on Art Dealing Chiefly with Literature, Painting and the Drama* (Cambridge: Harvard Univ. Press, 1960), pp. 42–43. Hereafter cited as *Crumbling Idols*.

22. Richard Chase, "Introduction" to Stephen Crane, *The Red Badge of Courage and Other Writings*, ed. Richard Chase (Boston: Houghton Mifflin, 1960), p. viii.

23. See, for example, Daniel Aaron, *The Unwritten War: American Writers and the Civil War* (New York: Alfred A. Knopf, 1973), p. 215.

24. Alfred Kazin, *On Native Grounds: An Interpretation of Modern American Prose Literature* (New York: Reynal & Hitchcock, 1942), p. 68.

25. Daniel G. Hoffman, *The Poetry of Stephen Crane* (New York: Columbia Univ. Press, 1957), p. x.

26. Joseph Katz, "Introduction" to *The Portable Stephen Crane*, ed. Joseph Katz (New York: The Viking Press, 1969), pp. viii–ix.

27. Thomas A. Gullason, "Introduction" to *The Complete Short Stories and Sketches of Stephen Crane*, ed. Thomas A. Gullason (New York: Doubleday, 1963), p. 45.

28. Thomas Beer, *Hanna, Crane, and the Mauve Decade* (New York: Alfred A. Knopf, 1941), pp. 280, 282, 324.

29. Harry Hartwick, *The Foregrounds of American Fiction* (New York: American Book Company, 1934), pp. 35–42.

30. Hartwick, pp. 35–42.

31. John Berryman, *Stephen Crane* (New York: World Publishing Co., 1962), p. 55.

32. Berryman, pp. 288–89, 292.

33. Charles Child Walcutt. *American Literary Naturalism: A Divided Stream* (Minneapolis: Univ. of Minnesota Press, 1956), pp. 22, 66.

34. R. W. Stallman. *Stephen Crane: An Omnibus* (New York: Alfred A. Knopf, 1961), p. 185. This volume hereafter cited as *Omnibus*.

35. *Omnibus*, p. 258.

36. Several additional items are of interest here. Jean Cazamajou, in *Stephen Crane (1871–1900): Ecrivain Journaliste, Etudes Anglaises*, No. 35 (Paris: Librairie Didier, 1969), pp. 501–05, gives the subject brief analysis. He adds little that is original to the discussion, however. Bert Bender, in "Hanging Stephen Crane in the Impressionistic Museum," *Journal of Aesthetics and Art Criticism*, 35 (1976), 47–55, brings confusion to Crane and Impressionism by misrepresenting the scholarship in rather serious ways and then refuting its contentions. He also suggests, erroneously, that Impressionism had exhausted itself by the early 1880s (p. 48). I have also eliminated from this discussion two of my own articles: "Impressionism in 'The Open Boat' and 'A Man and Some Others,'" *Research Studies*, 43 (1975), 27–37; and "Stephen Crane and the Narrative Methods of Impressionism," *Studies in the Novel*, 10 (1978), 76–85.

37. Sergio Perosa, "Naturalism and Impressionism in Stephen Crane's Fiction," *Stephen Crane: A Collection of Critical Essays*, ed. Maurice Bassan (Englewood Cliffs: Prentice-Hall, 1967), pp. 81–85. This volume hereafter cited as *Critical Essays*. Perosa's essay was translated by the author from "Stephen Crane fra naturalismo e impressionismo," *Anneli di Cá Foscari*, 3 (1964), 119–42, which was subsequently reprinted in *Le vie della narrativa americana* (Milano: Mursia, 1965).

38. *Americana Norvegica: Norwegian Contributions to American Studies*, I, eds. Sigmund Skard and Henry H. Wasser (Philadelphia: Univ. of Pennsylvania Press, 1966), p. 241. Hereafter cited as *Øverland*.

39. *Øverland*, pp. 251, 254, 263, 273–80.

40. Stanley Wertheim, "Crane and Garland: The Education of an Impressionist," *North Dakota Quarterly*, 35 (1967), 23–28.

41. Rodney O. Rogers, "Stephen Crane and Impressionism," *Career*, pp. 265, 276. Originally published in *Nineteenth-Century Fiction*, 24 (1969), 292–304.

42. Lionello Venturi, "Impressionism," *Art in America and Elsewhere*, 24, No. 3 (1936), 100.

43. John Rewald, *The History of Impressionism*, 4th ed. (New York: The Museum of Modern Art, 1973), p. 336.

44. See Herbert Muller, "Impressionism in Fiction: Prism vs. Mirror," *The American Scholar*, 7 (1938), 356.

45. Phoebe Pool, *Impressionism* (New York: Frederick A. Praeger, 1967), pp. 12, 14.

46. Todd K. Bender, "Literary Impressionism: General Introduction," *Literary Impressionism in Ford Madox Ford, Joseph Conrad and Related Writers* (Madison: Text Development Program, 1975), p. 2. Bender provides a useful overview of the philosophical backgrounds of Impressionism.

47. Quoted from Linda Nochlin, *Impressionism and Post-Impressionism 1874–1904: Sources and Documents* (Englewood Cliffs: Prentice-Hall, 1966), p. 25. This volume hereafter cited as Nochlin.

48. Nochlin, pp. 3, 5.

49. Quoted in Muller, p. 356.

50. See Nochlin, p. 95.

51. Benjamin D. Giorgio, "Stephen Crane: American Impressionist," Diss. Wisconsin, 1969, pp. 60–61.

52. Kenneth E. Bidle, "Impressionism in American Literature to the Year 1900," Diss. Northern Illinois, 1969, pp. 149–50.

53. See Giorgio, pp. 63, 77–80.

54. Cecelia Waern, "Some Notes on French Impressionism," *Atlantic*, 69 (1892), 535, 537.

55. See Giorgio, p. 13.

56. See Bidle, pp. 14–15.

57. *Crumbling Idols*, pp. 97–98, 109.

58. This comment is contained in a letter from Melvin H. Schoberlin to Joseph J. Kwiat. See Joseph J. Kwiat, "Stephen Crane and Painting," *Career*, p. 189n. Originally published in *American Quarterly*, 4 (1952), 331–38. Hereafter cited as Kwiat.

59. Lillian Gilkes, *Cora Crane: A Biography of Mrs. Stephen Crane* (Bloomington: Indiana Univ. Press, 1960), pp. 30–33.

60. *Biography*, pp. 336, 523.

61. Melvin H. Schoberlin to Joseph J. Kwiat, Jan. 1, 1949. See Kwiat, pp. 188–89n.

62. See Edwin H. Cady's "Introduction" to Corwin Knapp Linson, *My Stephen Crane*, ed. Edwin H. Cady (Syracuse: Syracuse Univ. Press, 1958), pp. xi–xiv. This volume hereafter cited as *My Stephen Crane*.

63. See *My Stephen Crane*, pp. 32, 33, 46–47, 66–67.

64. See *Heritage*, p. 155. Williams' interview with Crane first appeared in the *Illustrated American*, 20 (July 18, 1896), 126. See also *Biography*, p. 214.

65. Hoffman, p. 237.

66. *Omnibus*, p. 184.

67. See Kwiat, pp. 181–89.

68. Stephen Crane, "War Memories," *Tales of War*, Vol. VI of *The Works of Stephen Crane*, ed. Fredson Bowers, 10 vols. (Charlottesville: The University Press of Virginia, 1969–75), 254. Unless otherwise indicated, this edition is the source for all primary references. Subsequent documentation will be given within the text by volume number and page.

69. See, for example, Hoffman, p. 11.

70. See "The Seaside Assembly" (VIII, 551–54), and "Art at Avon-by-the-Sea" (VIII, 557–58).

71. Rewald, pp. 171–72, 430.

72. See. R. W. Stallman, *The Houses That James Built: And Other Literary Studies* (East Lansing: Michigan State Univ. Press, 1961). p. 83.

73. *My Stephen Crane*, pp. 18, 30–31.

74. Joseph Conrad, "Introduction" to Thomas Beer, *Stephen Crane: A Study in American Letters* (New York: Alfred A. Knopf, 1924), p. 23.

75. *Love Letters to Nellie Crouse*, p. 28.

76. *Biography*, p. 34.

77. See *Letters*, pp. 31–32, 78, 140n.

78. See *Career*, pp. 170–80. Colvert's essay originally published in *University of Texas Studies in English*, 34 (1955), 179–88.

79. See James E. Kilber, Jr., "The Library of Stephen and Cora Crane," *Proof*, 1 (1971), 199–246.

80. See *Letters*, pp. 250–51.

81. Ford Madox Ford, "Techniques," *Southern Review*, 1 (1935), 31.

82. Muller, pp. 357–58.

83. Michel Benamou, Herbert Howarth, Paul Ilie, Calvin S. Brown, Rémy Saisselin, "Symposium on Literary Impressionism," *Yearbook of Comparative and General Literature*, 17 (1968), 51. Hereafter cited as "Symposium."

84. Quoted in Giorgio, p. 42.

85. Perosa, p. 85.

86. See Rogers, p. 293.

87. Rogers, p. 265.

88. In American fiction, the concern for the truth-illusion theme in Impressionism represents, to some degree, a continuation of the theme of ambiguity in the works of the Romanticists, especially those of Poe, Melville, and Hawthorne. Edwin Cady attributes this theme to the Realists. However, since Cady makes no distinction between Realism and Impressionism, his view may not be inconsistent with my own. See Edwin H. Cady, *Stephen Crane* (New York: Twayne, 1962), p. 121. Hereafter cited as Cady.

89. H. Peter Stowell, "Chekhov's 'The Bishop': The Annihilation of Faith and Identity Through Time," *Studies in Short Fiction*, 12 (1975), 118–20.

90. Milne Holton, *Cylinder of Vision: The Fiction and Journalistic Writing of Stephen Crane* (Baton Rouge: Louisiana State Univ. Press, 1972), p. 9.

91. Marston LaFrance, *A Reading of Stephen Crane* (London: Oxford Univ. Press, 1971), p. 98.

92. Bidle, p. 57.

93. Bidle presents a number of helpful lists of Impressionistic techniques on pp. 93–94, 107–08, 226.

94. Ford is quoted in Seymour L. Weingart, "The Form and Meaning of the Impressionist Novel," Diss. Univ. of California, Davis, 1964, p. 16.

95. Weingart, p. 23.

96. For a discussion of this point, see Weingart, p. 119.

97. Crane was never to use either of them, choosing generally to avoid the difficulties of first person altogether. Hemingway used first person Impressionistically in *A Farewell to Arms*, although there are several reminders throughout that the narrative time is subsequent to the conclusion of the action. Faulkner employed a variation of the second method in both *The Sound and the Fury* and *As I Lay Dying*.

98. Orm Øverland is perceptive in discussing the implications of this device. See, especially, pp. 257, 265.

99. For a concurring analysis, see Maria Elisabeth Kronegger, *Literary Impressionism* (New Haven: College and University Press, 1973), p. 15.

100. Todd K. Bender, p. 4.

101. I am indebted here to Benamou, et al., "Symposium," p. 47.

102. Paul Ilie in "Symposium," p. 49.

103. As the mode of Impressionism develops historically, there is a tendency for it to move from objective to subjective forms. Impressionism begins close to Realism and moves toward ever greater internalization to psychological Realism and stream of consciousness. For a further comment on this point, see Giorgio, p. 2.

104. My use of the term "parallax" derives from Carol P. Knowle, "Impressionism and Arnold Bennett," in *Literary Impressionism in Ford Madox Ford, Joseph Conrad and Related Writers*, p. 45.

105. For a related comment on this point, see Øverland, p. 254.

106. Øverland, pp. 275–76.

107. See Bidle, p. 83.

108. Hulme and Pound are quoted by William Pratt in his "Introduction" to *The Imagist Poem: Modern Poetry in Miniature*, ed. William Pratt (New York: E. P. Dutton & Co., Inc., 1963), pp. 18, 25.

109. Giorgio, p. 37.

110. Lars Åhnebrink, *The Beginnings of Naturalism in American Fiction: A Study of the Works of Hamlin Garland, Stephen Crane and Frank Norris with Special Reference*

to *Some European Influences 1891–1903* (Cambridge: Harvard Univ. Press, 1950), p. 126.

111. See George J. Becker, "Realism: An Essay in Definition," *Modern Language Quarterly*, 10 (1949), 193, and Donald Pizer, "Nineteenth-Century American Naturalism: An Essay in Definition," *Bucknell Review*, 13, No. 3 (1965), 1–3.

112. Åhnebrink, pp. vi–vii.

113. John Berryman, "Stephen Crane: *The Red Badge of Courage,*" in *The American Novel: From James Fenimore Cooper to William Faulkner*, ed. Wallace Stegner (New York: Basic Books, 1965), p. 93.

114. See Pizer, "An Essay in Definition," p. 3, and Edwin H. Cady, *The Light of Common Day: Realism in American Fiction* (Bloomington: Indiana Univ. Press, 1971), p. 7.

115. W. S. Sichel, "Fathers of Literary Impressionism in England," *Quarterly Review*, 185 (Jan., 1897), 194.

116. Harold H. Kolb, Jr., *The Illusion of Life: American Realism as a Literary Form* (Charlottesville: Univ. Press of Virginia, 1969), p. 11.

117. Åhnebrink, p. vi.

118. Charles R. Metzger, "Realistic Devices in Stephen Crane's 'The Open Boat,' " *Midwest Quarterly*, 4 (1962), 48.

119. See Becker, pp. 185–87.

120. See "Mostly Relevant," *American Literary Realism*, 3 (Summer, 1968), 74.

121. Kolb would here disagree, attributing the truth-illusion theme to Realism. However, he makes no distinctions between Realism and Impressionism. See Kolb, p. 95.

122. See Kolb, pp. 40, 50.

123. See Kolb, p. 58.

124. *Omnibus*, p. xix.

Chapter II

1. See, for example, the review by Sydney Brooks in the *Saturday Review*, 81 (Jan. 11, 1896), 44–45. Brooks' review is reprinted in *Heritage*, pp. 99–103.

2. For concurrence on this point, see Frank Bergon, *Stephen Crane's Artistry* (New York: Columbia Univ. Press, 1975), p. 1.

3. See *Works*, VII, 134.

4. See *Works*, IV, 60, 62, 99, 130, 143.

5. Ford, "Techniques," p. 32.

6. Joseph X. Brennan, "Stephen Crane and the Limits of Irony," *Criticism*, 11 (1969), 184.

7. Stephen Crane to John Northern Hilliard, *Letters*, pp. 158–59.

8. See Pool, p. 20.

9. Øverland, p. 256.

10. Perosa, pp. 88–89.

11. Holton saw this restriction as so basic to Crane's fiction that he used the phrase as the title of his book *Cylinder of Vision*.

12. Weingart, p. 26.

13. For a similar interpretation of this passage, see Holton, pp. 48–49.

14. William Faulkner, *The Sound and the Fury* in *The Faulkner Reader* (New York: The Modern Library, 1954), pp. 42, 59.

15. Øverland gives a similar interpretation to another passage. See Øverland, p. 256.

16. Øverland, p. 256.

17. See *Heritage*, p. 329. Originally published in *American Mercury*, 1 (Jan., 1924), 11–14.

18. Perosa, p. 88.

19. For further comments on this point, see Bergon, pp. 2, 15, and Holton, p. 8.

20. See Perosa, p. 93.

21. J. C. Levenson gives a detailed and perceptive reading of this paragraph in his introduction to *The Red Badge, Works*, II, xiv.

22. See, for example, *Works*, II, 15.

23. See *Heritage*, p. 116. Originally published in the New York *Times* (Jan. 26, 1896), p. 22.

24. For further examples, see *Works*, II, 6, 10, 31, 50, 66, 67, 88, 129.

25. See *Works*, II, 15, 16, 20, 32, 35, 41, 42, 69.

26. See Cady, p. 120.

27. Levenson, p. xlvi.

28. Peter Sloat Hoff, an unpublished paper delivered at the Literary Impressionism session of the 1975 Modern Language Association convention.

29. See *Works*, II, 46, 47, 49, 67, 75, 87, for further examples.

30. For a similar comment on Crane's use of Impressionistic scenes, see Åhnebrink, p. 93.

31. Levenson, p. xxviii.

32. See Bergon, p. 19.

33. For a discussion of the composition and publication of *George's Mother*, see James B. Colvert's introduction in *Works*, I, 101–08.

34. For the earlier "swaggering" image, see I, 120–21.

35. To my knowledge, "parallax" was first used to describe the Impressionistic device of multiple perspectives by J. Theodore Johnson in a paper entitled "Towards a Definition of Literary Impressionism" delivered at the Midwest Modern Language Association meeting in 1970. My use of this term is essentially consistent with that of Carol P. Knowle, p. 45.

36. For a discussion of the multiple points of view in the Hemingway story, see my article "The Narrative Method of 'The Short Happy Life of Francis Macomber,'" *Research Studies*, 41 (1973), 18–27.

37. See Brennan, p. 184; Thomas A. Gullason, "A Stephen Crane Find: Nine Newspaper Sketches," *Southern Humanities Review*, 2 (1968), 1–37; and Rogers, p. 301.

38. See Rogers, pp. 264, 273, 276.

39. Rogers, p. 268.

40. I have explored the narrative method of this story in greater depth in "The Narrative Method of 'The Open Boat,'" *Revue des Langues Vivantes*, 39 (1973), 409–17, and "Impressionism in 'The Open Boat' and 'A Man and Some Others,'" *Research Studies*, 43 (1975), 27–37.

41. Bidle, p. 287.

42. See "Death and the Child," V, 121–41. For a somewhat different reading of the narrative method of the story, see Rogers, pp. 273–76.

43. See Leon Edel, *The Modern Psychological Novel* (New York: Grosset & Dunlap, 1964), pp. 35–62.

44. Gordon O. Taylor, *The Passages of Thought: Psychological Representation in the American Novel 1870–1900* (New York: Oxford Univ. Press, 1969), pp. 110–35.

45. Hoffman, p. 3.

46. Giorgio, p. 163.

47. Giorgio, p. 114.

48. Cady, p. 161.

49. See J. C. Levenson's introduction to *Works*, V, p. xcvi, and Perosa, p. 89, for related comments.

50. See Giorgio, pp. 109–10.

51. Rogers, p. 265.

Chapter III

1. Indeed, Rogers suggests that "Crane's sense of the nature of reality is what most convincingly implies his link with Impressionism" (p. 264).

2. James B. Colvert, "Introduction" to *Great Short Works of Stephen Crane*, ed. James B. Colvert (New York: Harper & Row, 1959), p. vii.

3. I was pleased to discover, after the initial draft of this discussion was completed, that Frank Bergon reaches many of the same conclusions in his book. See pp. 25, 46.

4. See Giorgio, p. 98, and Holton, p. 9.

5. See *Works*, VIII, 683.

6. See Stallman's comments in *Omnibus*, p. 288.

7. See John W. Rathbun, "Structure and Meaning in *The Red Badge of Courage*," *Ball State University Forum*, 10, No. 1 (1969), 12–13, for a similar observation.

8. Pizer, "Nineteenth-Century American Naturalism: An Essay in Definition," p. 14.

9. Kronegger, p. 89.

10. James B. Colvert, "Structure and Theme in Stephen Crane's Fiction," *Modern Fiction Studies*, 5 (1959), 200.

11. See Colvert, "Structure and Theme," pp. 203–04.

12. I am indebted in my analysis of this point to Donald Pizer's perceptive discussion in "Stephen Crane's 'Maggie' and American Naturalism," *Criticism*, 7 (1965), 169.

13. Pizer, "Stephen Crane's 'Maggie,' " p. 169.

14. See Philip H. Ford, "Illusion and Reality in Crane's *Maggie*," *Arizona Quarterly*, 25 (1969), 296.

15. See William T. Lenehan, "The Failure of Naturalistic Techniques in Stephen Crane's *Maggie*," *Stephen Crane's Maggie: Text and Context*, ed. Maurice Bassan (Belmont: Wadsworth Publishing Co., 1966), p. 171.

16. *Biography*, p. 75.

17. *Letters*, p. 14.

18. Donald Pizer develops a similar reading in "Stephen Crane's 'Maggie.' "

19. Malcolm Cowley, "Naturalism in American Literature," *Maggie: Text and Context*, p. 120. Originally published in *Evolutionary Thought in America*, ed. Stow Persons (New Haven: Yale Univ. Press, 1950), pp. 300–33.

20. See LaFrance, p. 40.

21. See *The O'Ruddy*, *Works*, IV, 143–44.

22. Åhnebrink, p. 219.

23. See Hoffman, p. 217, and Florence Leaver, "Isolation in the Work of Stephen Crane," *South Atlantic Quarterly*, 61 (1962), 521.

24. Hoffman, pp. 9–10.

25. Kronegger, p. 67.

26. See Bidle, p. 326, and Pizer, "Nineteenth-Century American Naturalism: An Essay in Definition," p. 16.

27. I am indebted here to Donald B. Gibson, *The Fiction of Stephen Crane* (Carbondale: Southern Illinois Univ. Press, 1968), p. xvii.

28. See Walcutt, p. 67, and Cowley, "Naturalism in American Literature," p. 120.

29. See *Works*, I, 9, 35, 45, 52 for examples.

30. Holton, p. 54. For related comments, see Larzer Ziff, *The American 1890s: Life and Times of a Lost Generation* (New York: The Viking Press, 1966), p. 192; Pizer, "Stephen Crane's 'Maggie,' " pp. 172–73; and Marston LaFrance, "Stephen Crane in Our Time," *The Chief Glory of Every People*, ed. Matthew J. Bruccoli (Carbondale: Southern Illinois Univ. Press, 1973), p. 35.

31. LaFrance, *A Reading of Stephen Crane*, p. 152.

Chapter IV

1. A. G. Sedgwick [Review of *The Red Badge of Courage*], *Heritage*, p. 133. Reprinted from *Nation*, 63 (July 2, 1896), 15.

2. See Frederic's review in *Heritage*, p. 117. Reprinted from the New York *Times* (Jan. 26, 1896), 22.

3. Edwin Cady discusses these matters, with somewhat different conclusions, in *The Light of Common Day*, pp. 23–52.

4. See *Heritage*, p. 104. Reprinted from *National Observer*, 15 (Jan. 11, 1896), 272.

5. It is also possible to describe this method as a "stylistic" trait, as Orm Øverland does, p. 259.

6. See *Biography*, p. 69.

7. See J. C. Levenson, "Introduction" to *Works*, II, lxxvii.

8. Berryman, *Stephen Crane*, p. 290.

9. See *Letters*, pp. 154–56.

10. See Bergon, p. 99, for a similar formulation of this concept.

11. Taylor, p. 6.

12. Thomas A. Gullason, "Thematic Patterns in Stephen Crane's Early Novels," *Nineteenth-Century Fiction*, 16 (1961), 59–67.

13. J. C. Levenson, "Introduction" to *Works*, II, xxxviii.

14. Holton, p. 216.

15. James B. Colvert has demonstrated the stages of Henry's development in "Structure and Theme in Stephen Crane's Fiction," p. 204.

16. See Beverly Jean Gibbs, "Impressionism as a Literary Movement," *Modern Language Journal*, 36 (1952), 175–83.

17. See *Biography*, p. 176.

18. H. L. Mencken, "Introduction: Major Conflicts," *The Work of Stephen Crane*, ed. Wilson Follett, (New York: Alfred A. Knopf, Inc., 1926), X, xii.

19. Berryman, *Stephen Crane*, p. 286.

20. For related comments, see Giorgio, p. 39; Levenson, "Introduction" to *Works*, V, xv; Wertheim, p. 25.

21. For related comments, see Katz, "Introduction" to *The Portable Stephen Crane*, p. ix; and Bergon, p. 63.

22. See Eric Solomon, *Stephen Crane in England: A Portrait of the Artist* (Columbus: Ohio State Univ. Press, 1964), p. 101.

23. See Ford Madox Ford, *Joseph Conrad: A Personal Remembrance* (London: 1924), p. 210.

24. I am indebted here to C. B. Ives, "Symmetrical Design in Four of Stephen Crane's Stories," *Ball State University Forum*, 10, No. 1 (1969), 17–26.

25. Rathbun, p. 9, and Ives, pp. 22–23, both give the novel a similar division although with a somewhat differing thematic emphasis.

26. See Thomas M. Lorch, "The Cyclical Structure of *The Red Badge of Courage*," *College Language Association Journal*, 10 (1967), 232.

27. William P. Safranek, "Crane's *The Red Badge of Courage*," *Explicator*, 26 (1967), Item 21.

28. See Matthew J. Bruccoli, "Maggie's Last Night," *Stephen Crane Newsletter*, 2, No. 1 (1967), 10, on this point.

29. See Perosa, p. 85.

30. *Letters*, p. 41.

31. Ives, pp. 21–22, gives the novel a differing structural analysis.

32. Colvert, "Introduction," *Great Short Works of Stephen Crane*, p. xiv.

33. Ives, pp. 25–26, develops a similar interpretation.

34. For a more detailed analysis of the story, see my article "Structure and Theme in Crane's 'An Experiment in Misery,'" *Studies in Short Fiction*, 10 (1973), 169–74.

35. For related comments on Crane's ironic endings, see Gibson, pp. 96–97, and Colvert, "Structure and Theme in Stephen Crane's Fiction," p. 201.

36. James B. Colvert, "Introduction" to *Reports of War*, *Works*, IX, xxii.

37. See Maurice Bassan, "The Design of Stephen Crane's Bowery 'Experiment,'" *Stephen Crane: A Collection of Critical Essays*, ed. Maurice Bassan (Englewood Cliffs: Prentice Hall, 1967), p. 122.

38. For a more detailed analysis of this point, see "Structure and Theme in Crane's 'An Experiment in Misery,'" pp. 169–74.

39. This key passage was curiously deleted from the Bowers edition of *Works* and placed in the textual notes (I, 86). Joseph Katz has given this matter considered examination, including the implications of the imagery, in his fine essay "The *Maggie* Nobody Knows," *Modern Fiction Studies*, 12 (1966), 200–12.

40. See I, 15, 17, 48, 67, 74, 75.

41. A number of critics have discussed these and other aspects of the imagery in *Maggie*, among them Pizer, "Stephen Crane's 'Maggie' and American Naturalism," pp. 168–75, and Milne Holton, "The Sparrow's Fall and the Sparrow's Eye: Crane's *Maggie*," *Studia Neophilologica*, 41 (1969), 115–29.

42. See Joseph X. Brennan, "The Imagery and Art of *George's Mother*," *College Language Association Journal*, 4 (1960), 106–15. My reading is consistent with Brennan's with regard to the church-humanism conflict but differs in its assessment of the values of the saloon and the meaning of the images of the clock and the "hideous crabs."

43. For examples, see I, 124, 127, 129, 146, 156, 161.

44. See James Trammel Cox, "Stephen Crane as Symbolic Naturalist: An Analysis of 'The Blue Hotel,'" *Modern Fiction Studies*, 3 (1957), 147–58.

45. A. J. Liebling, "The Dollars Damned Him," *Crane: Critical Essays*, p. 23. Reprinted from *New Yorker*, 37 (August, 1961), 48–60, 63–66, 69–72.

46. Cady, *Stephen Crane*, pp. 139–40.

47. See Perosa, p. 88.

48. *Heritage*, p. 95. Reprinted from *Critic*, 24 (Nov. 30, 1895), 363.

49. See Solomon, *Stephen Crane in England*, p. 9. Solomon quotes from the *Indianapolis Journal* (Sept. 9, 1896).

50. Holton, p. 77.

51. Øverland, p. 248.

52. *Omnibus*, p. 186.

53. See Richard P. Adams, "Naturalistic Fiction: 'The Open Boat,'" *Tulane Studies in English*, 4 (1954), 143, and Melvin Schoberlin, "Introduction" to *The Sullivan County Sketches of Stephen Crane*, ed. Melvin Schoberlin (Syracuse: Syracuse Univ. Press, 1949), p. 15.

54. See Nochlin, pp. 15, 17.

55. Robert L. Hough, "Crane and Goethe: A Forgotten Relationship," *Career*, p. 192. Reprinted from *Nineteenth-Century Fiction*, 17 (1962), 135–48.

56. Hough, p. 202.

57. My discussion of Goethe's theories and their influence on Crane is in accord with Hough. Opposed to this view is Jean Cazemajou, who argues that Crane's sense of color derived from other sources in *Stephen Crane (1871–1900): Ecrivain Journaliste*, pp. 501–05.

58. See *Stephen Crane's Love Letters to Nellie Crouse*, p. 65.

59. I am indebted here to Hough, p. 195. Milne Holton, also influenced by Hough, discusses this matter in a similar way in Holton, p. 93.

60. My conclusions here parallel those of Hough (see especially pp. 193, 197, 200–01). However, he regards Crane's color images as "symbolic" whereas I regard them as either literal or as functioning in the manner of objective correlatives.

61. Pound's comment is quoted in Pratt, *The Imagist Poem*, p. 18.

62. See James W. Tuttleton, "The Imagery of *The Red Badge of Courage*," *Modern Fiction Studies*, 8 (1963), 414.

63. See Rathbun, p. 10, for a similar observation.

64. *Omnibus*, p. 199. My discussion of Stallman's analysis of *The Red Badge* refers to this account.

65. See Edward Stone, "The Many Suns of *The Red Badge of Courage*," *American Literature*, 29 (1957), 325, and Jean Cazemajou, "*The Red Badge of Courage*: The 'Religion of Peace' and the War Archetype," in *Transition*, p. 62.

66. See Jean G. Marlowe, "Crane's Wafer Image: Reference to an Artillery Primer?" *American Literature*, 43 (1972), 645–47.

67. Scott C. Osborn, "Stephen Crane's Imagery: 'Pasted Like a Wafer,'" *American Literature*, 23 (1951), 362.

68. LaFrance, *A Reading of Stephen Crane*, p. 100.

69. Here, LaFrance, p. 99, would agree.

70. Edmond Louis Antoine Huot de Goncourt, *Paris and the Arts, 1851–1896: From the Goncourt Journal,* edited and translated by George J. Becker and Edith Philips (Ithaca: Cornell Univ. Press, 1971), pp. 91, 221.

71. See Rudyard Kipling, *The Light That Failed* (New York: Albatross Library, n.d.), pp. 9, 23, 46.

72. Waern, pp. 535–41.

73. Crane used similar sun images on numerous occasions, and many of them express the emotions of a character. None of them refer to Christian rites. In "The Little Regiment," for example, there is the image of the "red round eye of the sun" which carries no symbolic values (VI, 19). In "Nebraska's Bitter Fight for Life" the image of the sun as a "burning disc" reveals the way it is perceived but again is not symbolic (VIII, 410).

74. See *Works,* II, 62, 64, 66, 67.

75. See *Works,* II, 108, 123, 124, 131.

76. James Trammel Cox, in "The Imagery of 'The Red Badge of Courage,'" *Modern Fiction Studies,* 5 (1959), 210, interprets these images in much the same way.

77. See Kolb, pp. 116, 122, and Cady, p. 139, for concurrence on these points.

78. See Hoffman, p. 260, and Holton, pp. 90–91.

Chapter V

1. Daniel G. Hoffman, "Stephen Crane's First Story," *Bulletin of the New York Public Library,* 64 (1960), 273.

2. See *Letters,* p. 14.

3. Here Pizer, "Stephen Crane's 'Maggie' and American Naturalism," p. 168, would agree.

4. *Omnibus,* p. xxv.

5. See *Omnibus,* p. 17.

6. Here Hoffman, *The Poetry of Stephen Crane,* p. 93, would agree.

7. See Kazin, p. 68; Richard Chase, "Introduction" to Stephen Crane, *The Red Badge of Courage and Other Writings,* ed. Richard Chase (Boston: Houghton Mifflin Co., 1960), p. vii; Hartwick, *Foreground,* pp. 17–44; R. W. Stallman, "Crane's 'Maggie': A Reassessment," *Modern Fiction Studies,* 5 (1959), 215–59.

8. See Cady, *The Light of Common Day,* pp. 74–75, for a related comment.

9. See Berryman, *Stephen Crane,* p. 37, and Gibson, p. 3.

10. Øverland, p. 241.

11. Colvert, p. 204.

12. Ernest Hemingway, "Chapter V," *The Short Stories of Ernest Hemingway* (New York: Charles Scribner's Sons, 1966), p. 127.

13. Carl Sandburg, "Stevie Crane," *Chicago Poems* (New York: Henry Holt and Co., 1916), p. 176.

14. See Vernon L. Parrington, *Main Currents in American Thought, III: The Beginnings of Critical Realism in America: 1860–1920* (New York: Harcourt, Brace & World, Inc., 1958), p. 328, and Fred Lewis Pattee, "Stephen Crane," *The New American Literature 1890–1930* (New York: Cooper Square Publishers, Inc., 1968), p. 64.

15. Carl Van Doren, "Stephen Crane," *American Mercury,* 1 (1924), 11.

16. Joseph Conrad, "His War Book," *Critical Essays,* p. 123. Reprinted from Conrad's *Last Essays* (New York: Doubleday, Page, 1926).

Index

DATE DUE

			PRINTED IN U.S.A.